Dear Readers:

Welcome to a very special project: the twin companion *BEAUTY AND THE BEAST* manga set! This particular manga is *THE BEAST'S TALE*, where we relive the classic story from the Beast's perspective.

Creating a manga image for such a ubiquitous and enigmatic character such as the Beast is a challenge unto itself. Fortunately, we were blessed with an extremely talented team of artists in Japan who ended up with the perfect manga look. To do so, the artists balanced extensive notes and guidance from the Disney team with inherent manga sensibility – and you can experience that process a bit by studying the Concept Art bonus pages near the end of this book.

Further, adapting the gorgeous production design from the film into hand-drawn illustrations in the manga was an exhilarating experience. Our goal was always to satisfy your innate curiosity about this classic world and characters while keeping the manga aesthetic relevant to your reading experience. Hopefully you'll enjoy the visuals as much as we do.

And of course adapting this world-renowned story for the page was critical, especially honing in on the Beast's point of view, which is particularly unique to this book. While BEAUTY AND THE BEAST is famously Belle's story, we wanted to demystify the Beast in a personal and intimate way.

So, in this manga you can dive in and experience this side of the Beast from within – his true emotions, his soul. Join us on a journey into the Beast's mind – and see what Belle saw, and who she fell in love with.

TOKYOPOP is proud to bring you *THE BEAST'S TALE*!!

—Team TOKYOPOP

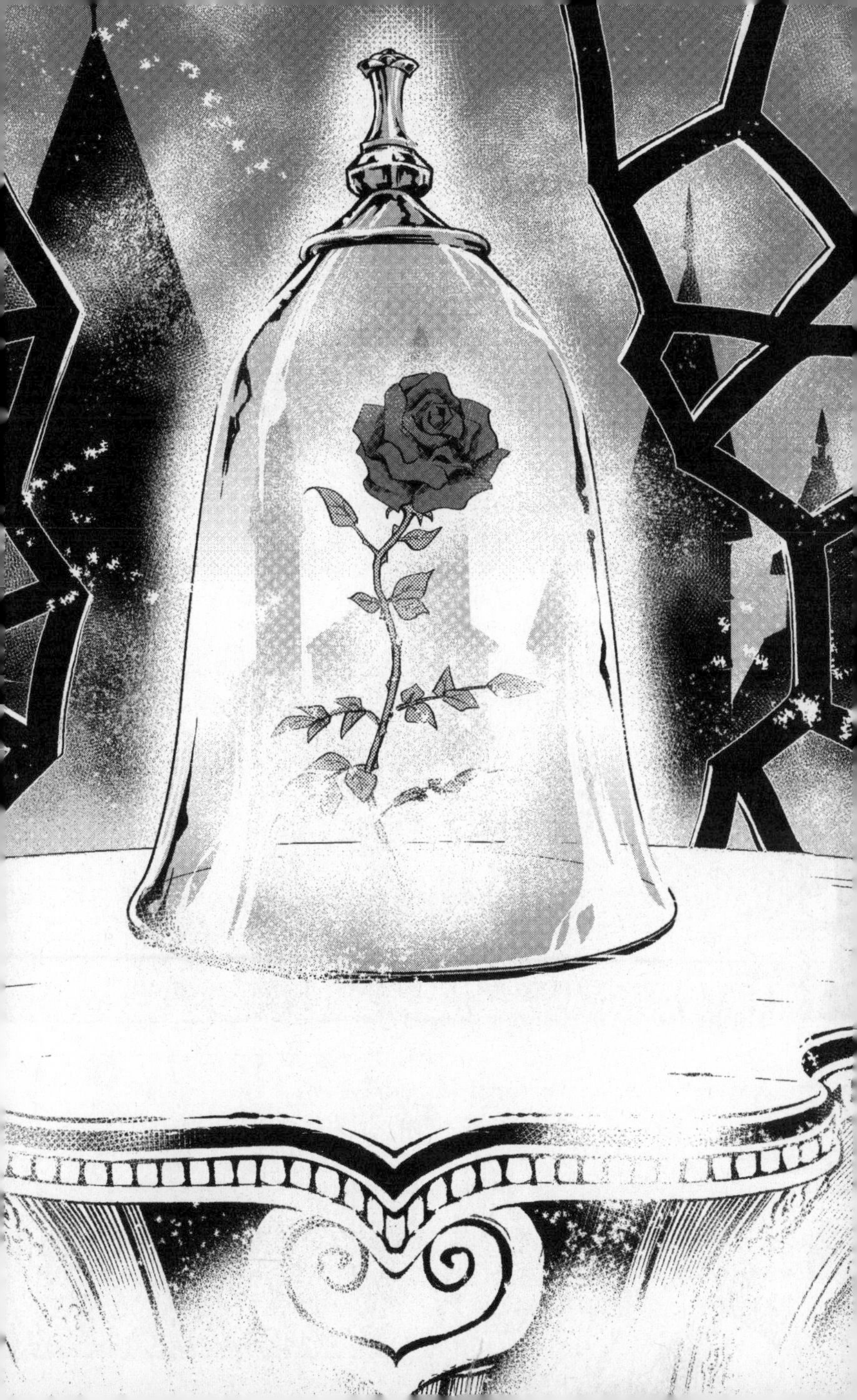

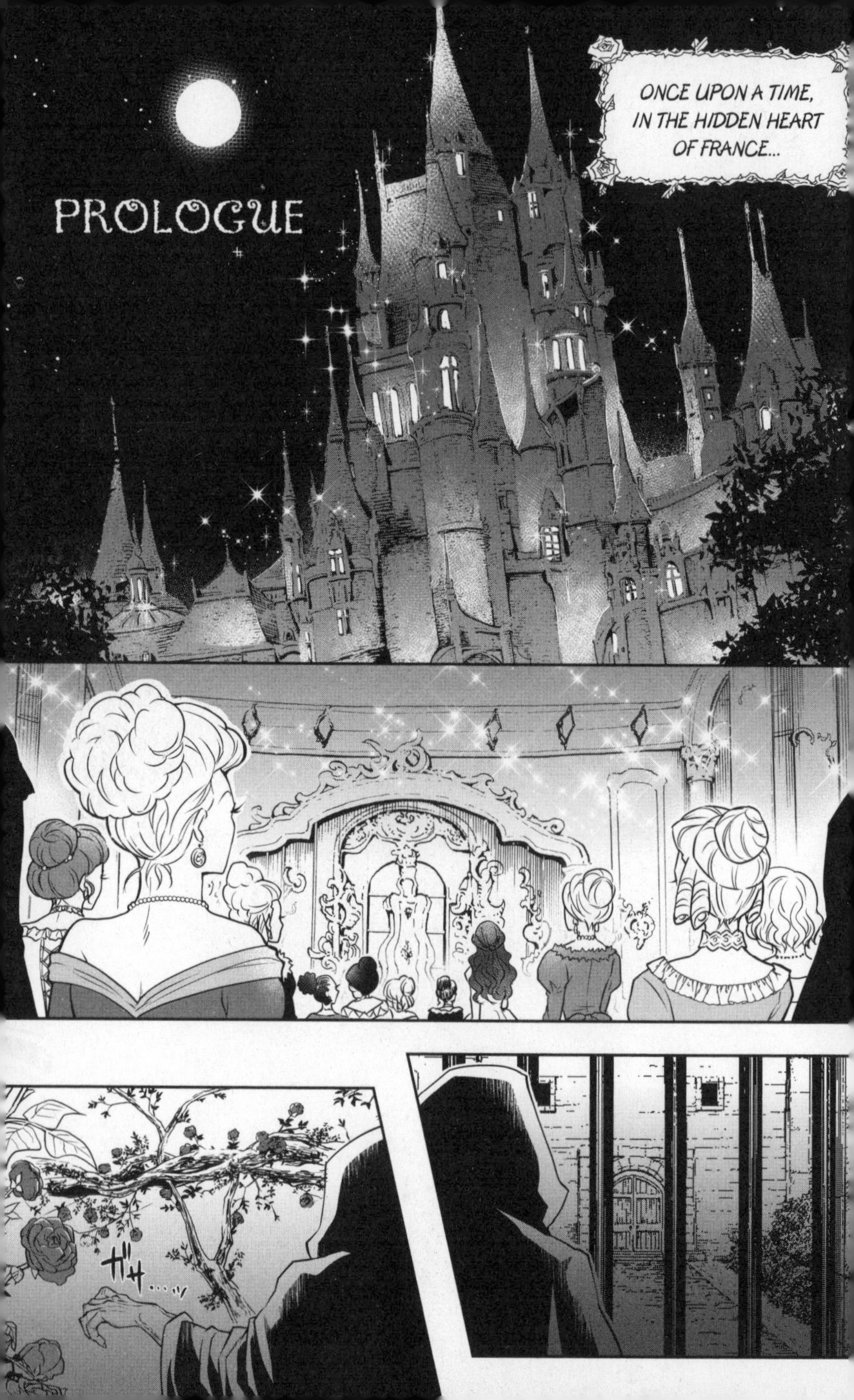
ONCE UPON A TIME, IN THE HIDDEN HEART OF FRANCE...
PROLOGUE

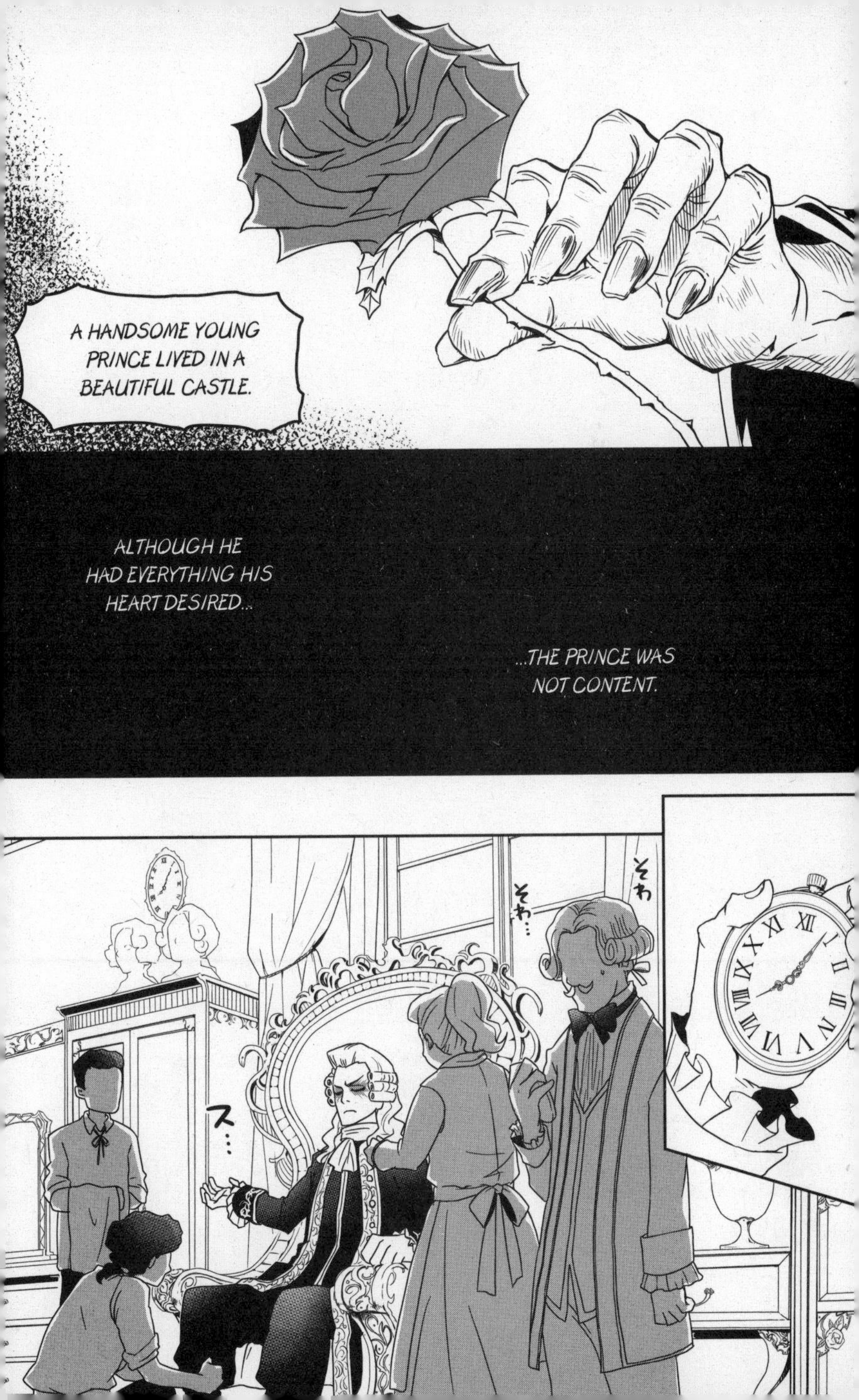
A HANDSOME YOUNG PRINCE LIVED IN A BEAUTIFUL CASTLE.
ALTHOUGH HE HAD EVERYTHING HIS HEART DESIRED...
...THE PRINCE WAS NOT CONTENT.
そわ
そわ…
ス…

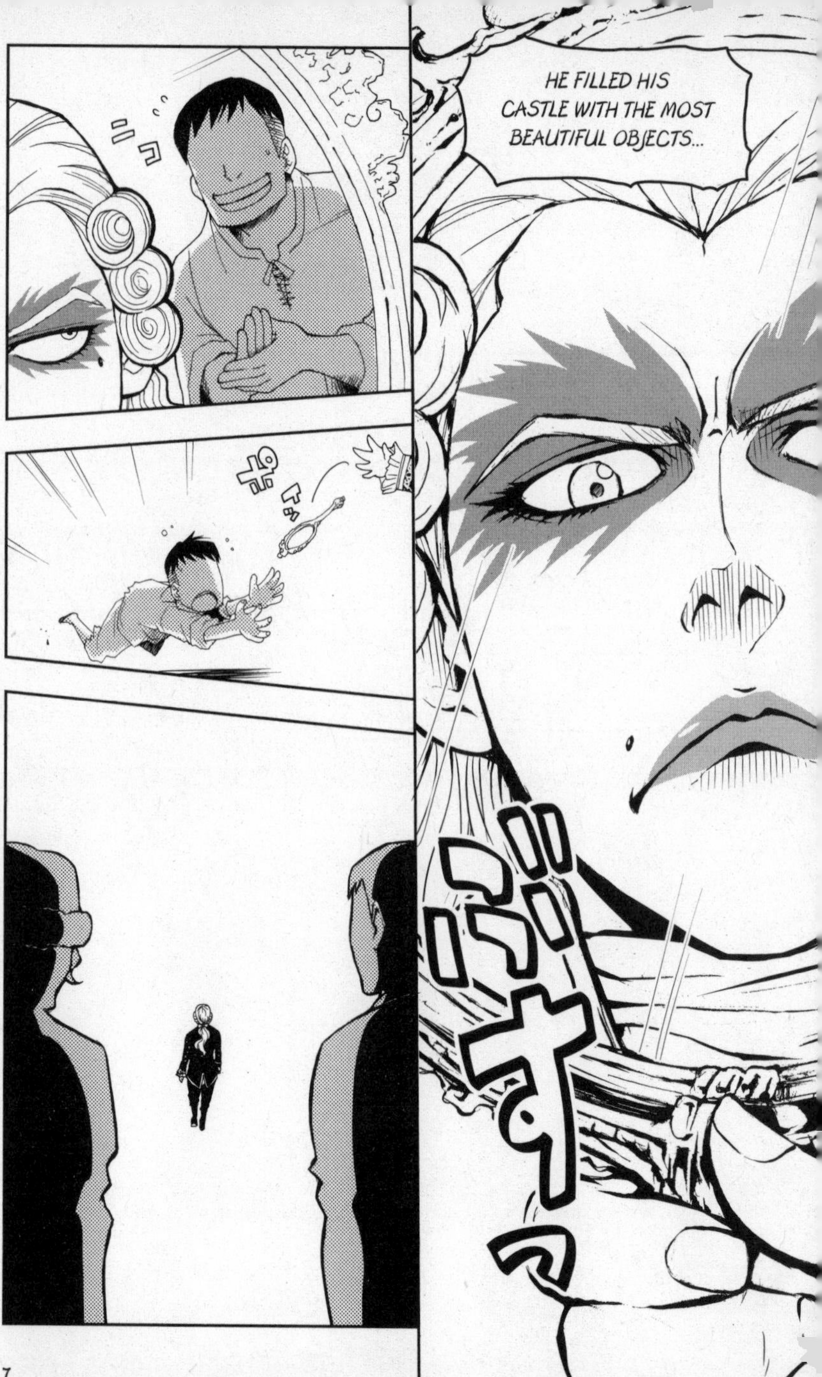
HE FILLED HIS CASTLE WITH THE MOST BEAUTIFUL OBJECTS...

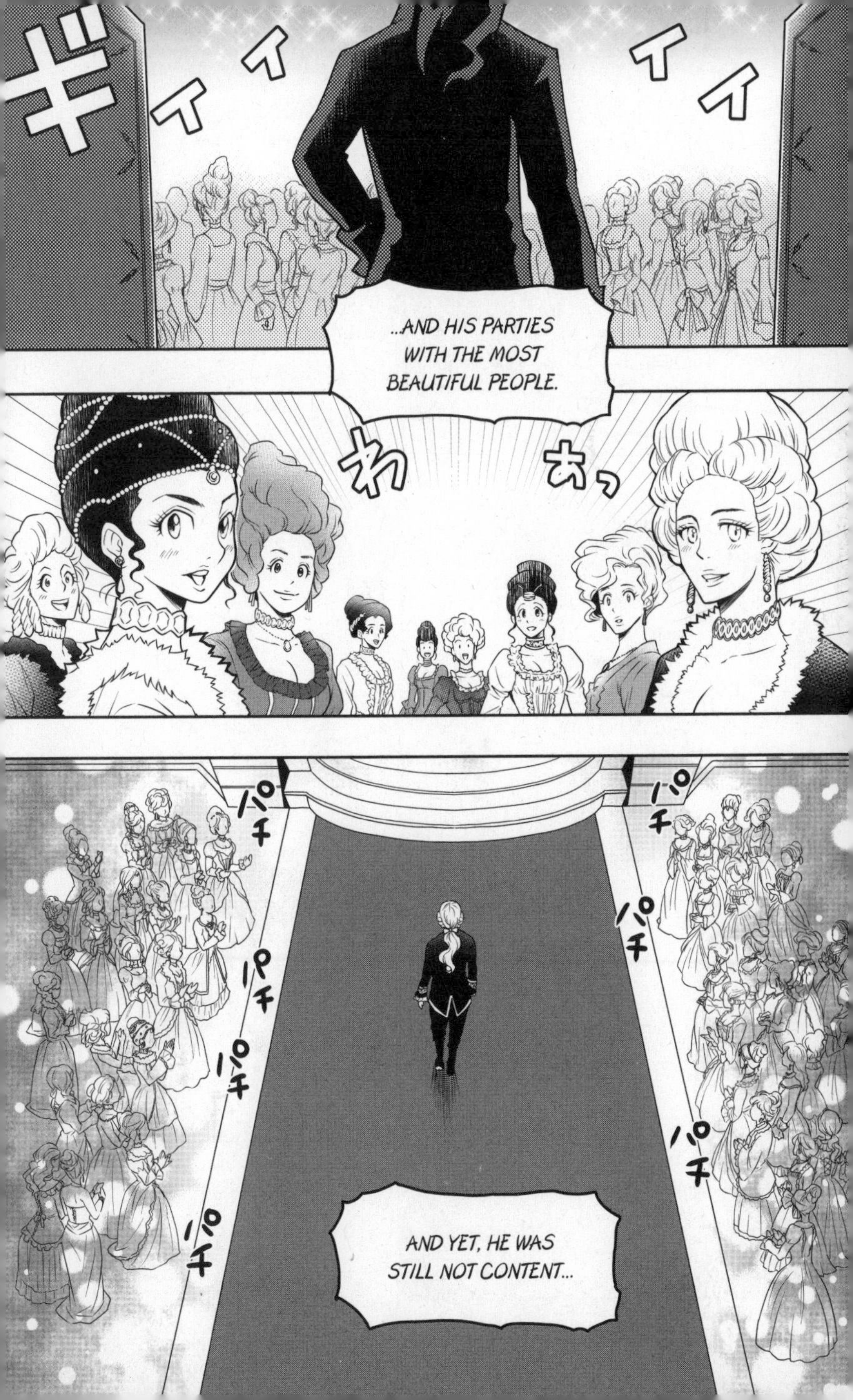
ギィィ
イィ
...AND HIS PARTIES WITH THE MOST BEAUTIFUL PEOPLE.
あっ
わ
パチ
パチ
パチ
パチ
パチ
パチ
AND YET, HE WAS STILL NOT CONTENT...

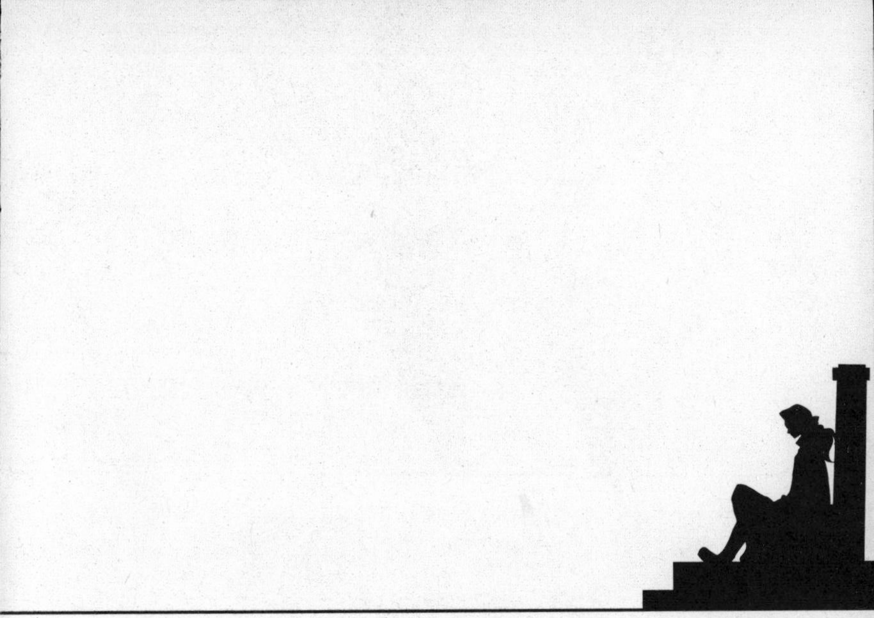

THAT IS NOT HOW THE STORY ENDS.

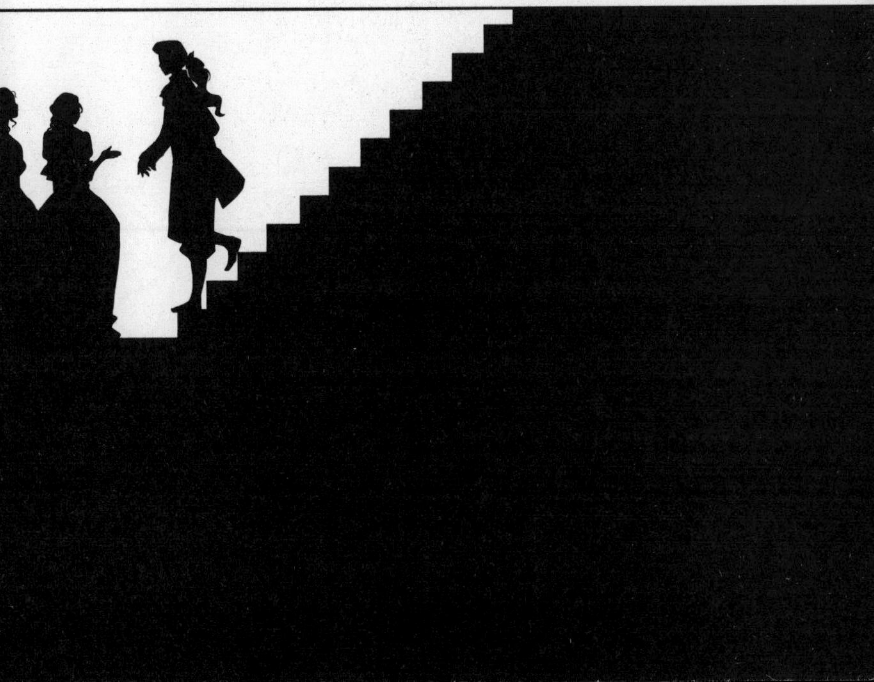

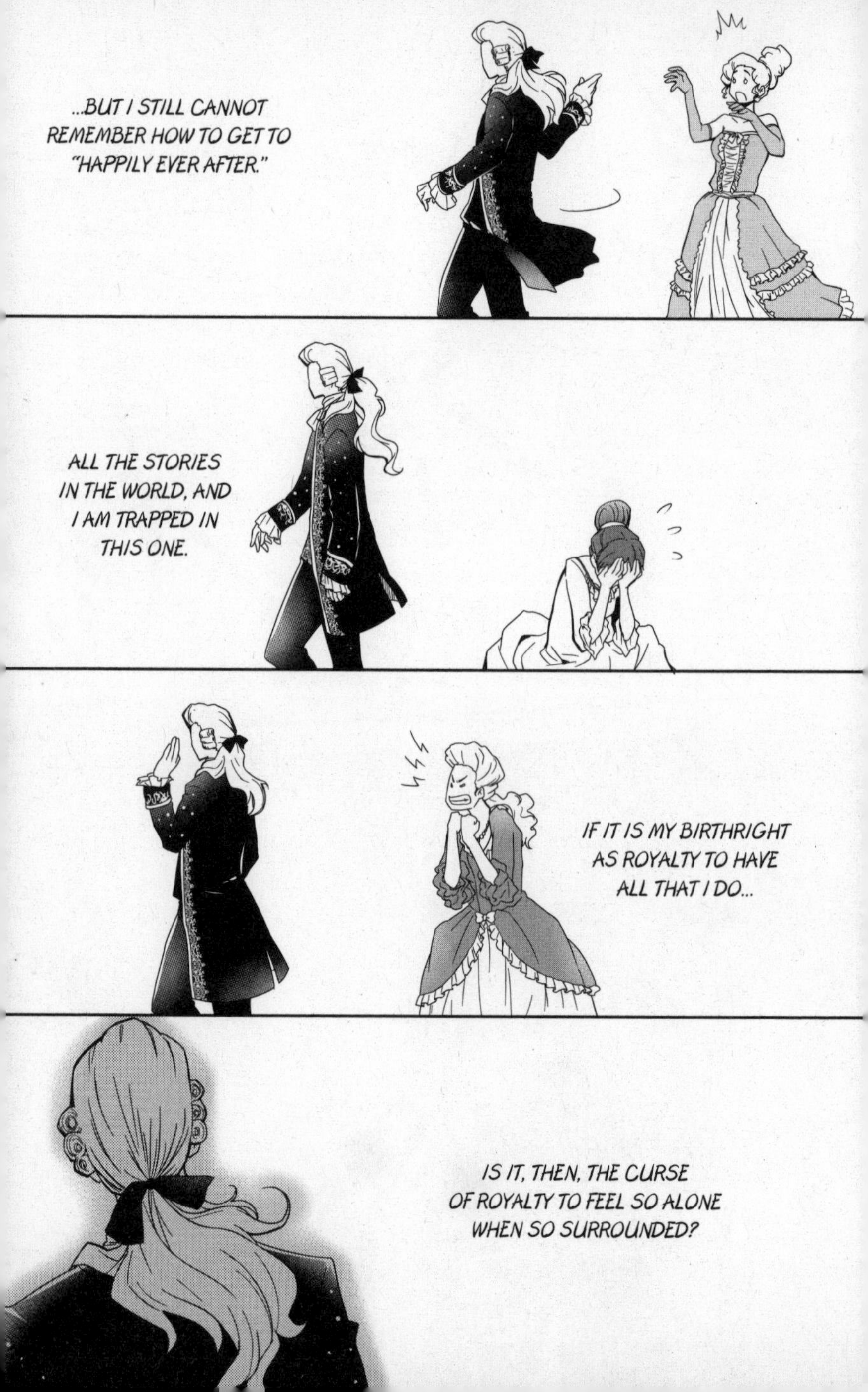

...BUT I STILL CANNOT REMEMBER HOW TO GET TO "HAPPILY EVER AFTER."
ALL THE STORIES IN THE WORLD, AND I AM TRAPPED IN THIS ONE.
IF IT IS MY BIRTHRIGHT AS ROYALTY TO HAVE ALL THAT I DO...
IS IT, THEN, THE CURSE OF ROYALTY TO FEEL SO ALONE WHEN SO SURROUNDED?

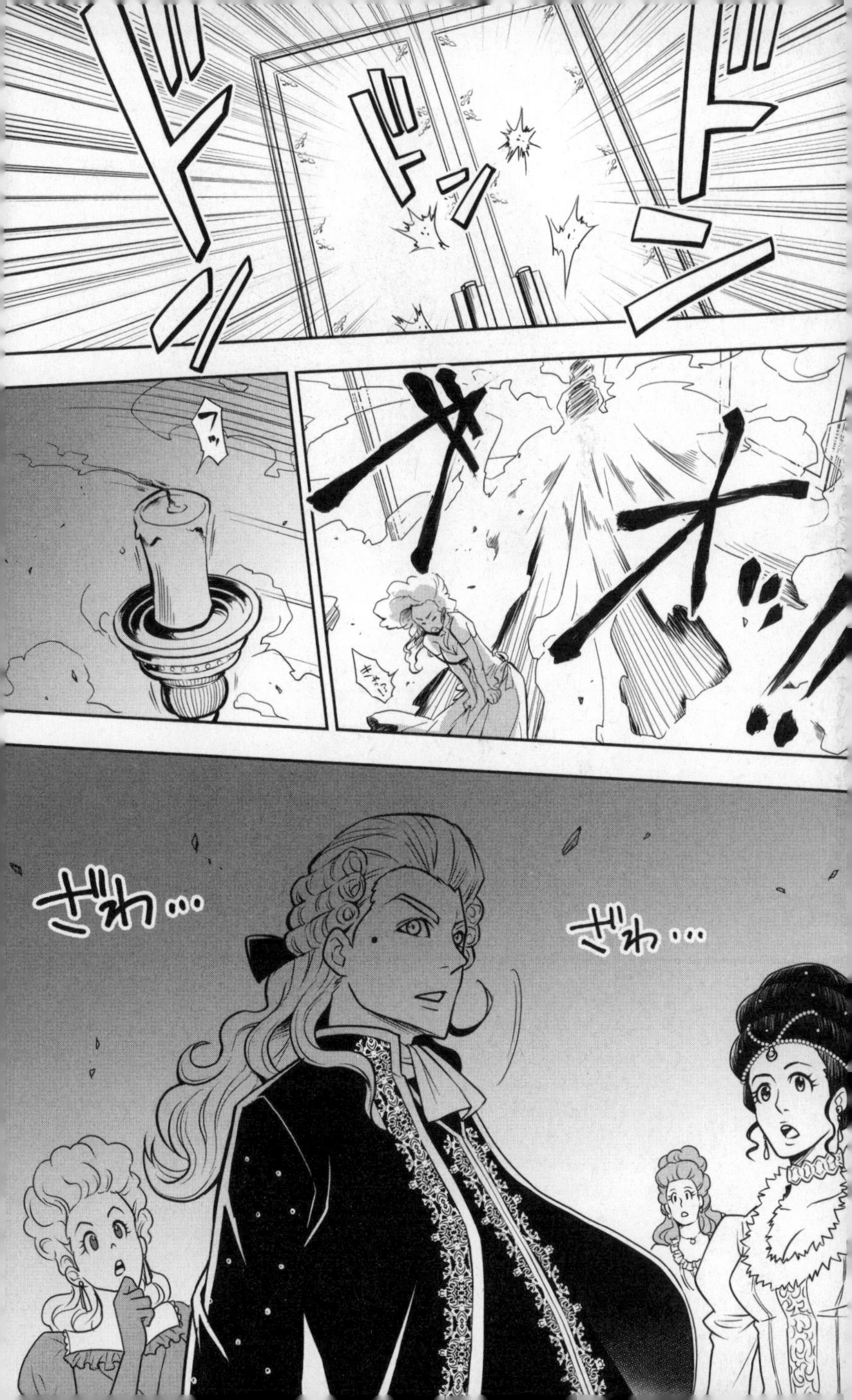

ドドーン
ドドーン
ドドン
ゴオッ!!
きゃあー!
フッ
ざわ…
ざわ…

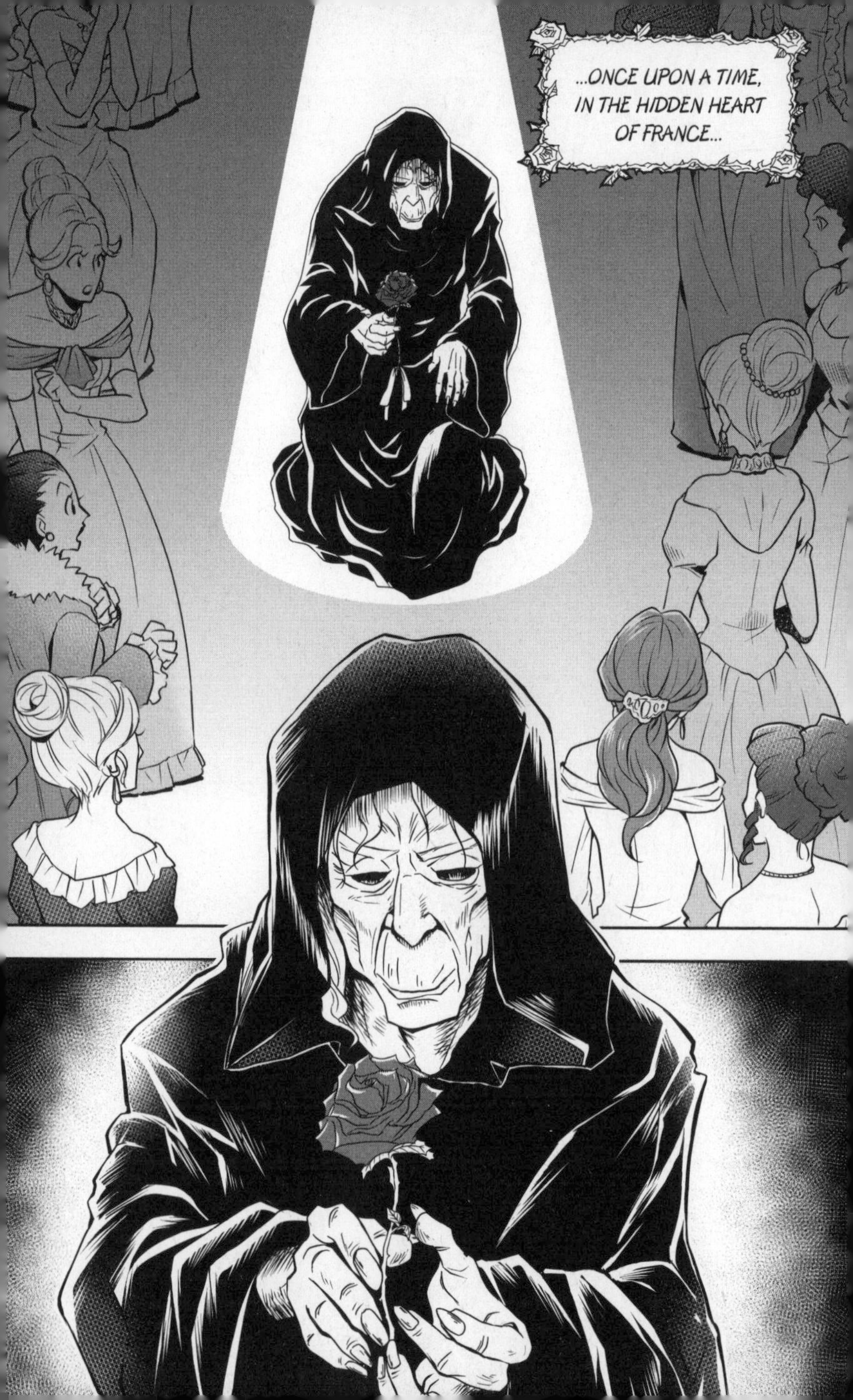
...ONCE UPON A TIME,
IN THE HIDDEN HEART
OF FRANCE...

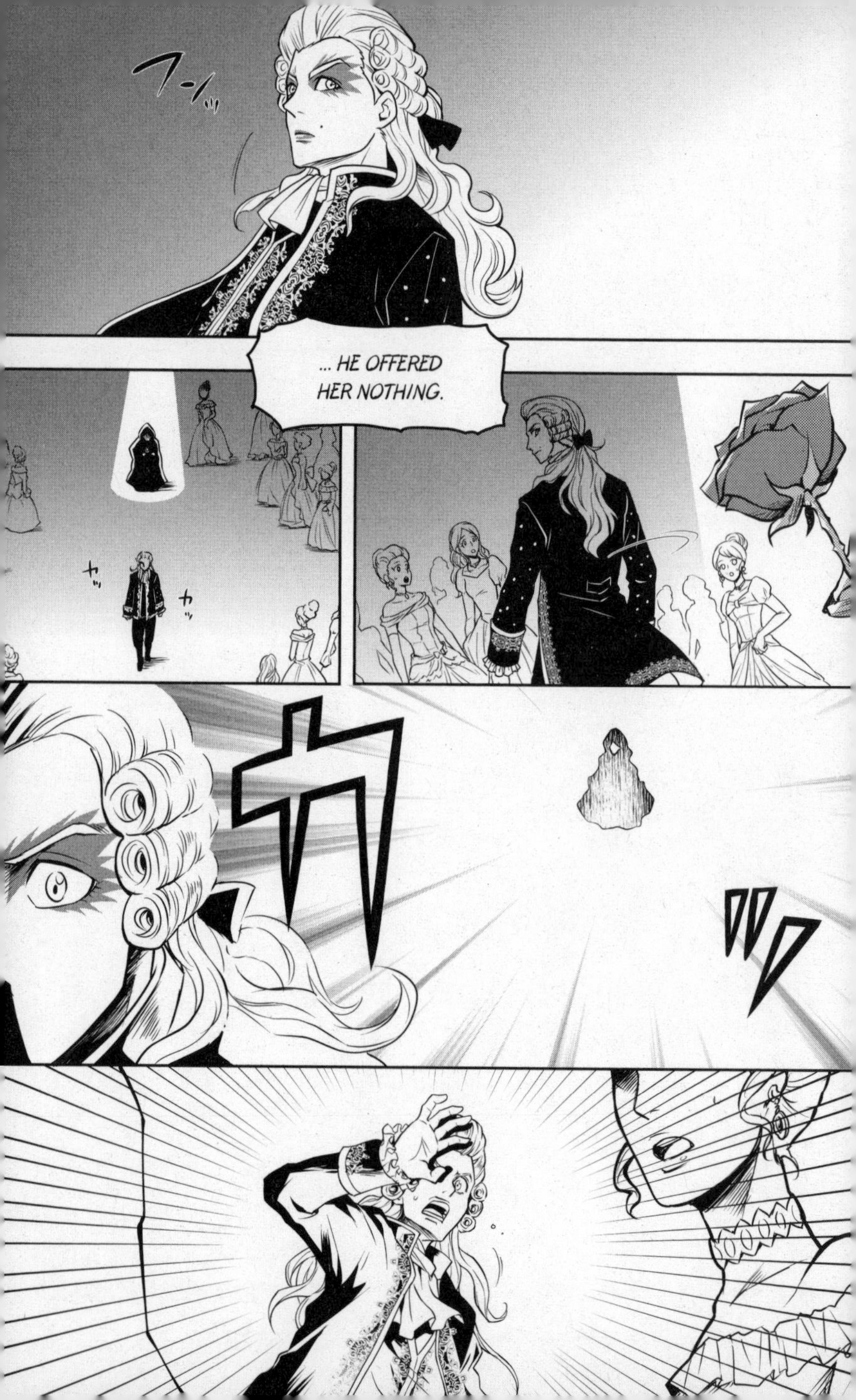
... HE OFFERED HER NOTHING.

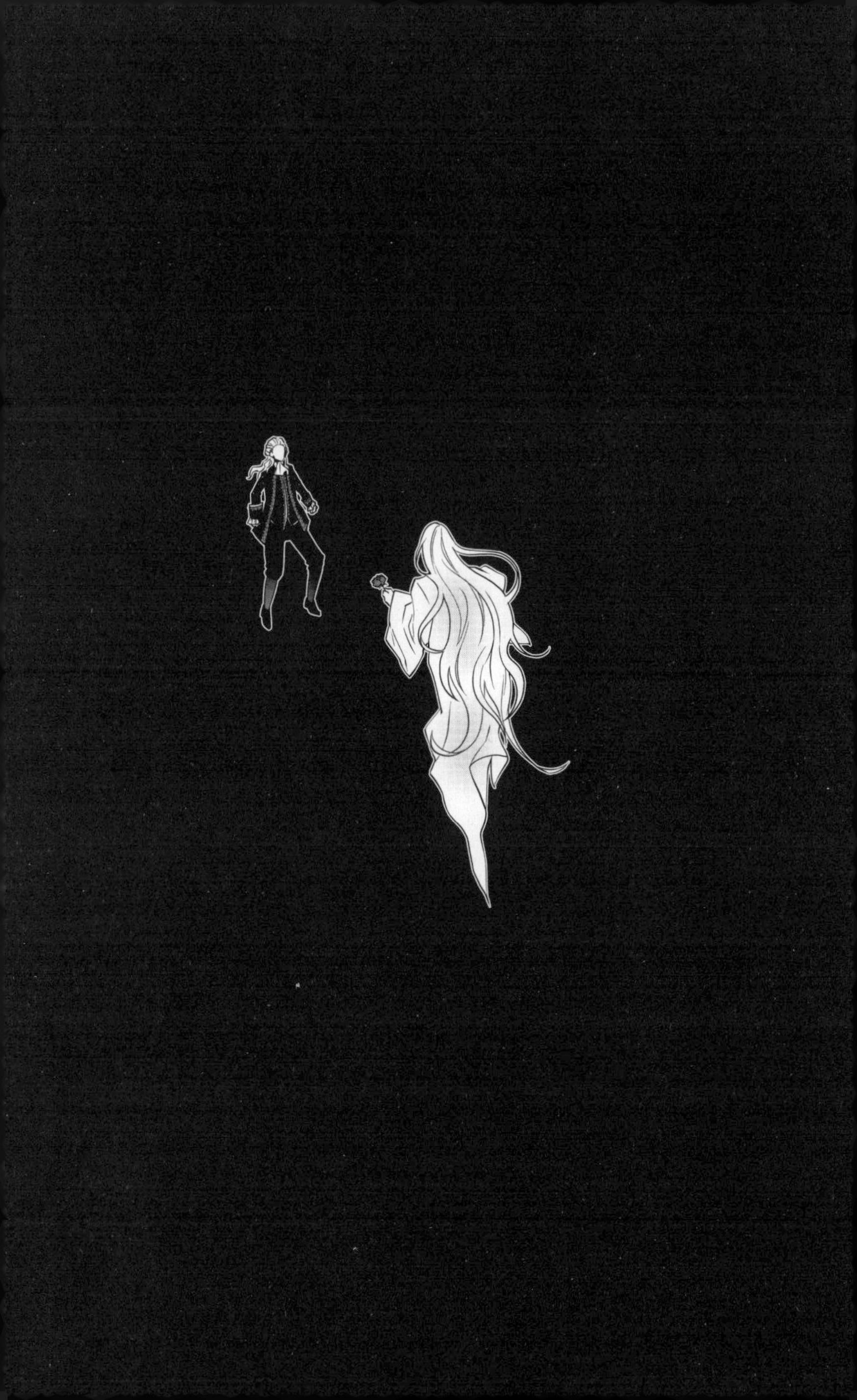

HER PLEA FOR HELP
HAD BEEN NOTHING...

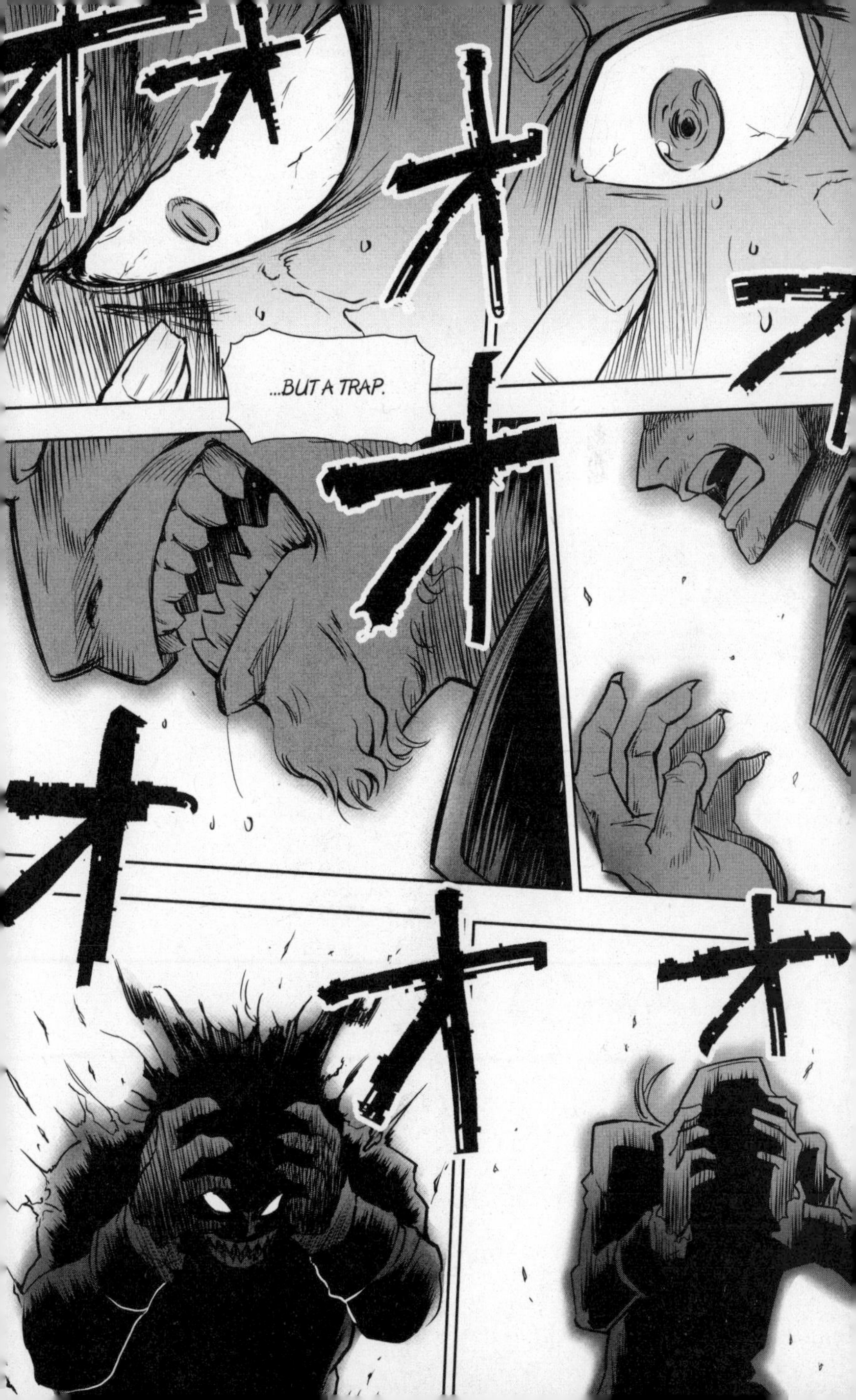
...BUT A TRAP.

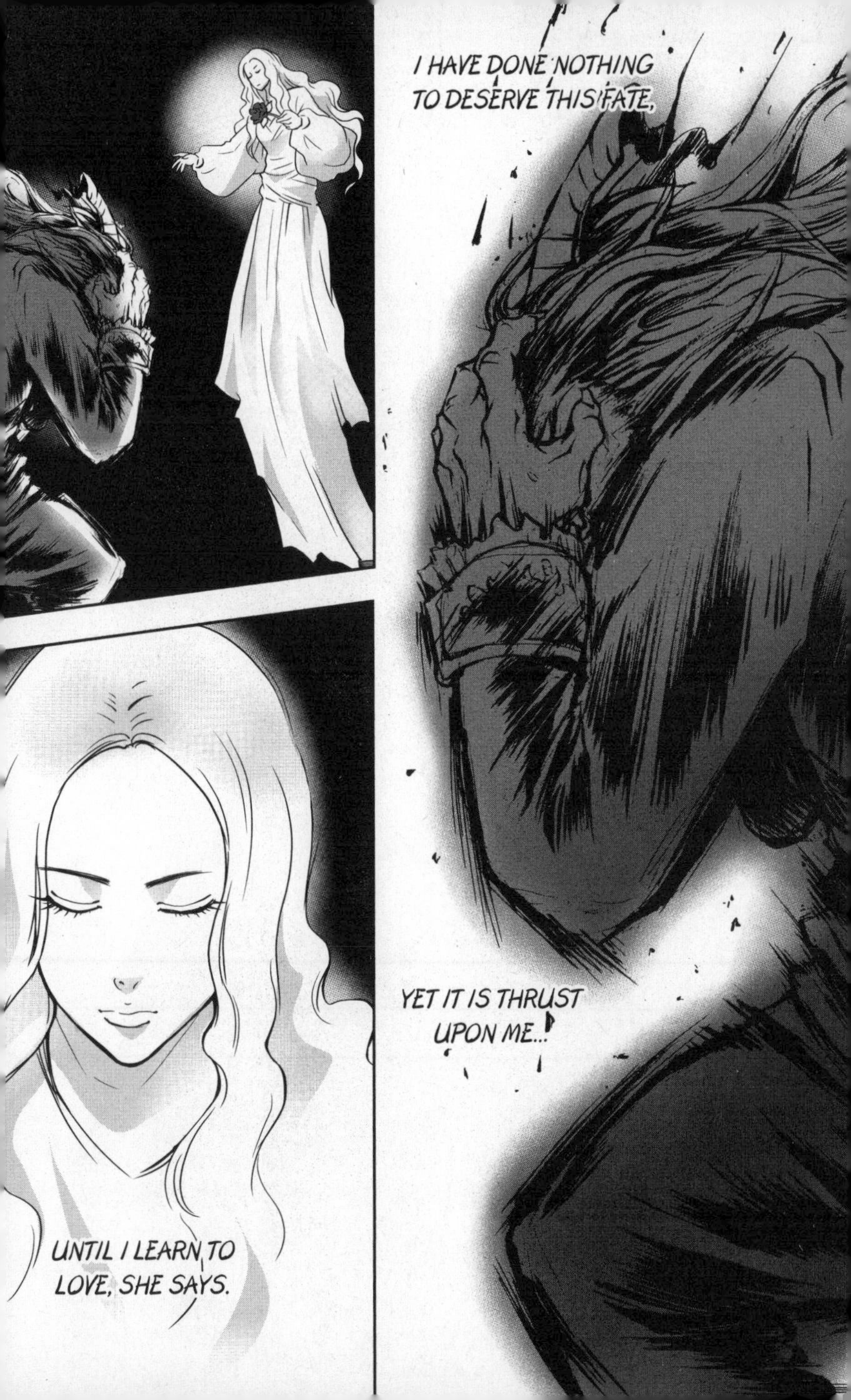
I HAVE DONE NOTHING TO DESERVE THIS FATE,
YET IT IS THRUST UPON ME...!
UNTIL I LEARN TO LOVE, SHE SAYS.

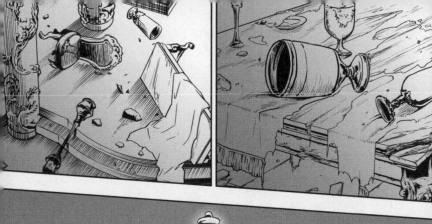

AND THE ROSE SHE OFFERED WAS JUST ANOTHER CURSE...

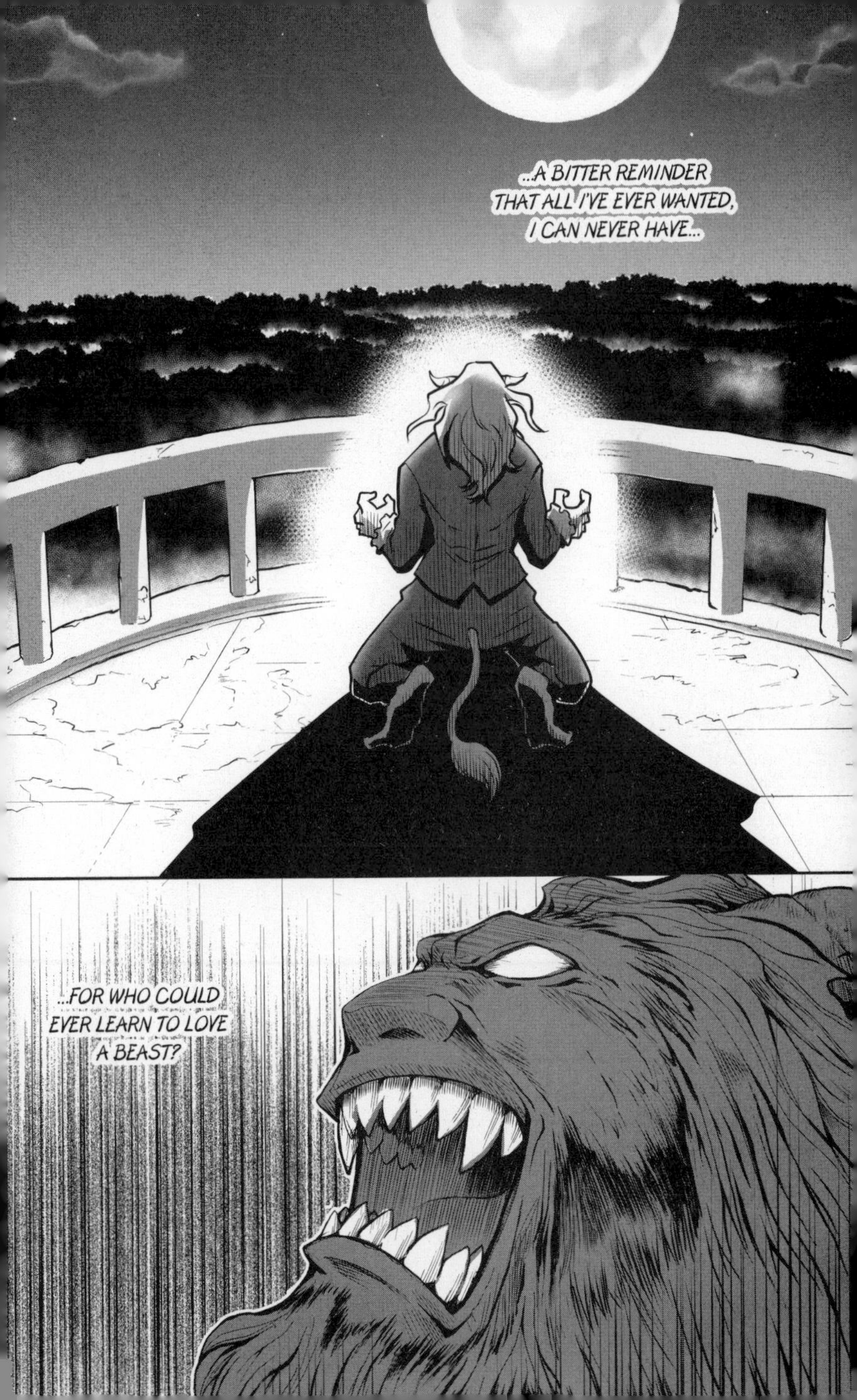
...A BITTER REMINDER THAT ALL I'VE EVER WANTED, I CAN NEVER HAVE...
...FOR WHO COULD EVER LEARN TO LOVE A BEAST?

CHAPTER 1

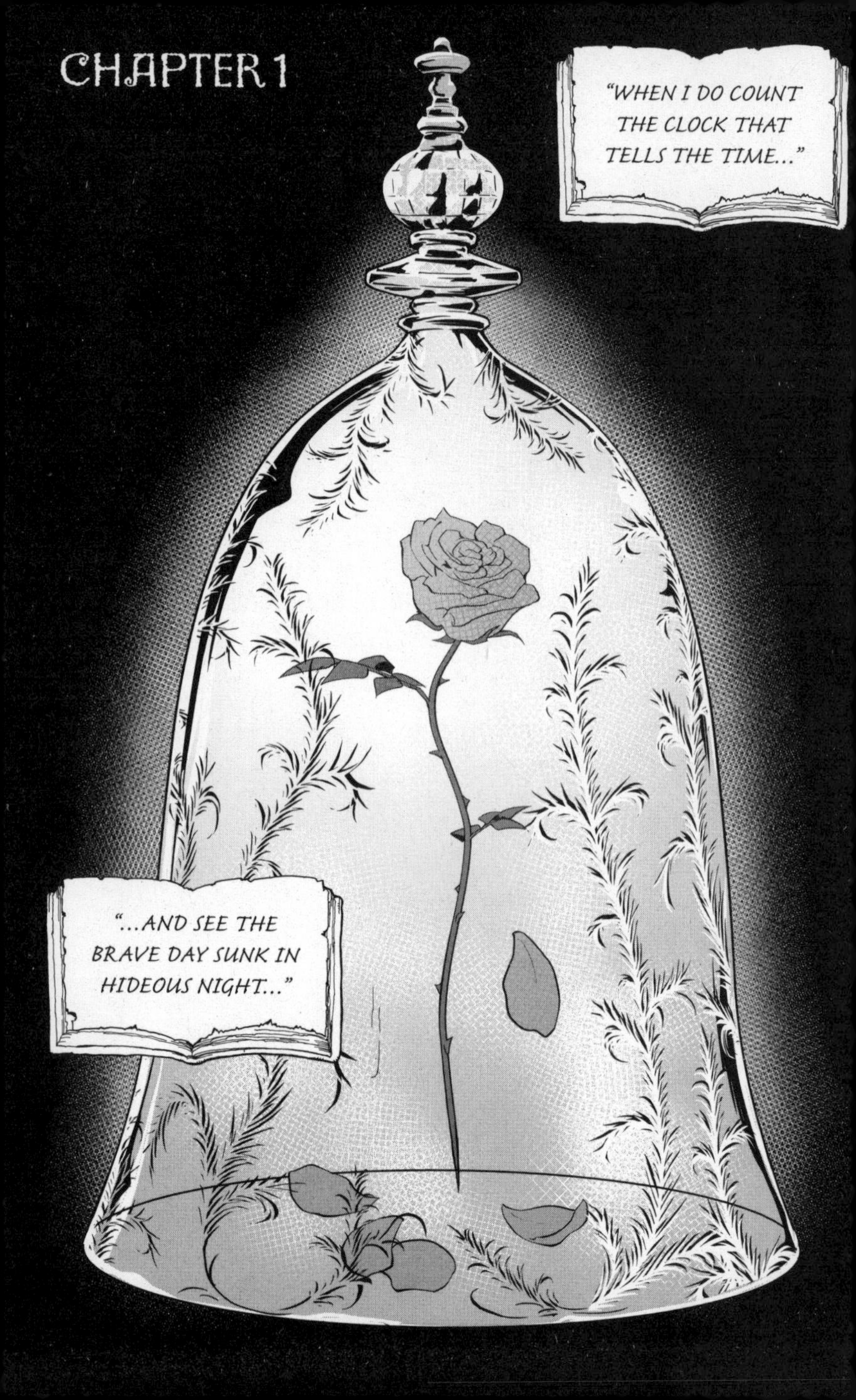
"WHEN I DO COUNT THE CLOCK THAT TELLS THE TIME..."
"...AND SEE THE BRAVE DAY SUNK IN HIDEOUS NIGHT..."

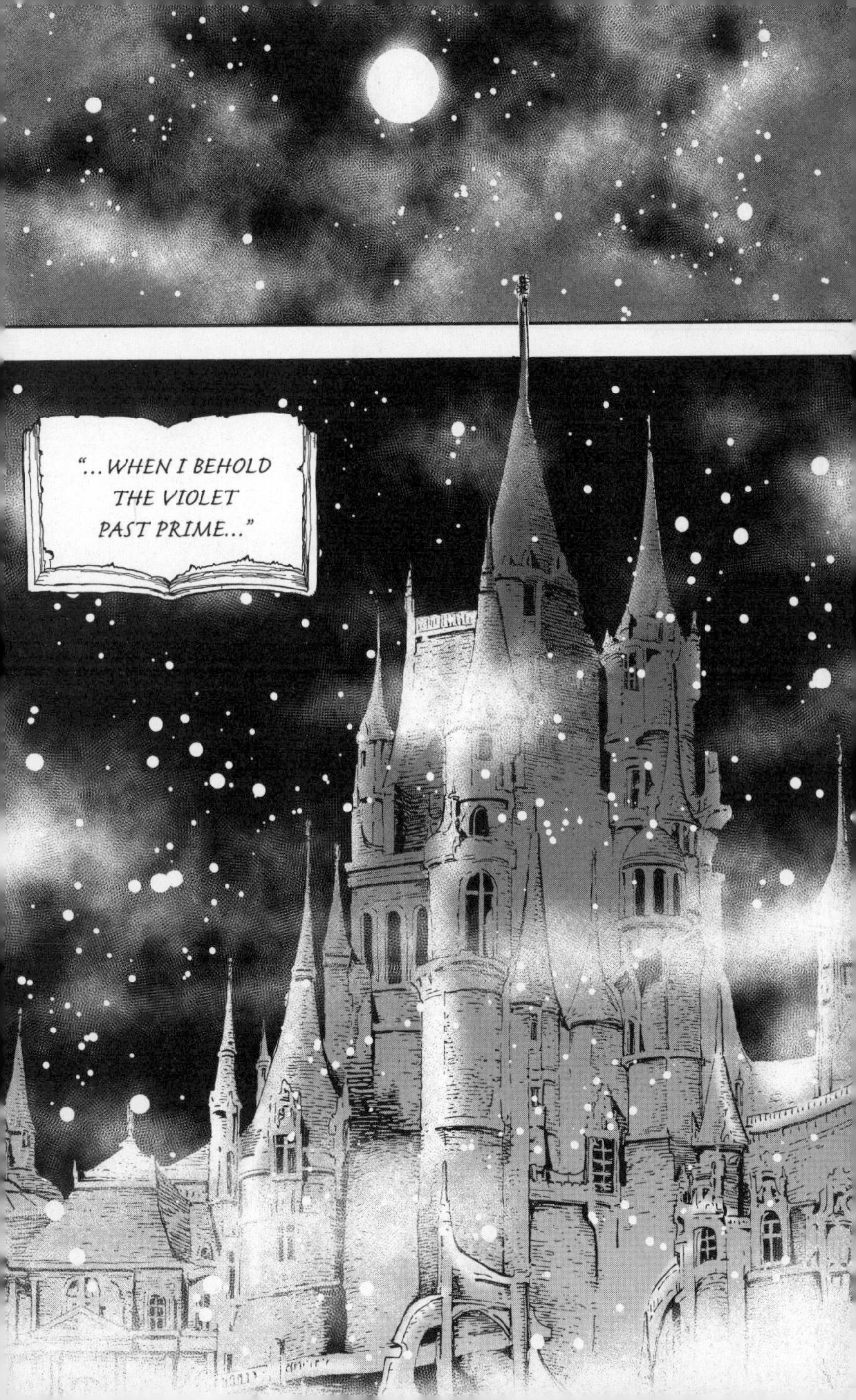
"...WHEN I BEHOLD THE VIOLET PAST PRIME..."

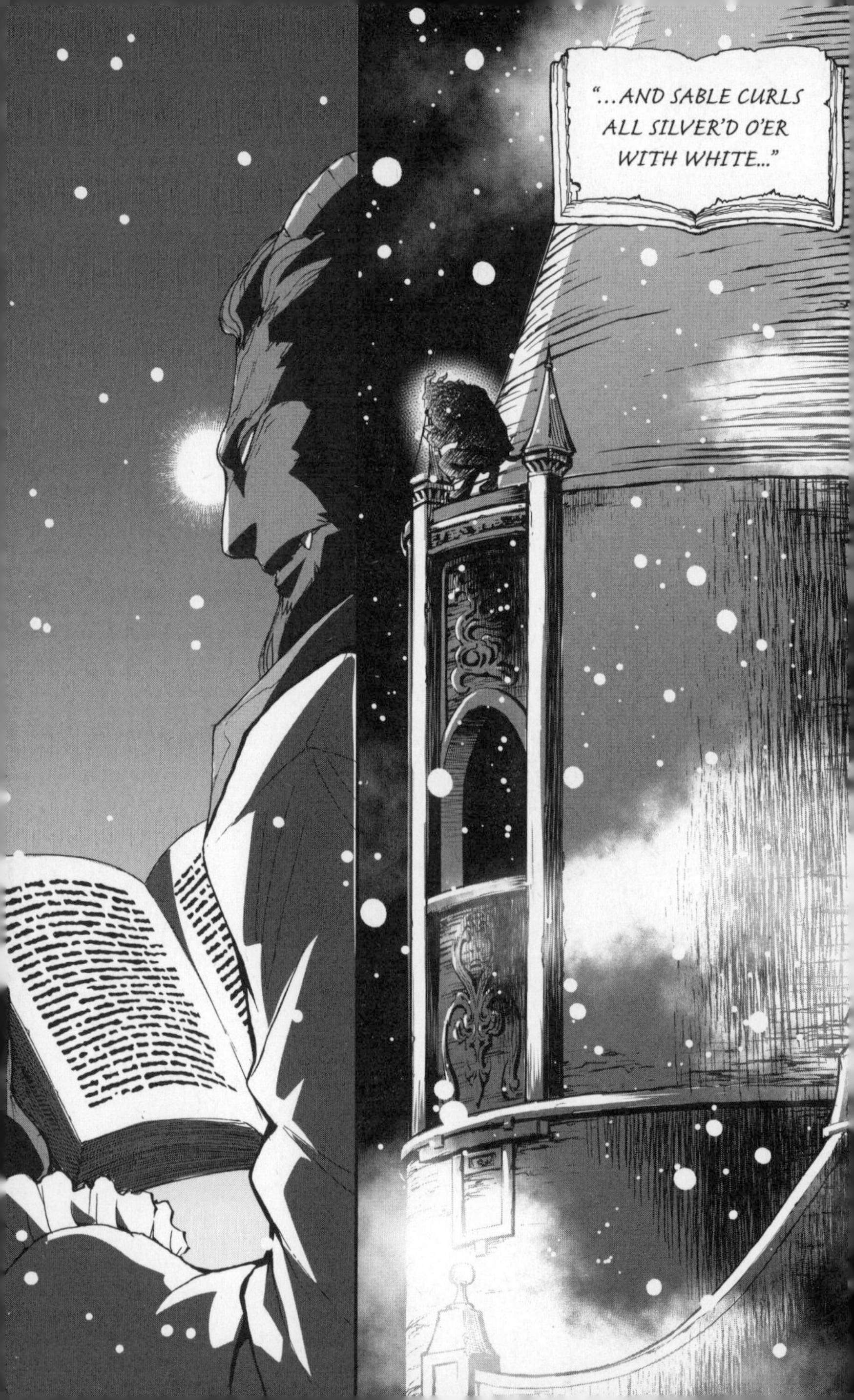
"...AND SABLE CURLS ALL SILVER'D O'ER WITH WHITE..."

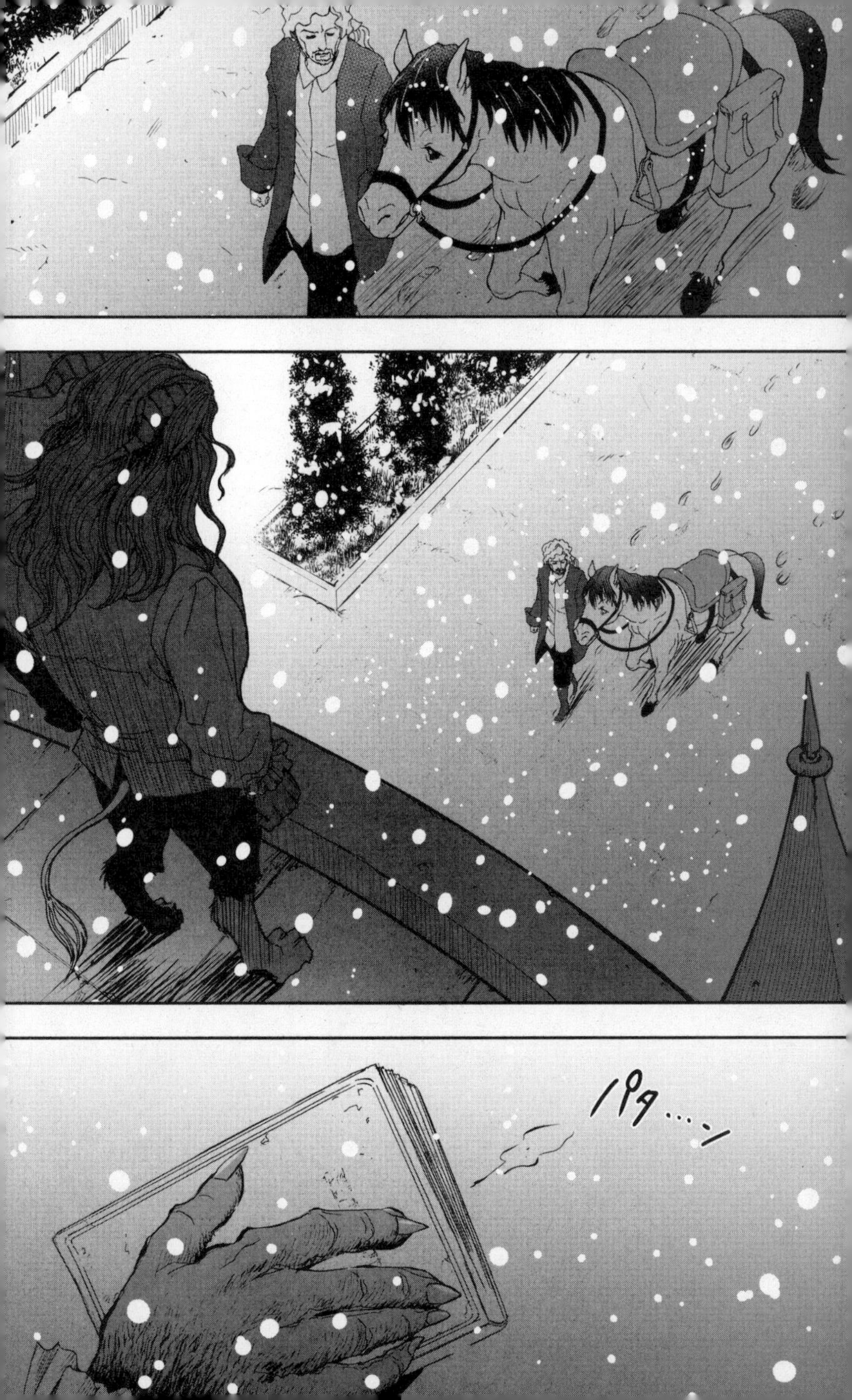
パタ…ン

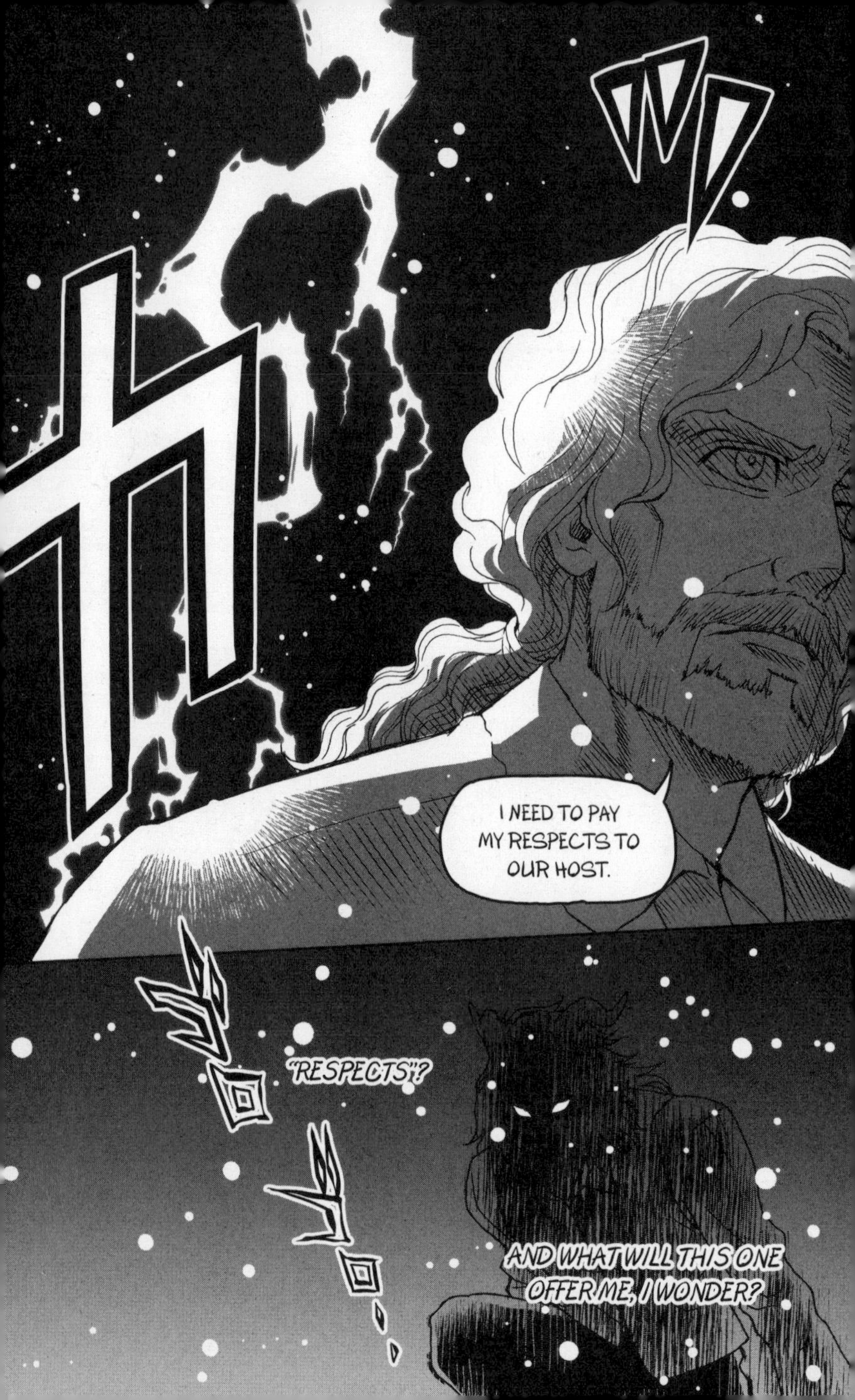
I NEED TO PAY MY RESPECTS TO OUR HOST.
"RESPECTS"?
AND WHAT WILL THIS ONE OFFER ME, I WONDER?

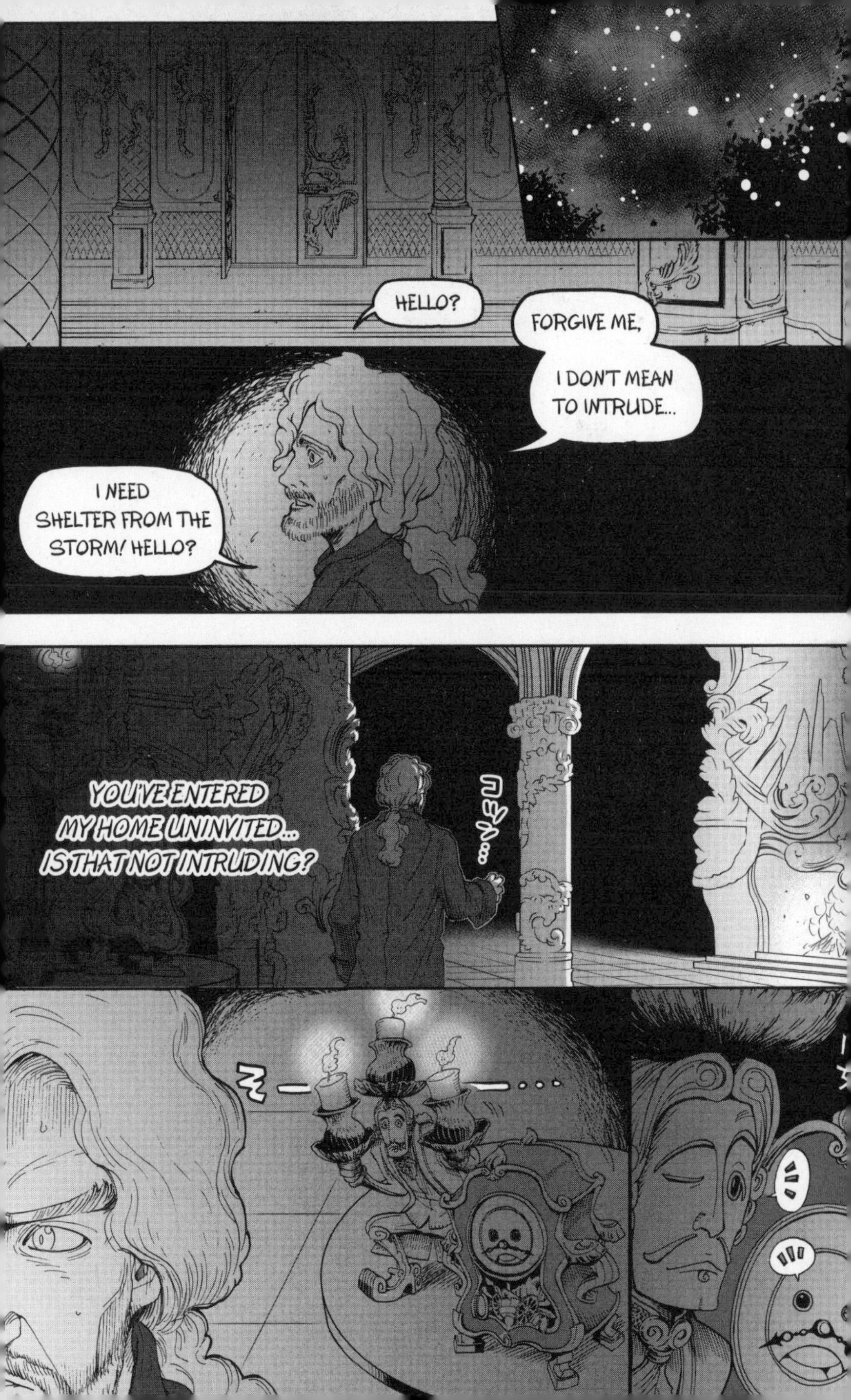
HELLO?
FORGIVE ME,
I DON'T MEAN TO INTRUDE...
I NEED SHELTER FROM THE STORM! HELLO?
YOU'VE ENTERED MY HOME UNINVITED... IS THAT NOT INTRUDING?

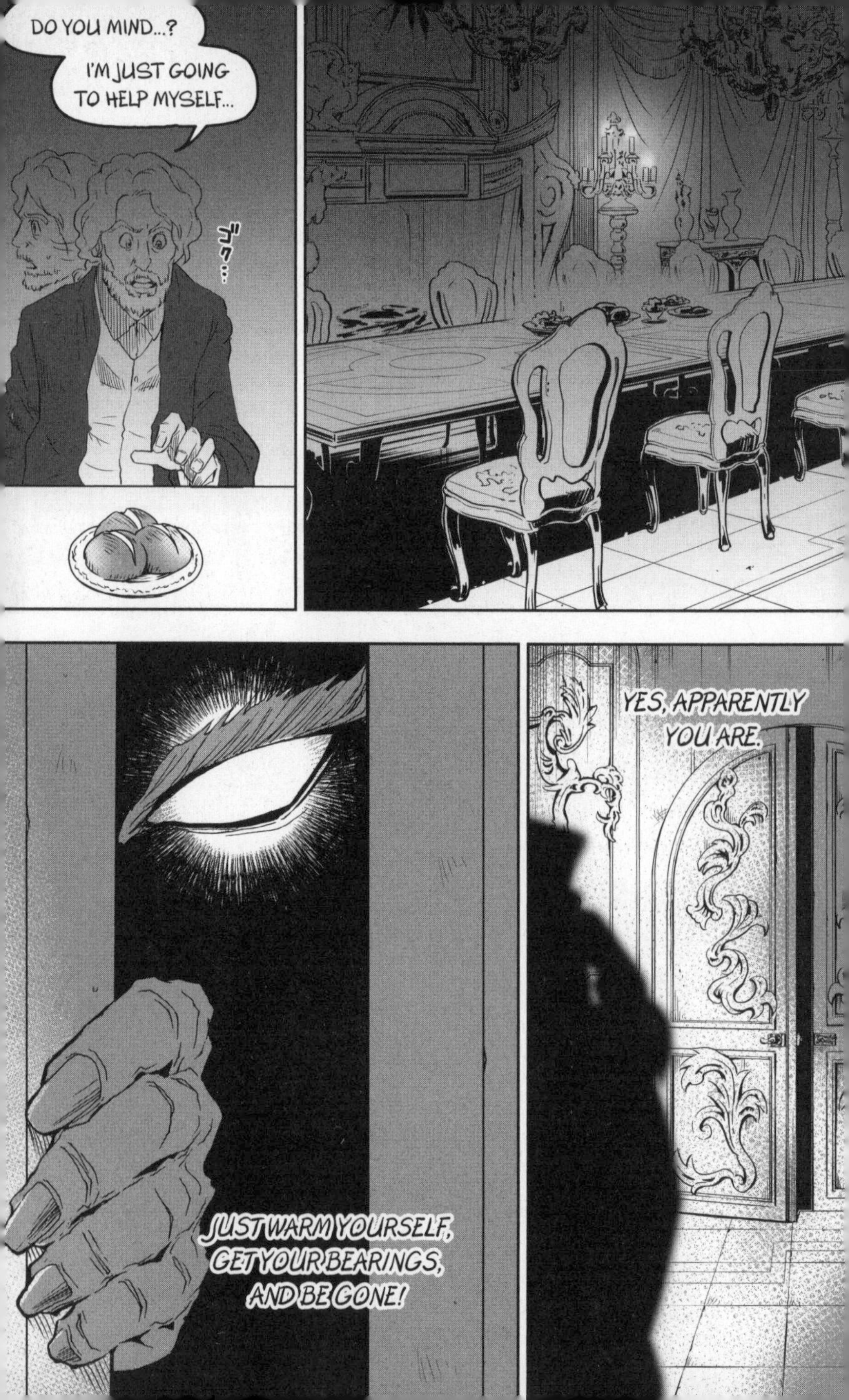
DO YOU MIND...?
I'M JUST GOING TO HELP MYSELF...
ゴク…
YES, APPARENTLY YOU ARE.
JUST WARM YOURSELF, GET YOUR BEARINGS, AND BE GONE!

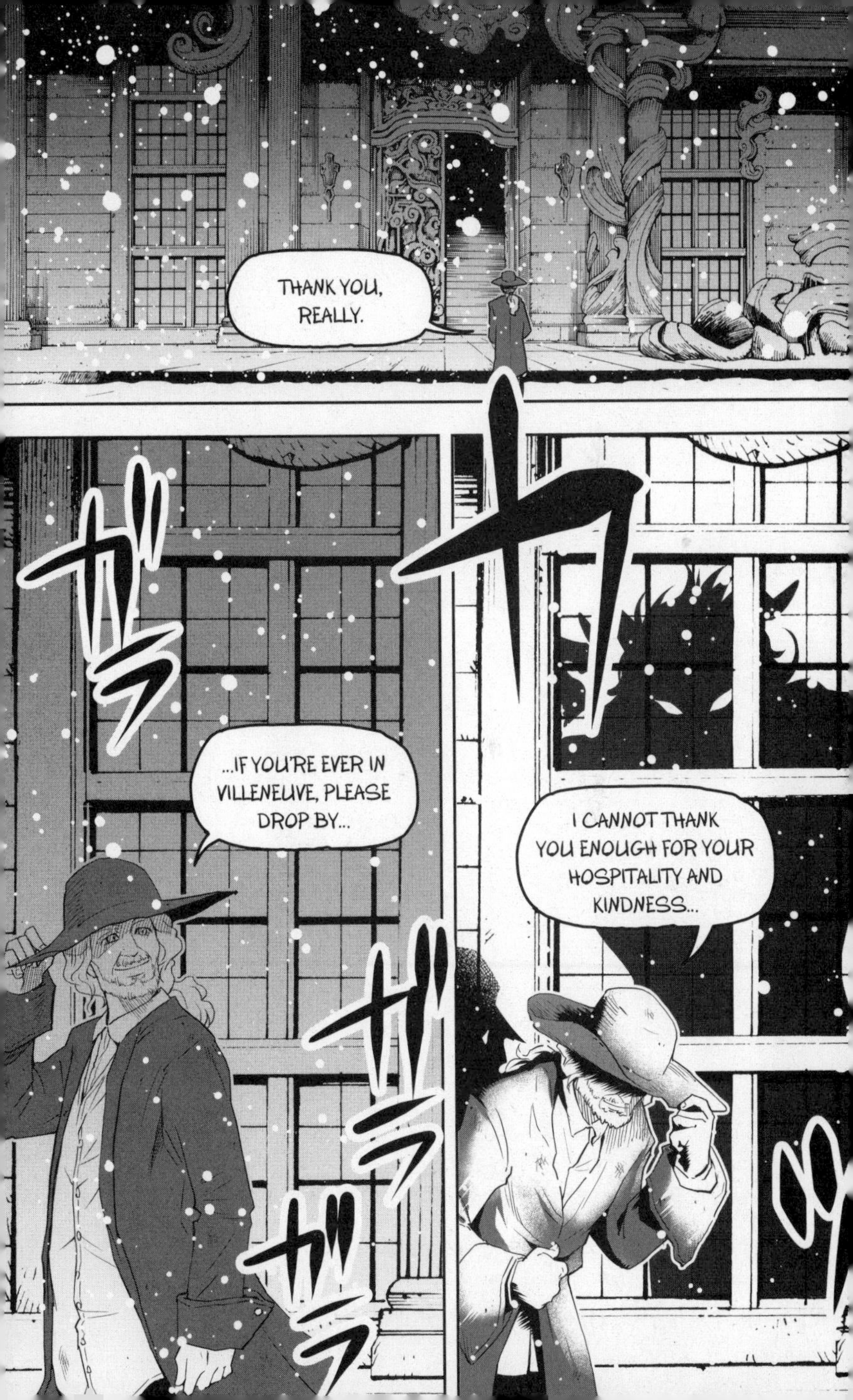
THANK YOU, REALLY.
I CANNOT THANK YOU ENOUGH FOR YOUR HOSPITALITY AND KINDNESS...
...IF YOU'RE EVER IN VILLENEUVE, PLEASE DROP BY...

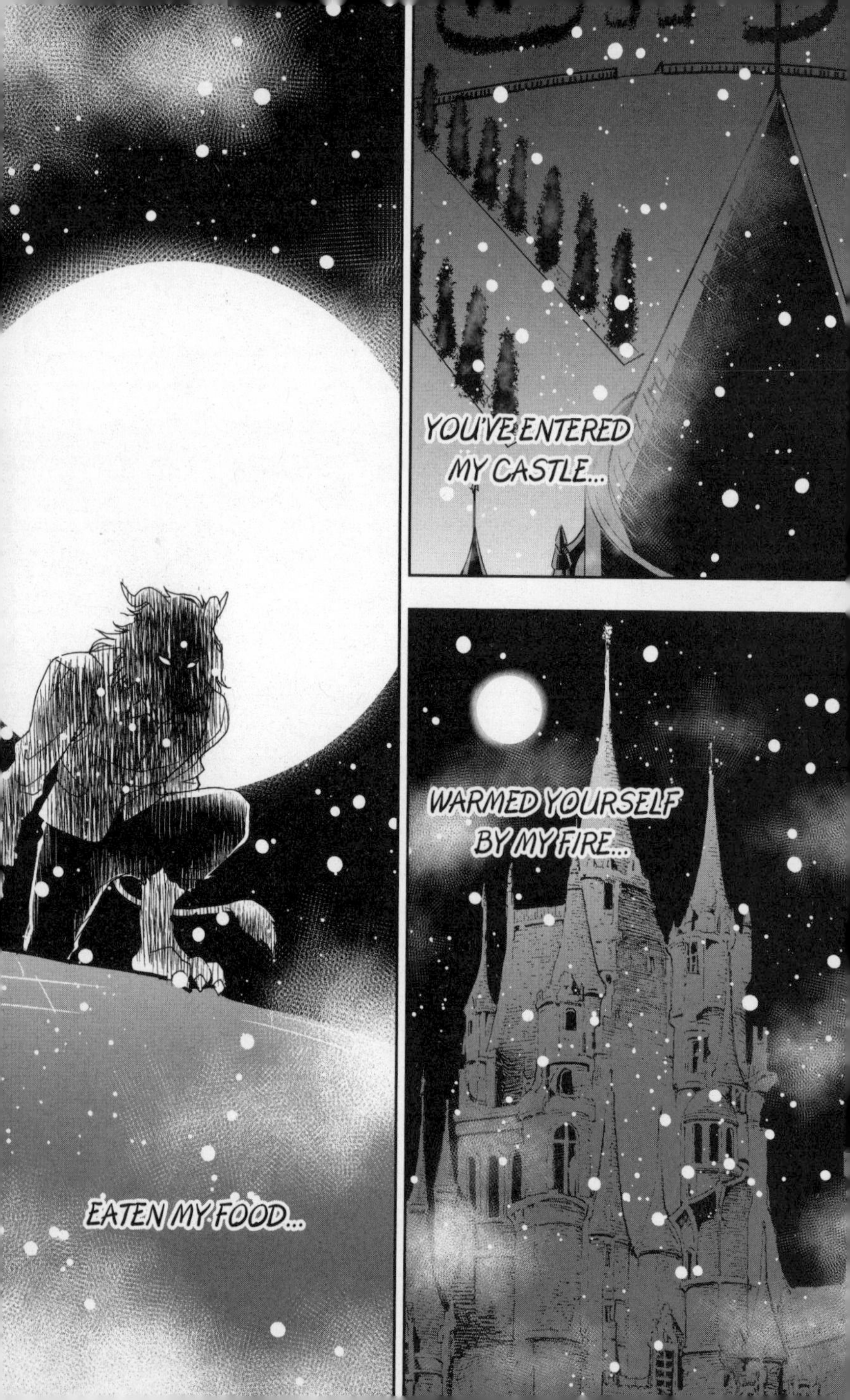
YOU'VE ENTERED MY CASTLE...
WARMED YOURSELF BY MY FIRE...
EATEN MY FOOD...

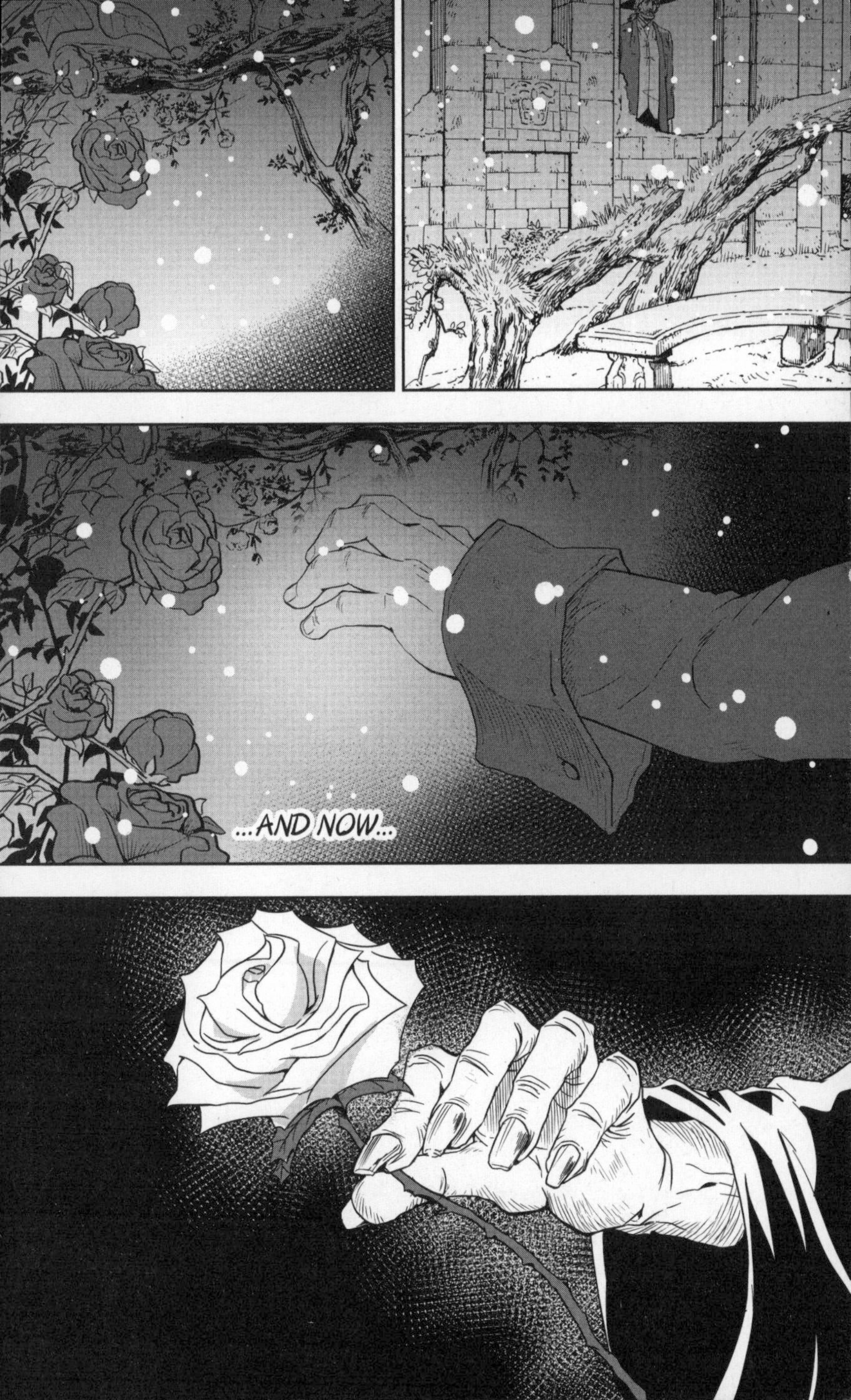
...AND NOW...

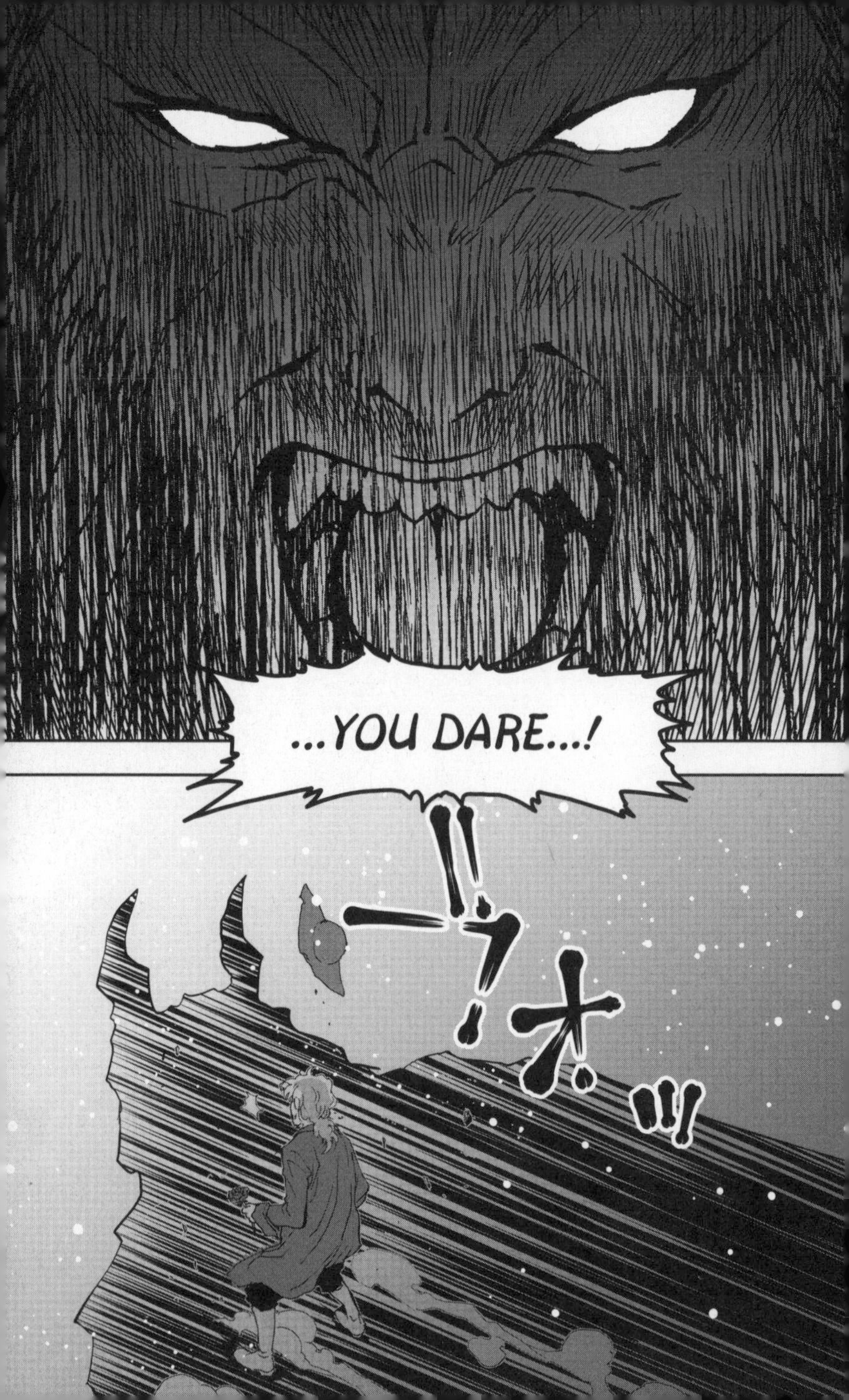
...YOU DARE...!

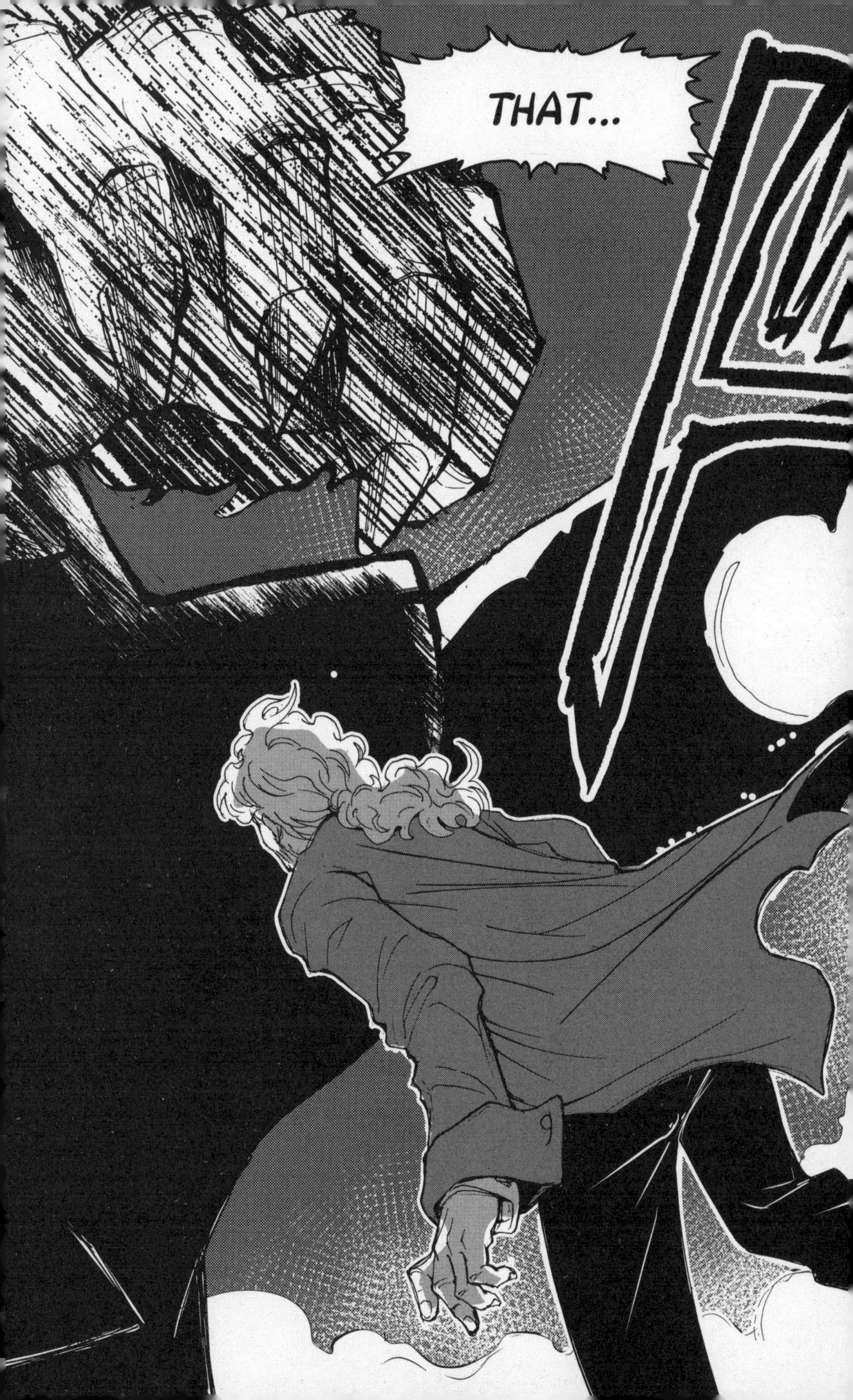
THAT...

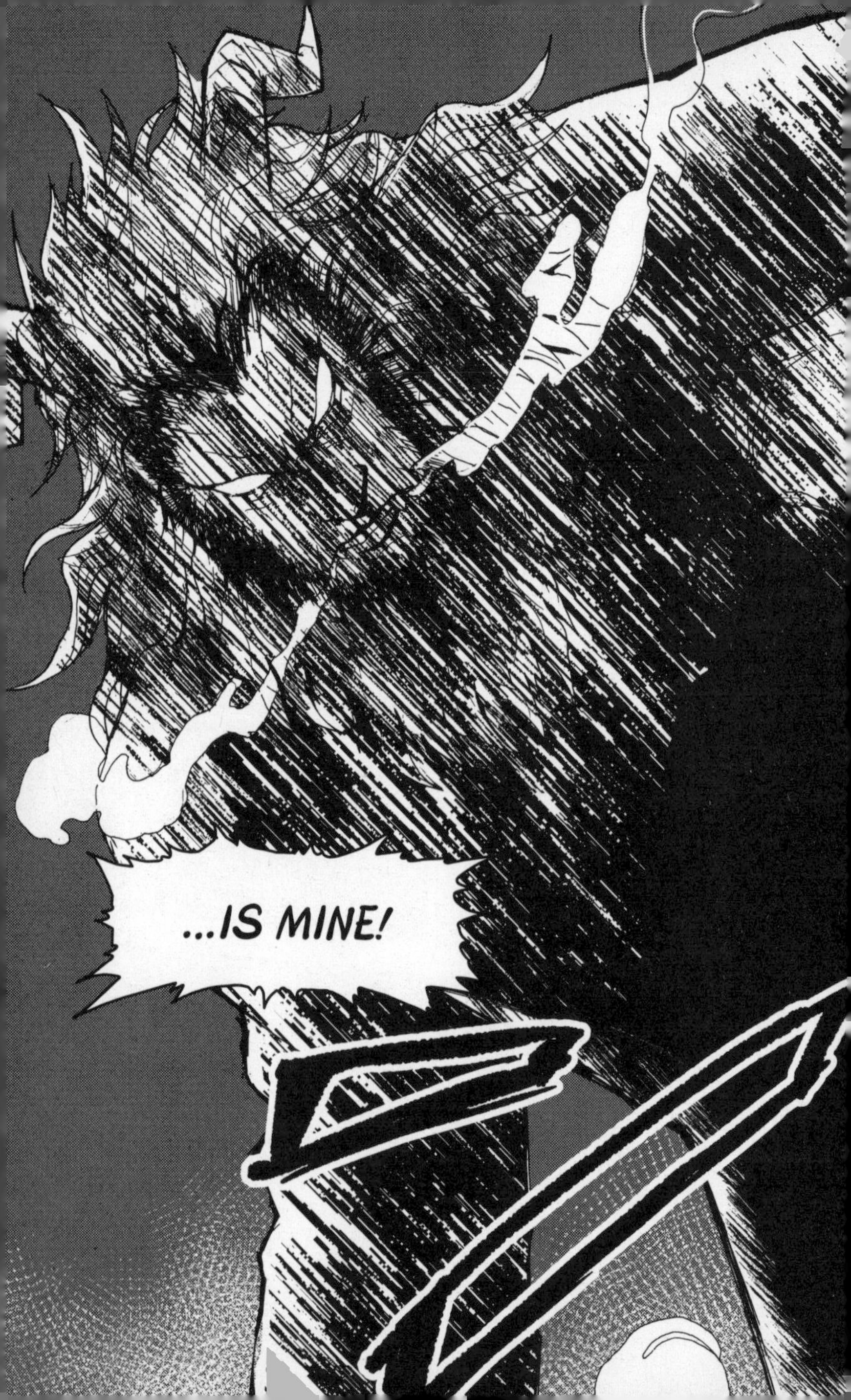
...IS MINE!

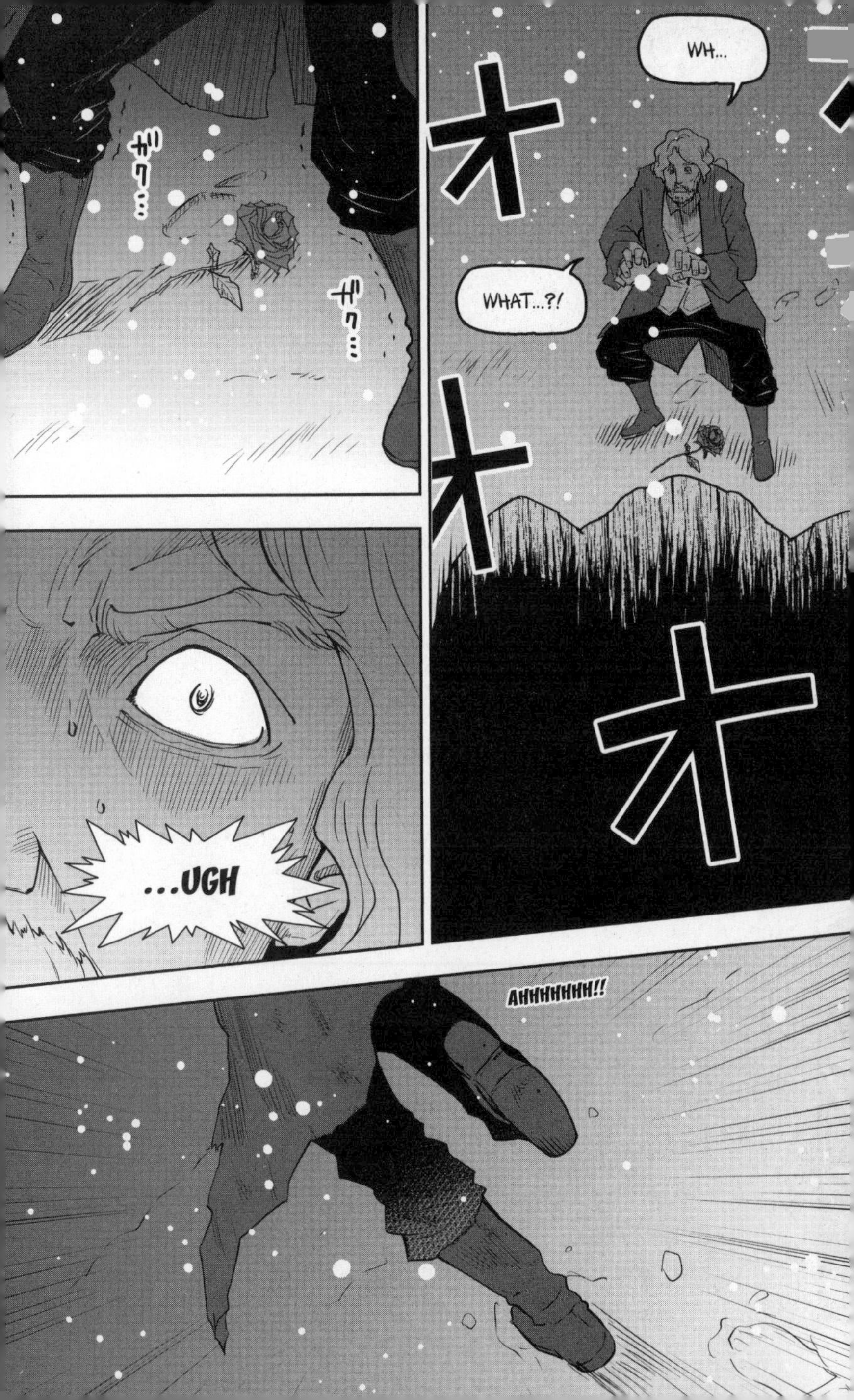
WH...
オ
WHAT...?!
オ
オ
ガク…
ガク…
...UGH
AHHHHHHH!!

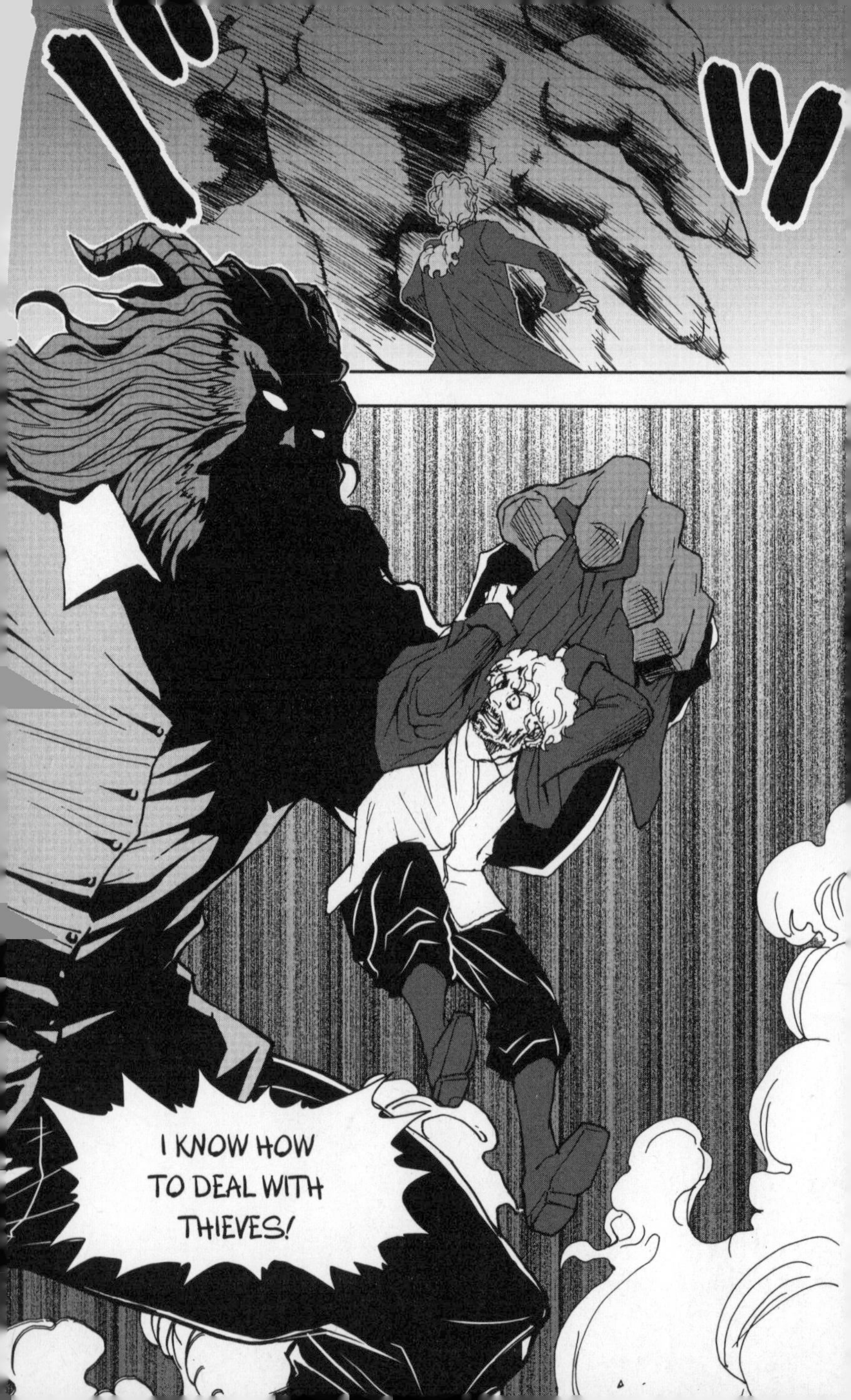
I KNOW HOW TO DEAL WITH THIEVES!

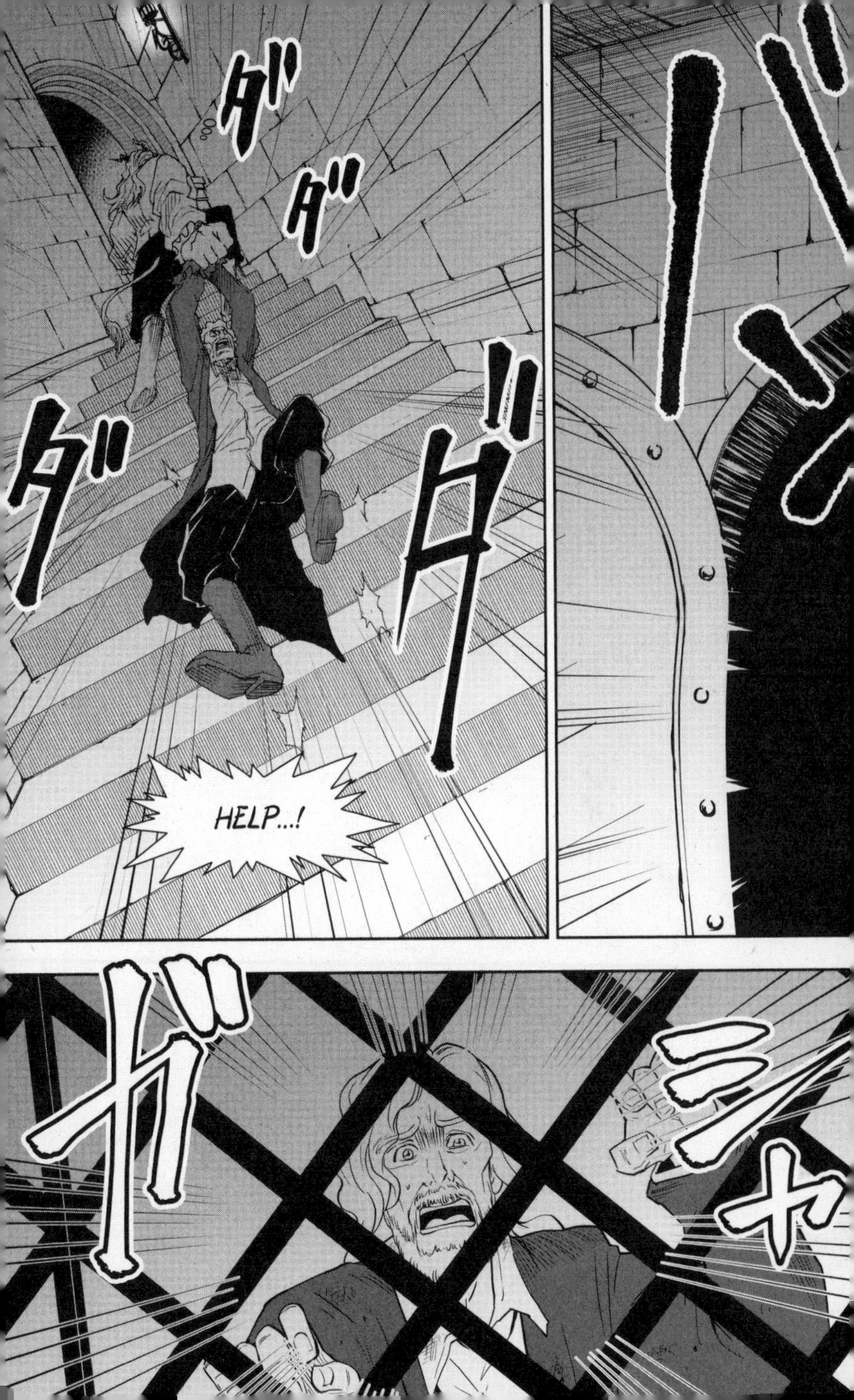
バン
ダダダダ
HELP...!
ガシャ

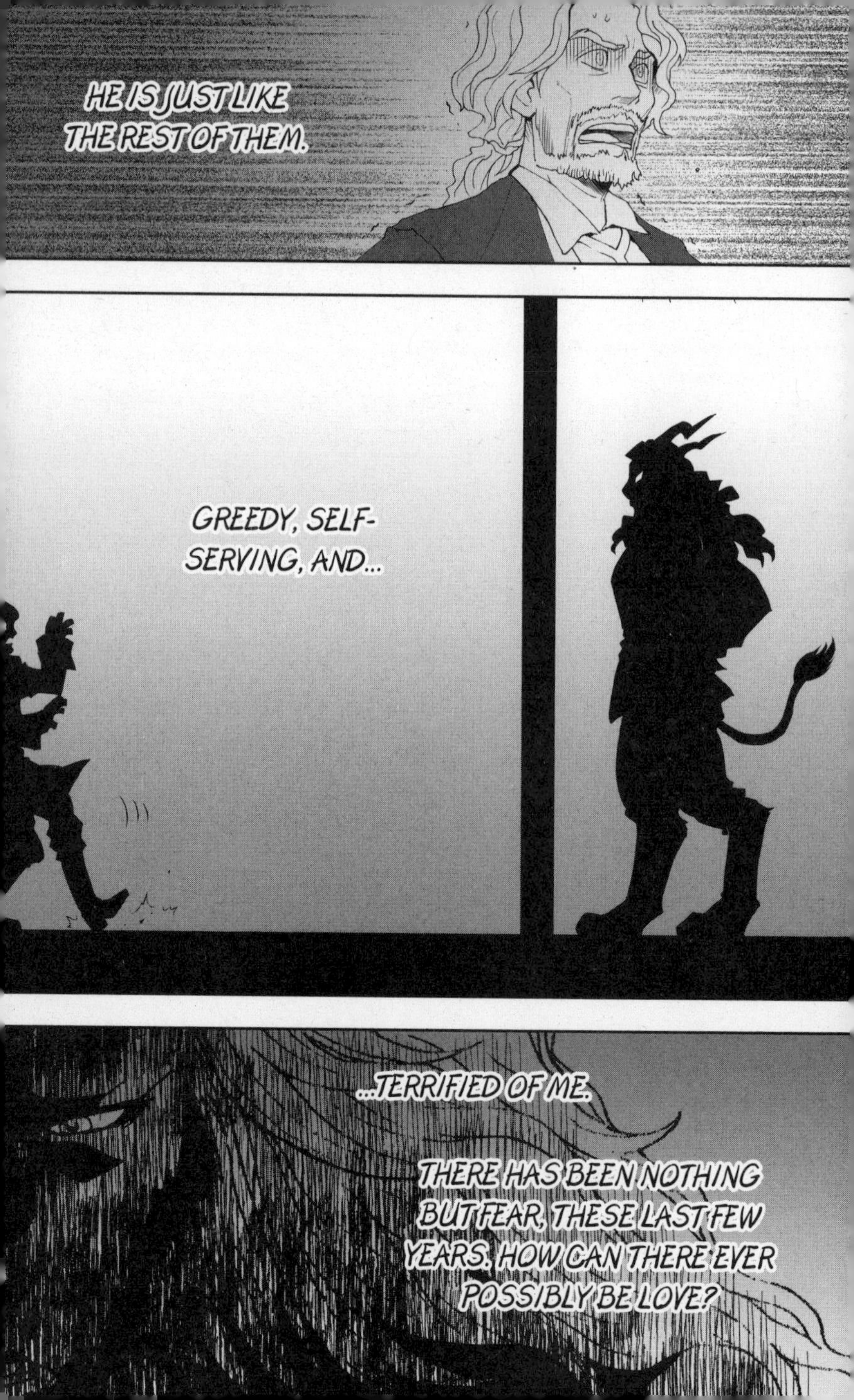
HE IS JUST LIKE THE REST OF THEM.
GREEDY, SELF-SERVING, AND...
...TERRIFIED OF ME.
THERE HAS BEEN NOTHING BUT FEAR, THESE LAST FEW YEARS. HOW CAN THERE EVER POSSIBLY BE LOVE?

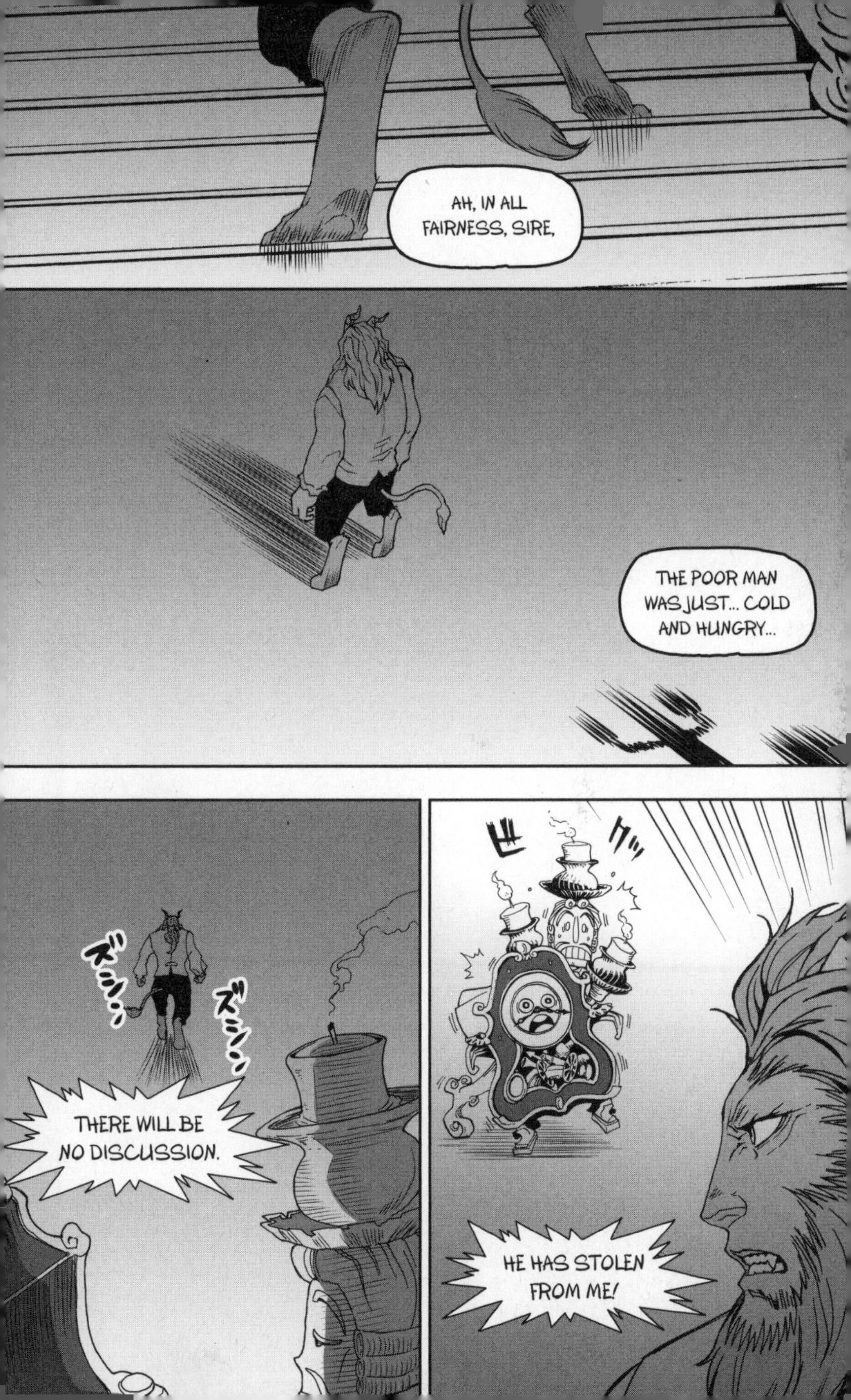
AH, IN ALL FAIRNESS, SIRE,
THE POOR MAN WAS JUST... COLD AND HUNGRY...
ビクッ
HE HAS STOLEN FROM ME!
ズシン、
ズシン、
THERE WILL BE NO DISCUSSION.

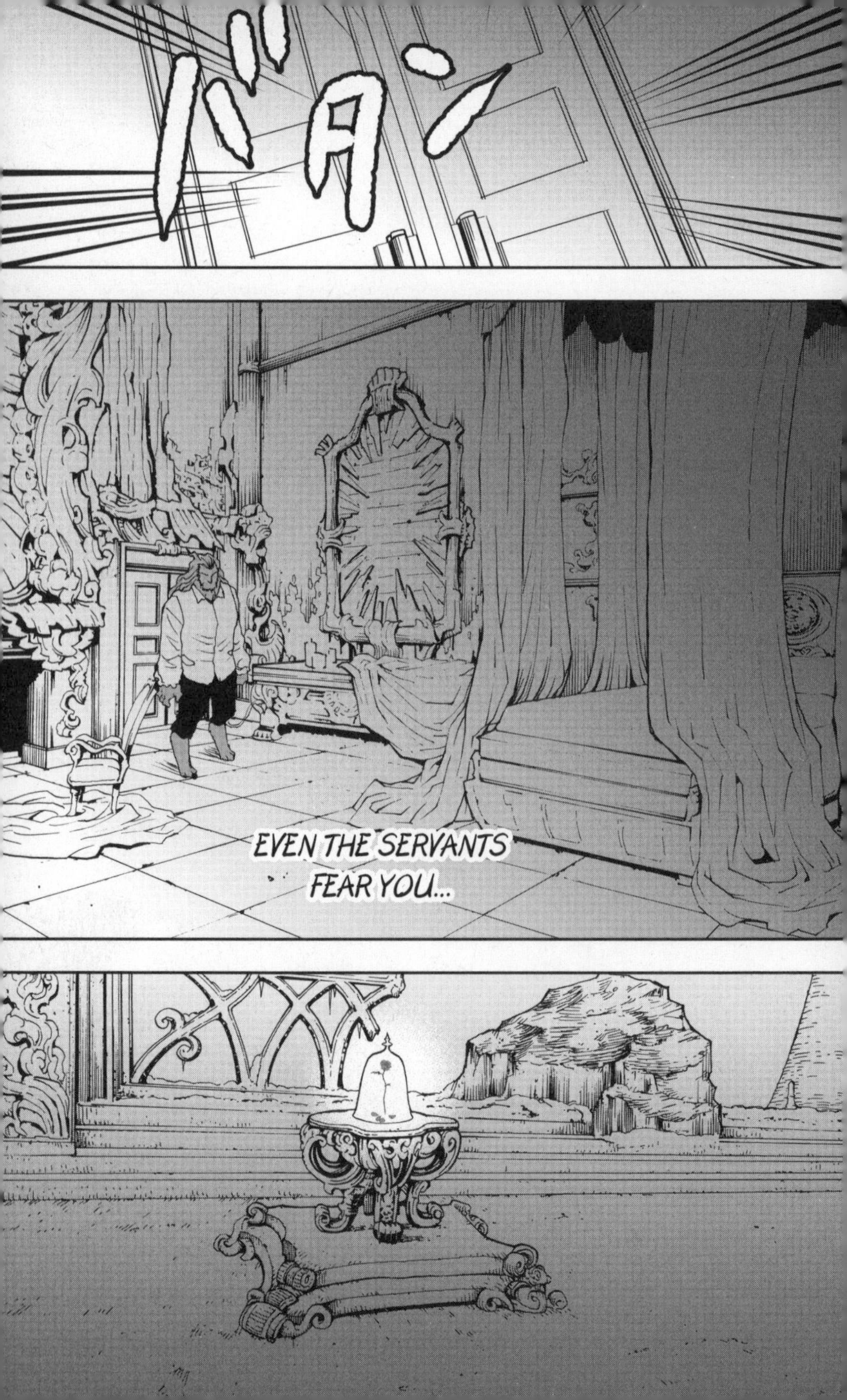
バタン
EVEN THE SERVANTS FEAR YOU...

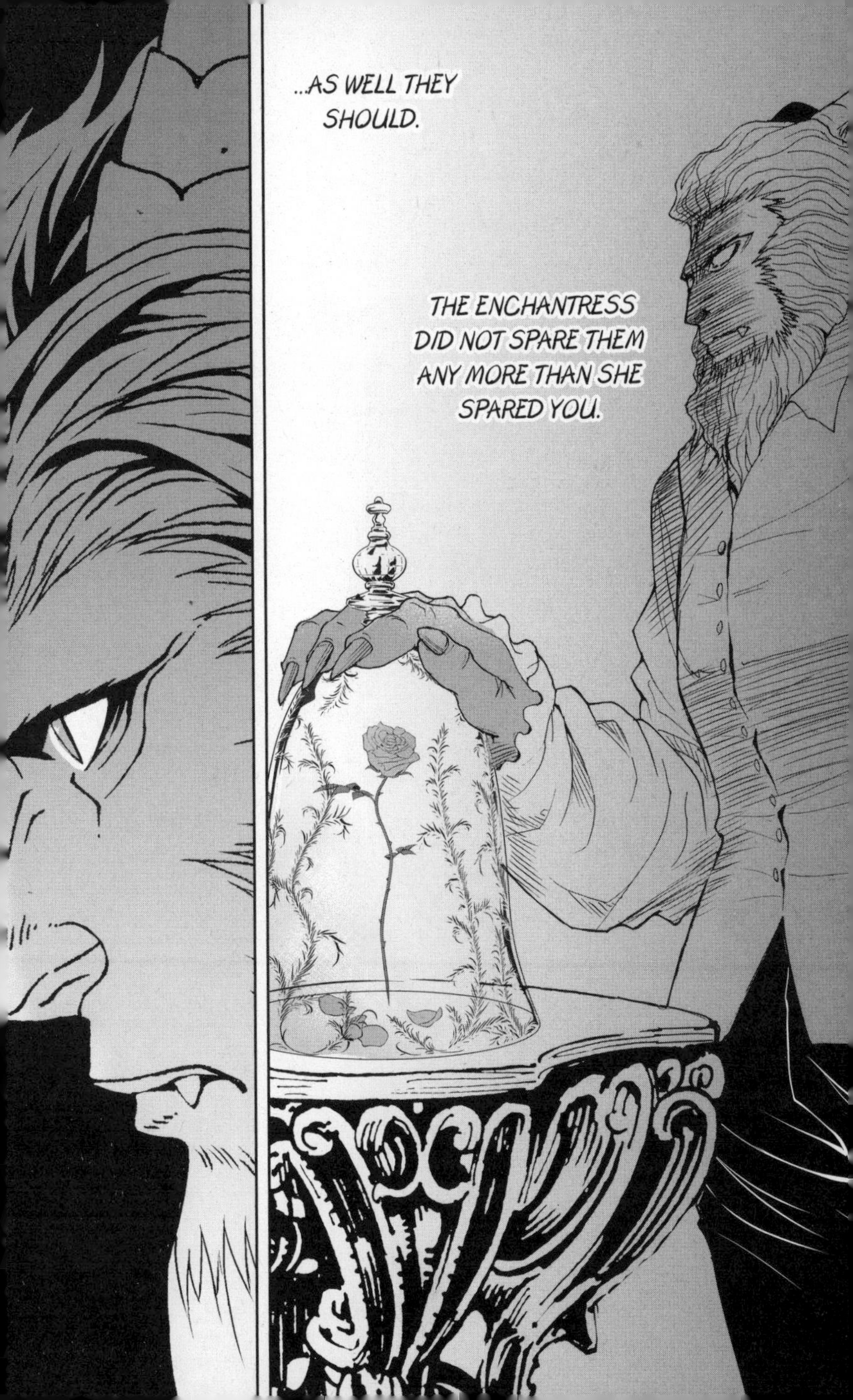
...AS WELL THEY SHOULD.
THE ENCHANTRESS DID NOT SPARE THEM ANY MORE THAN SHE SPARED YOU.

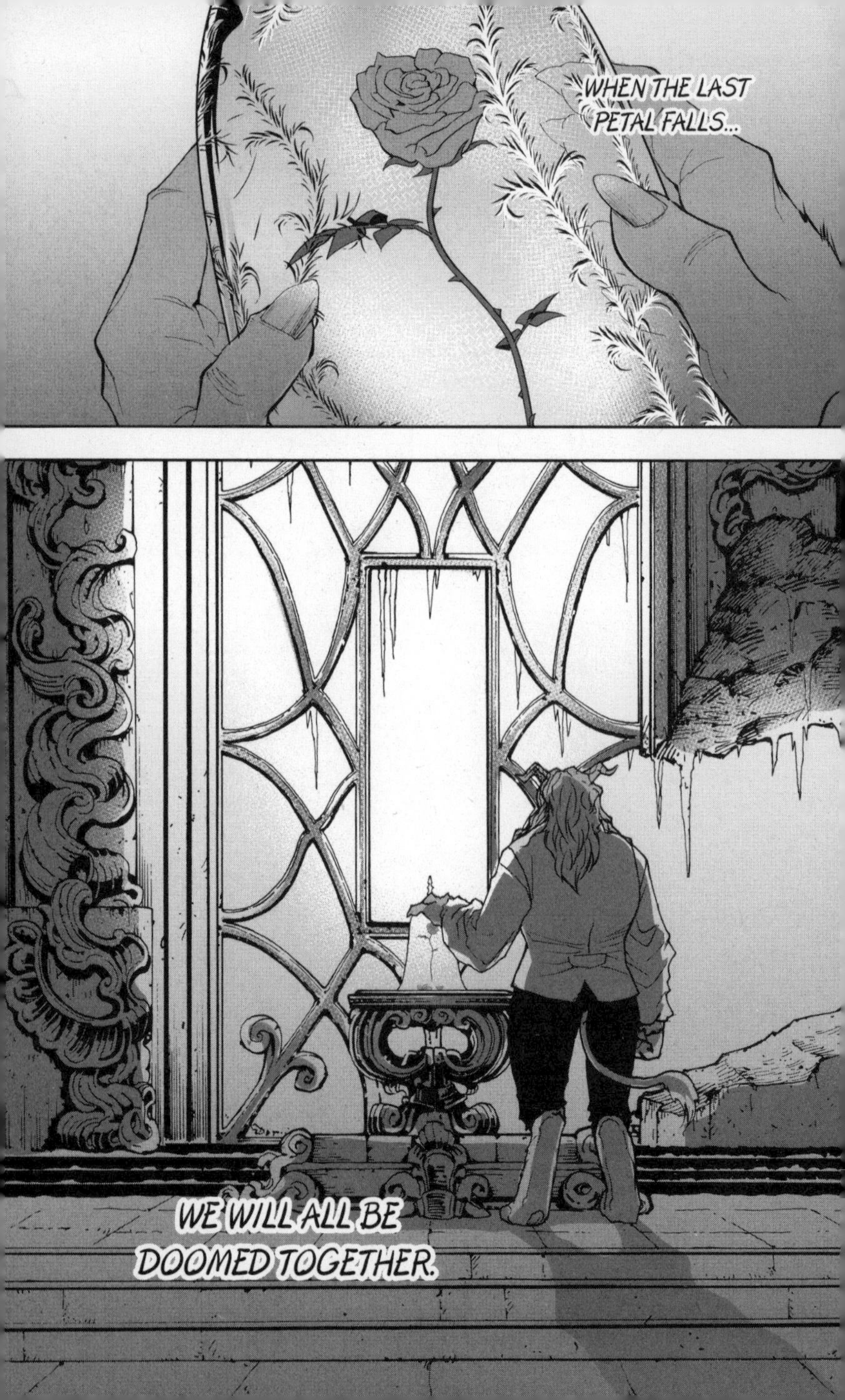
WHEN THE LAST PETAL FALLS...
WE WILL ALL BE DOOMED TOGETHER.

Disney
Beauty and the Beast

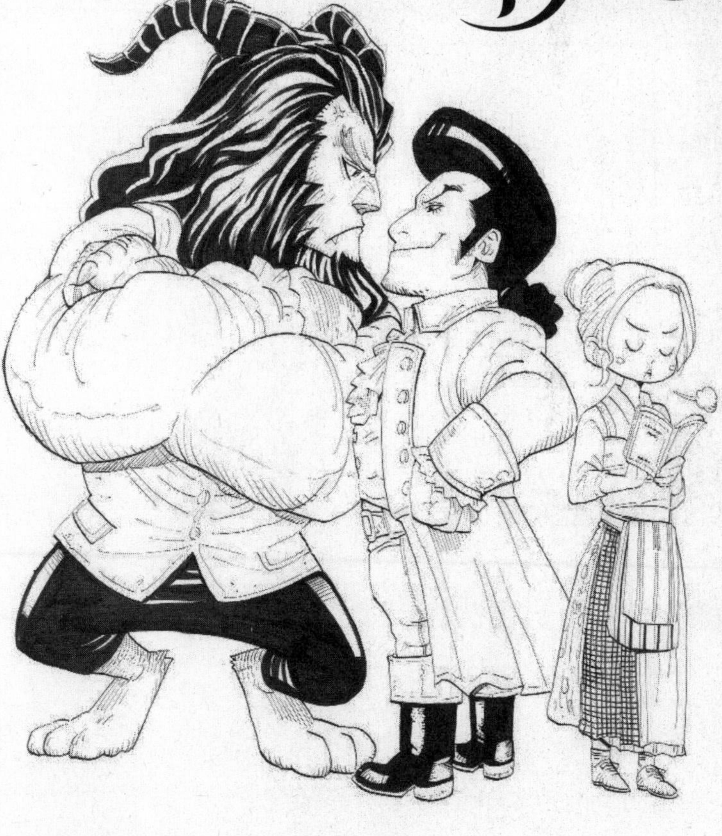

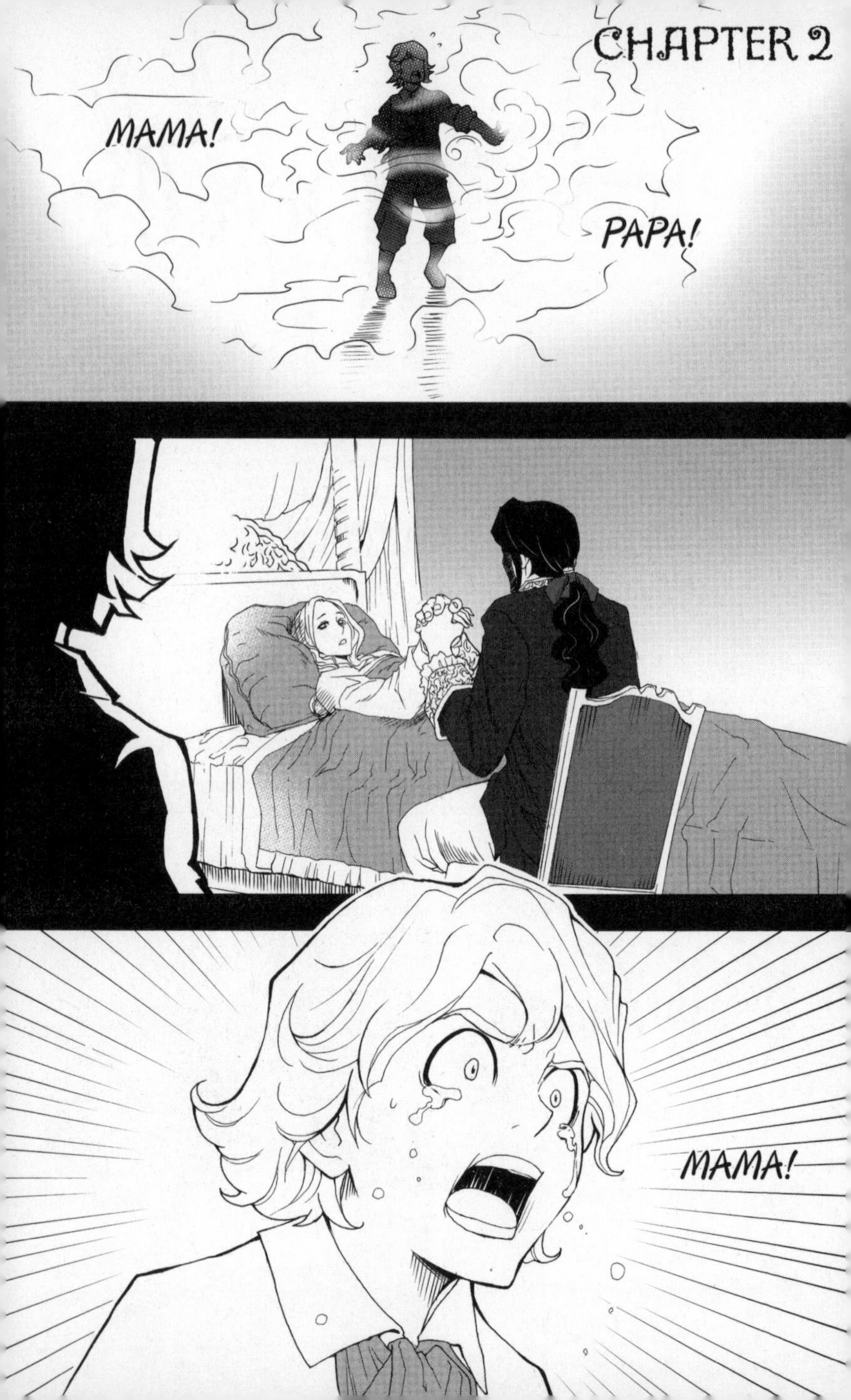
CHAPTER 2
MAMA!
PAPA!
MAMA!

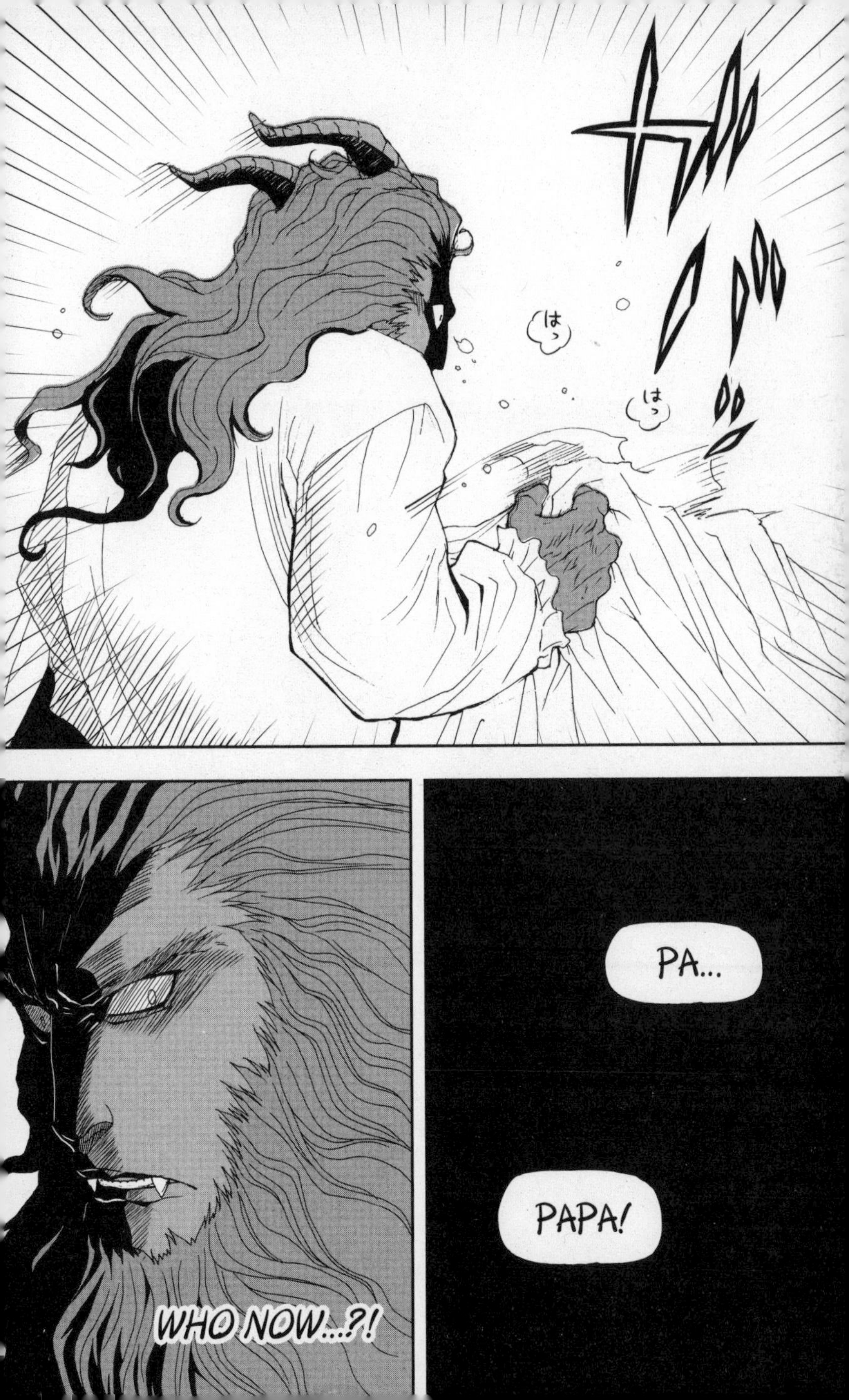
はっ
はっ
PA...
PAPA!
WHO NOW...?!

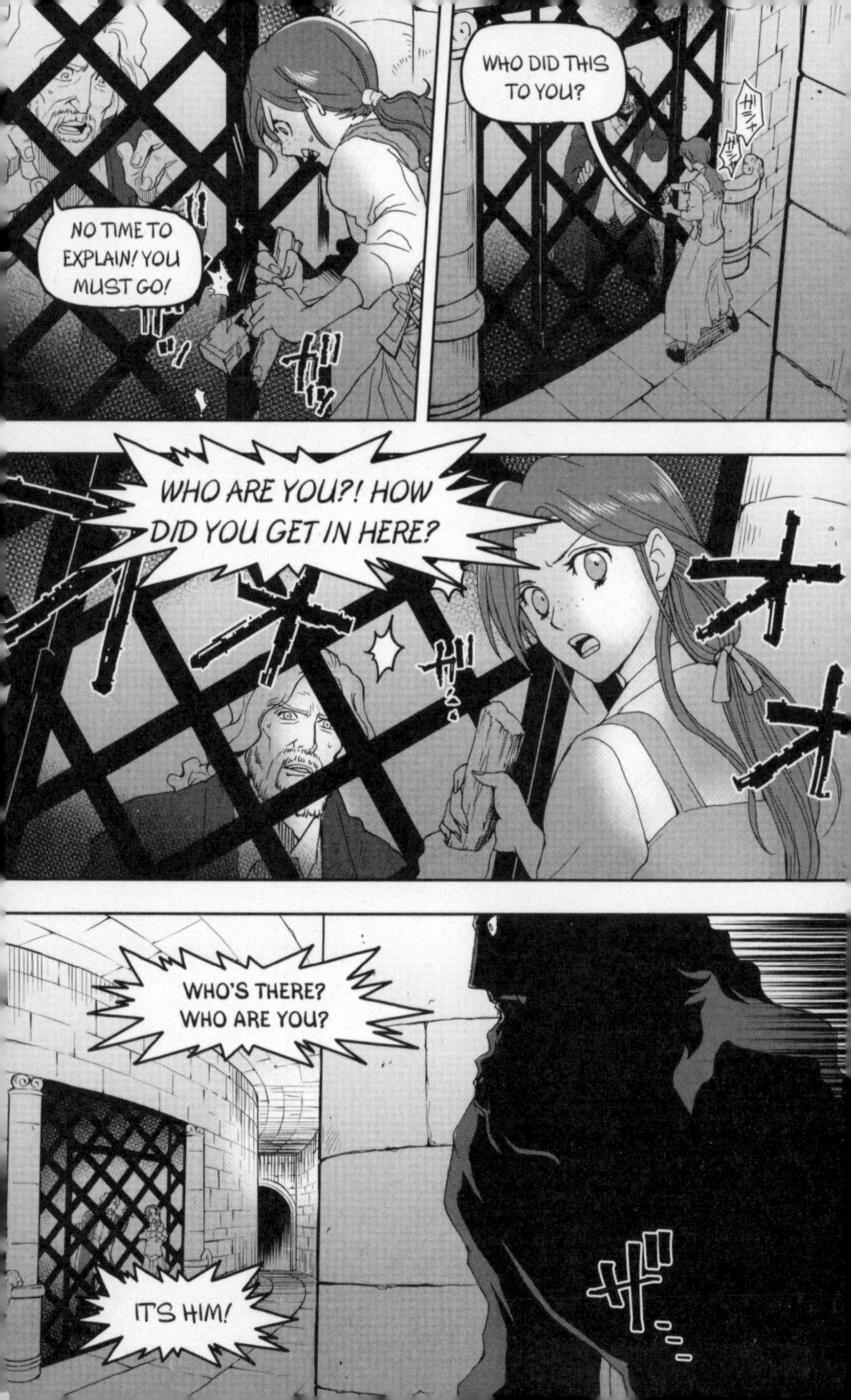
WHO DID THIS TO YOU?
NO TIME TO EXPLAIN! YOU MUST GO!
WHO ARE YOU?! HOW DID YOU GET IN HERE?
WHO'S THERE? WHO ARE YOU?
IT'S HIM!

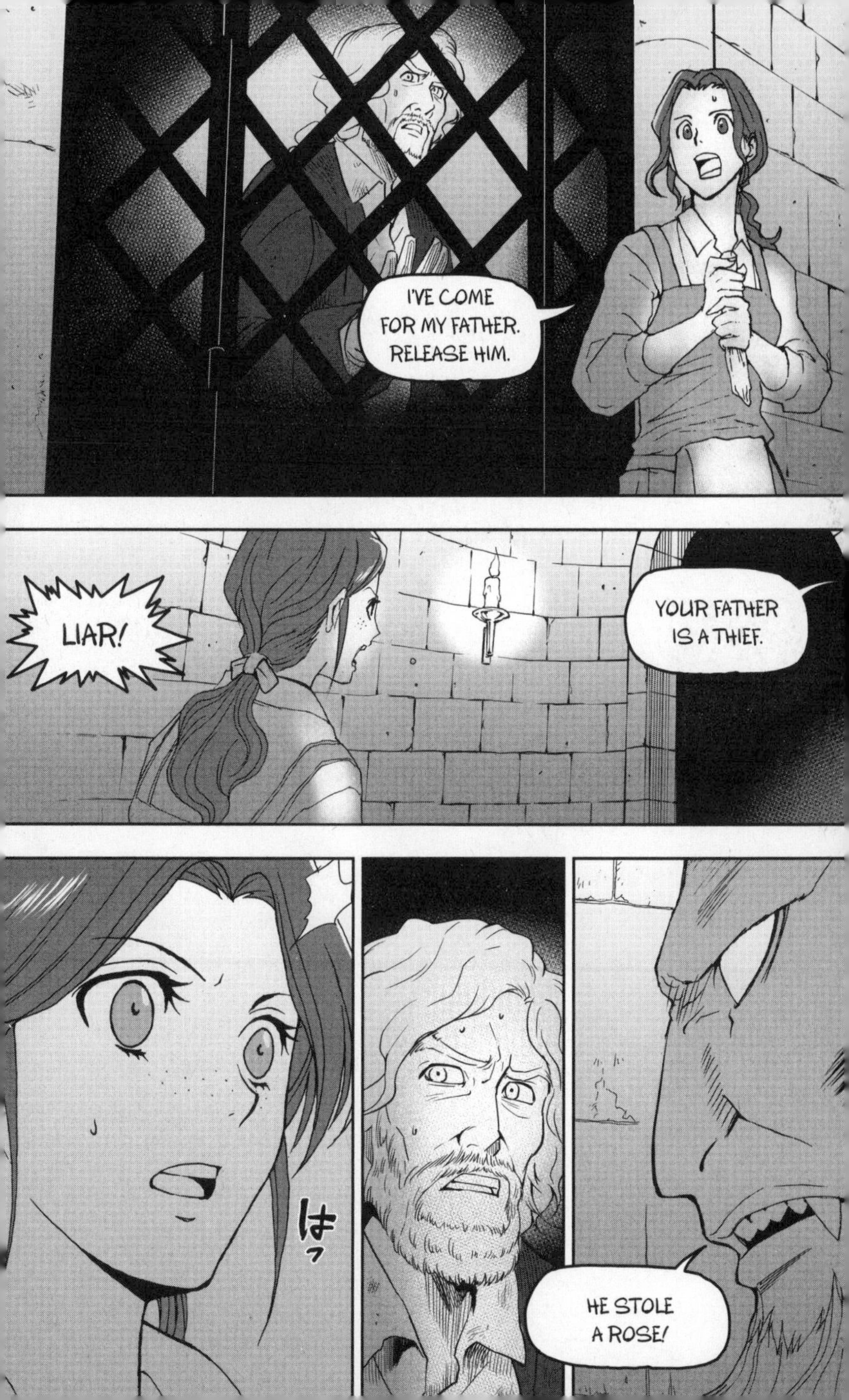
I'VE COME FOR MY FATHER. RELEASE HIM.
YOUR FATHER IS A THIEF.
LIAR!
HE STOLE A ROSE!
はっ

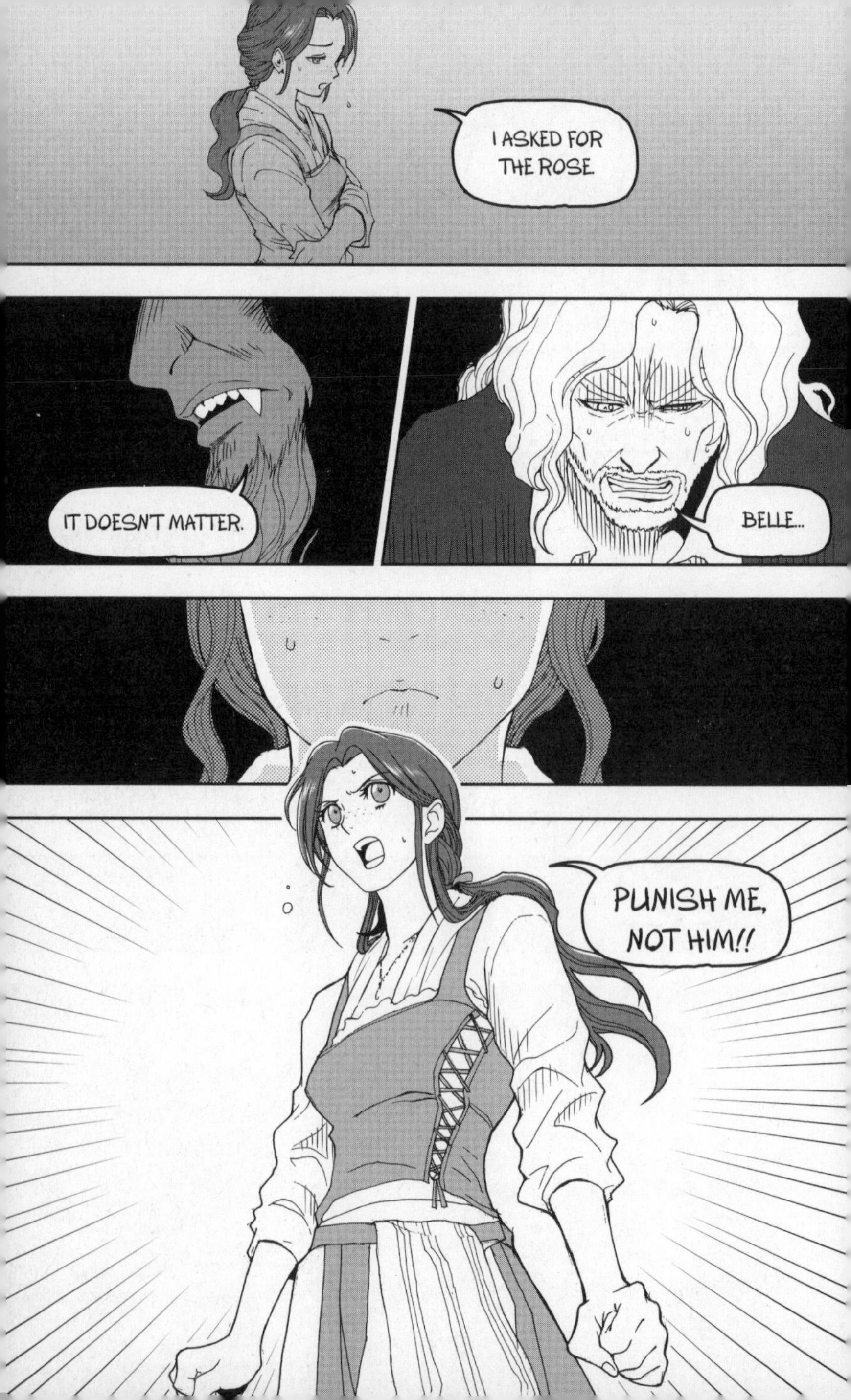
I ASKED FOR THE ROSE.
BELLE...
IT DOESN'T MATTER.
PUNISH ME, NOT HIM!!

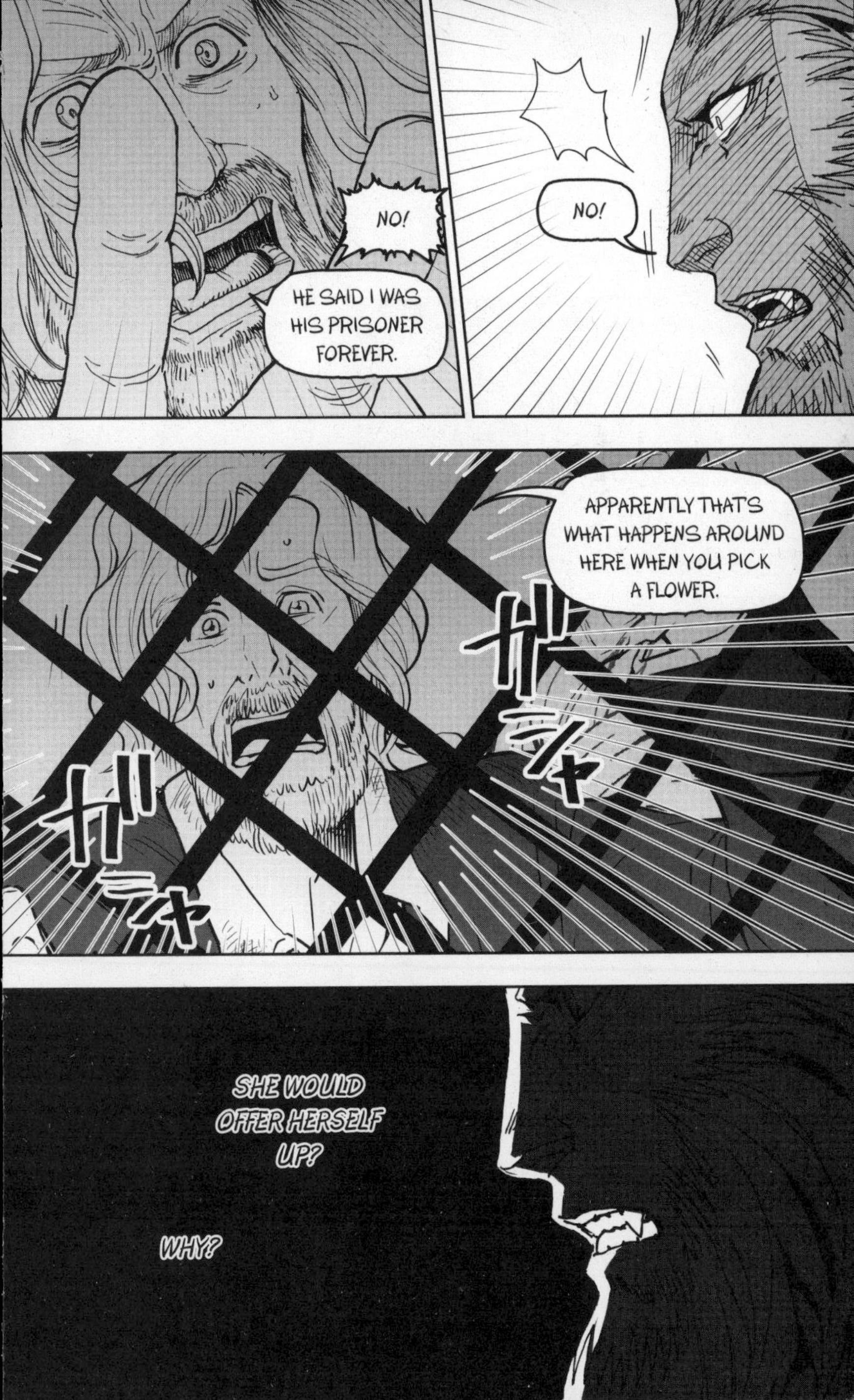
NO!
NO!
HE SAID I WAS HIS PRISONER FOREVER.
APPARENTLY THAT'S WHAT HAPPENS AROUND HERE WHEN YOU PICK A FLOWER.
ガシャ
ガシャ
SHE WOULD OFFER HERSELF UP?
WHY?

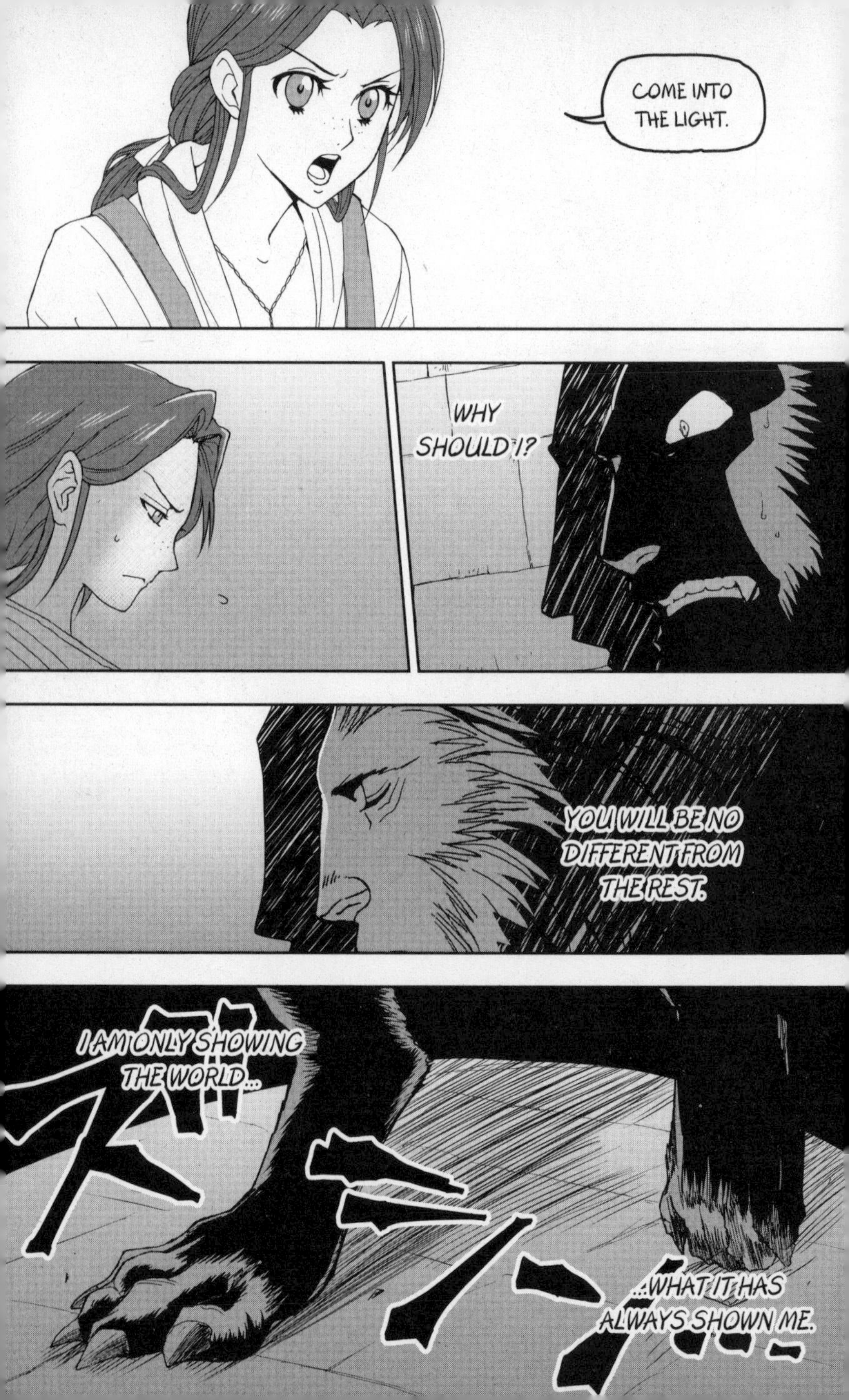
COME INTO THE LIGHT.
WHY SHOULD I?
YOU WILL BE NO DIFFERENT FROM THE REST.
I AM ONLY SHOWING THE WORLD...
...WHAT IT HAS ALWAYS SHOWN ME.

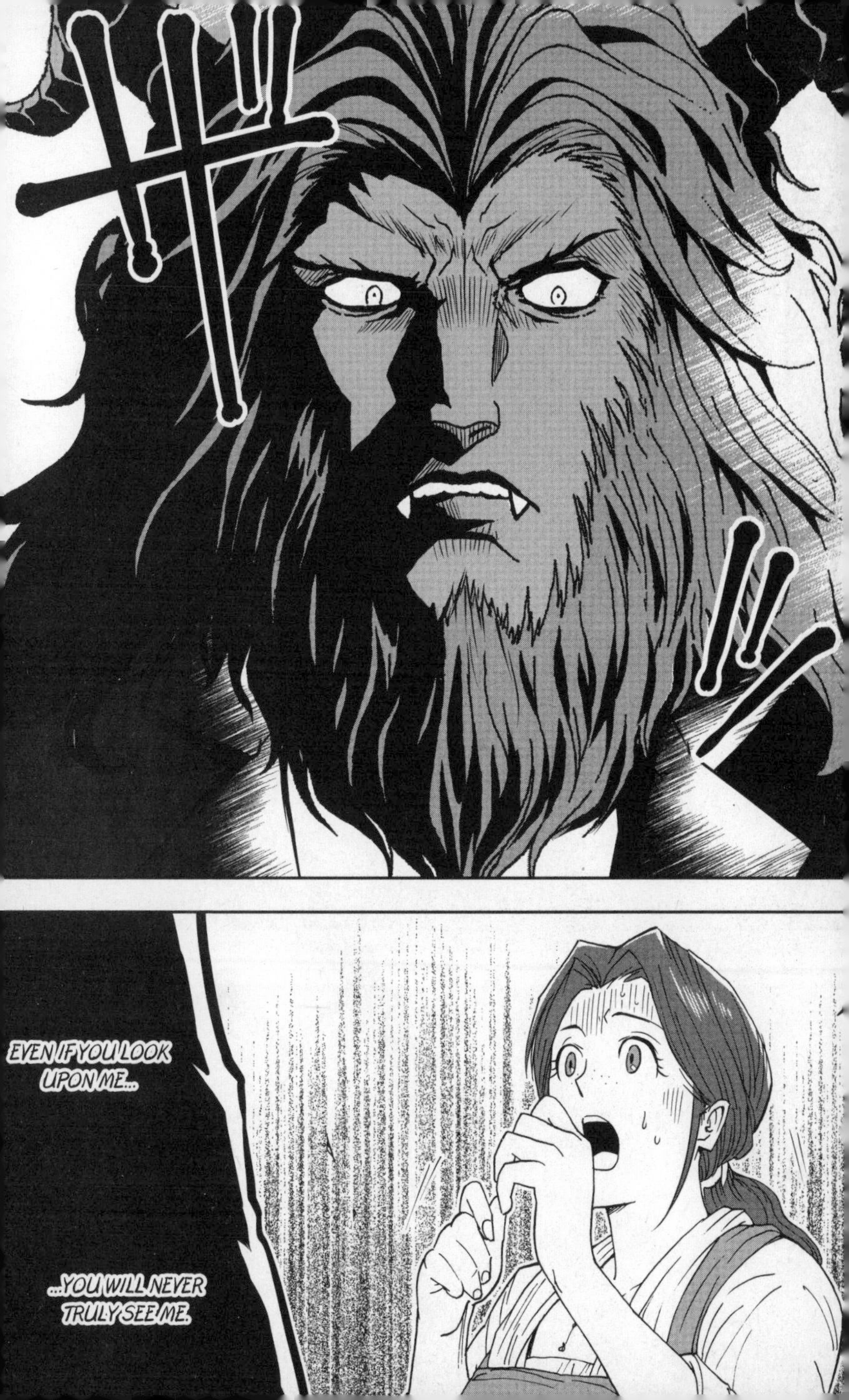
EVEN IF YOU LOOK UPON ME...
...YOU WILL NEVER TRULY SEE ME.

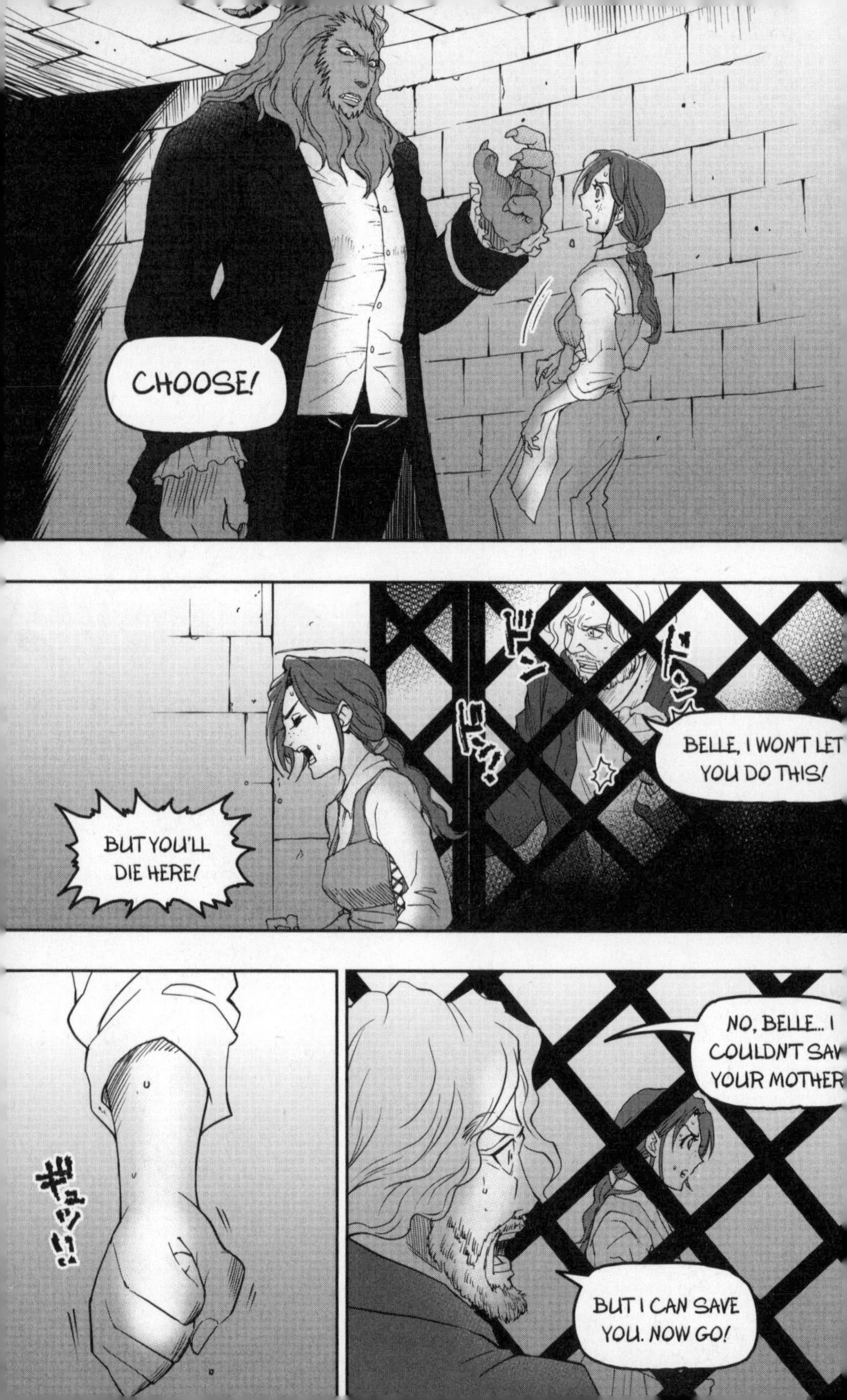

CHOOSE!
BELLE, I WON'T LET YOU DO THIS!
BUT YOU'LL DIE HERE!
NO, BELLE... I COULDN'T SAV YOUR MOTHER
BUT I CAN SAVE YOU. NOW GO!
ギュッ!!

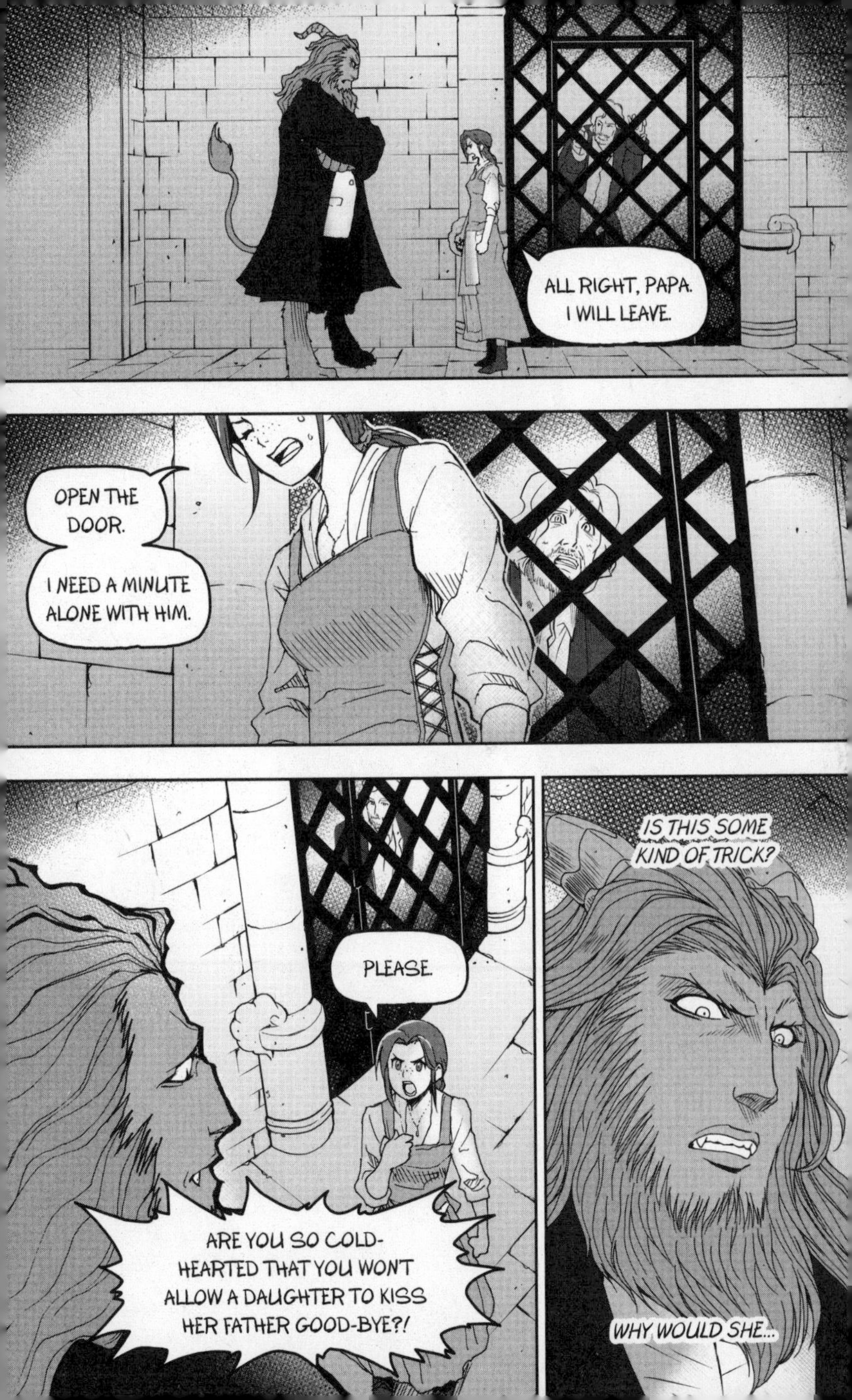
ALL RIGHT, PAPA. I WILL LEAVE.
OPEN THE DOOR.
I NEED A MINUTE ALONE WITH HIM.
IS THIS SOME KIND OF TRICK?
WHY WOULD SHE...
PLEASE.
ARE YOU SO COLD-HEARTED THAT YOU WON'T ALLOW A DAUGHTER TO KISS HER FATHER GOOD-BYE?!

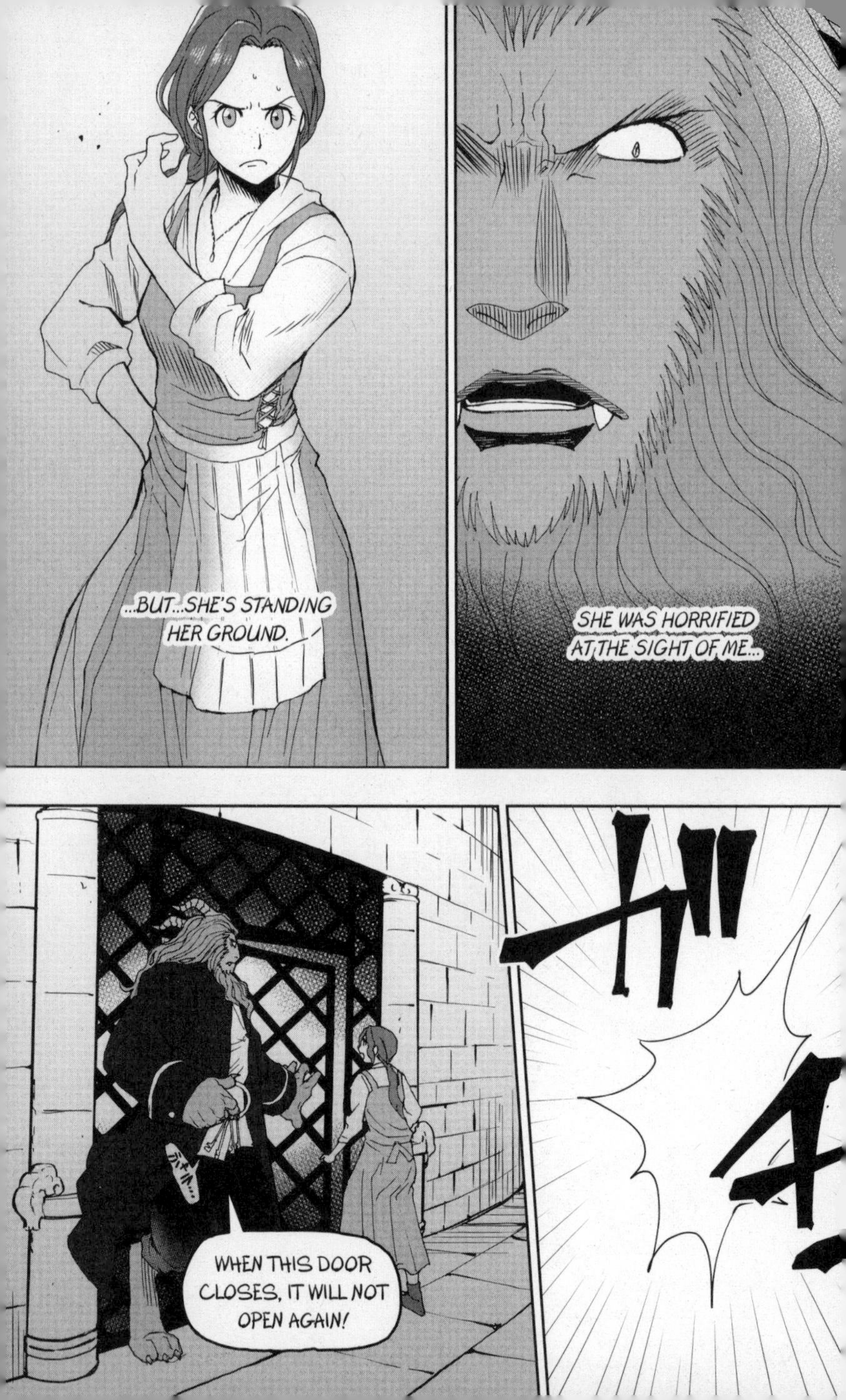
SHE WAS HORRIFIED AT THE SIGHT OF ME...
...BUT...SHE'S STANDING HER GROUND.
WHEN THIS DOOR CLOSES, IT WILL NOT OPEN AGAIN!

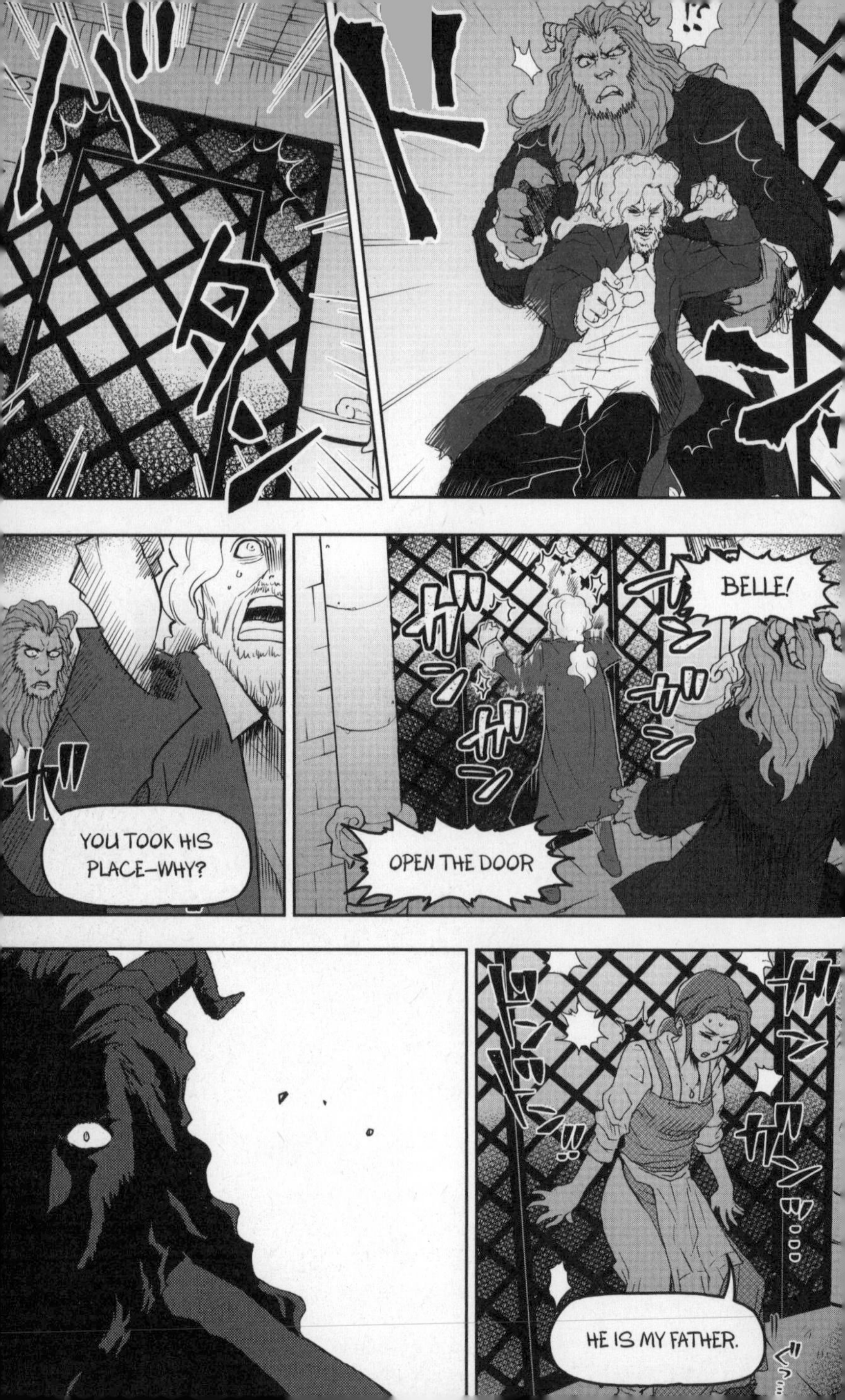
!?
BELLE!
OPEN THE DOOR
YOU TOOK HIS PLACE—WHY?
HE IS MY FATHER.

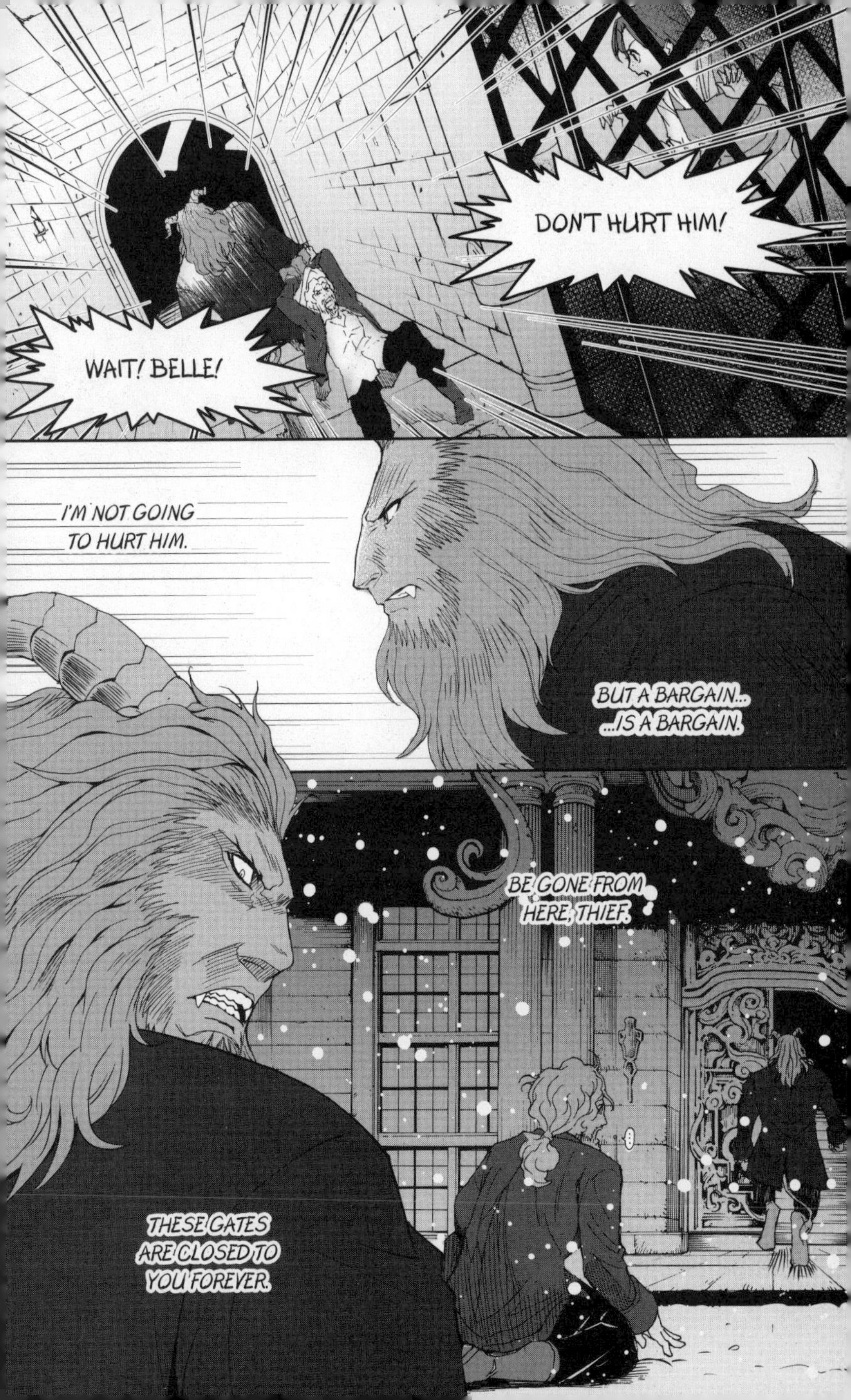
DON'T HURT HIM!
WAIT! BELLE!
I'M NOT GOING TO HURT HIM.
BUT A BARGAIN... ...IS A BARGAIN.
BE GONE FROM HERE, THIEF.
...
THESE GATES ARE CLOSED TO YOU FOREVER.

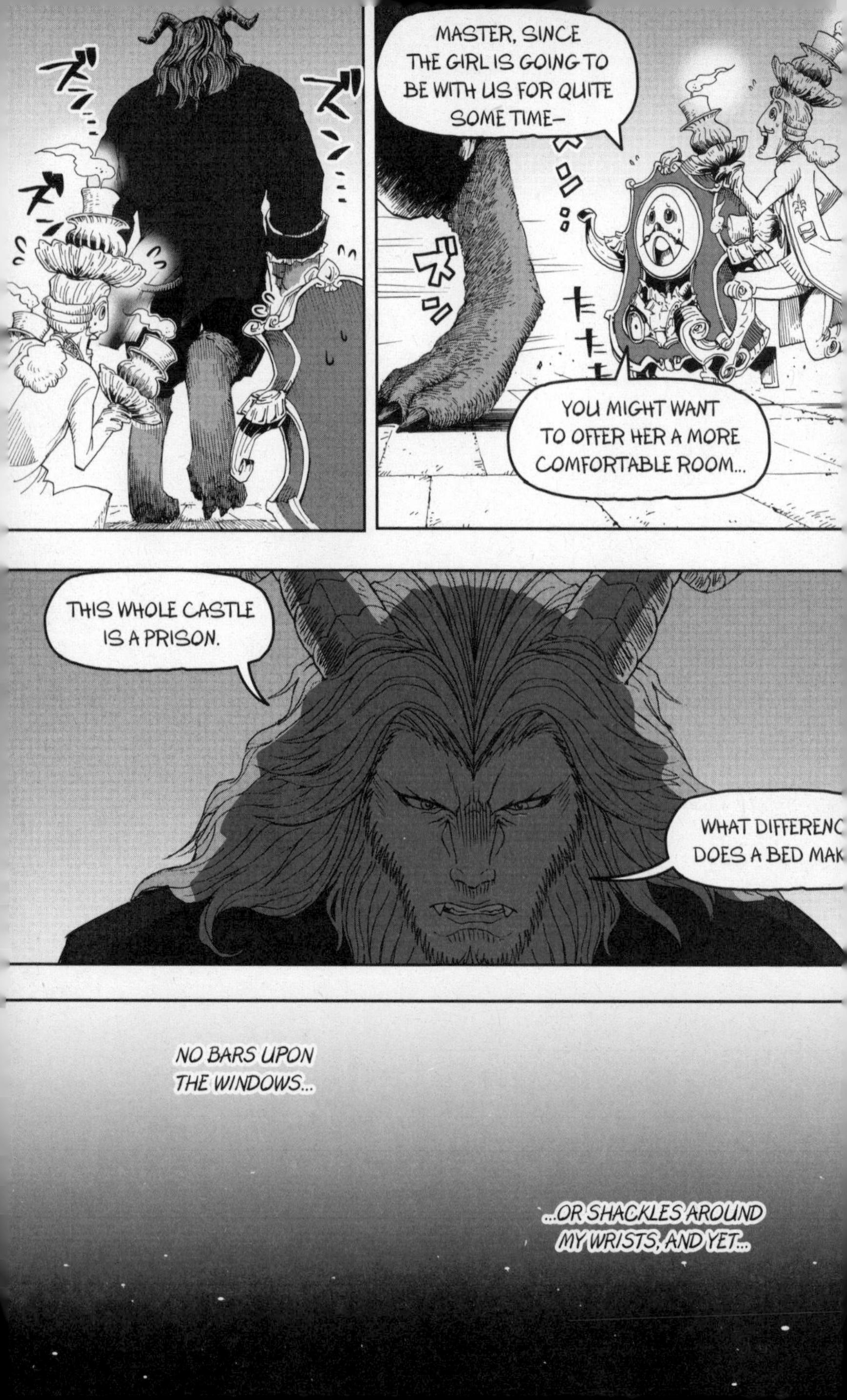
MASTER, SINCE THE GIRL IS GOING TO BE WITH US FOR QUITE SOME TIME–
YOU MIGHT WANT TO OFFER HER A MORE COMFORTABLE ROOM...
ズン
ズン
ズン
WHAT DIFFERENC DOES A BED MAK
THIS WHOLE CASTLE IS A PRISON.
NO BARS UPON THE WINDOWS...
...OR SHACKLES AROUND MY WRISTS, AND YET...

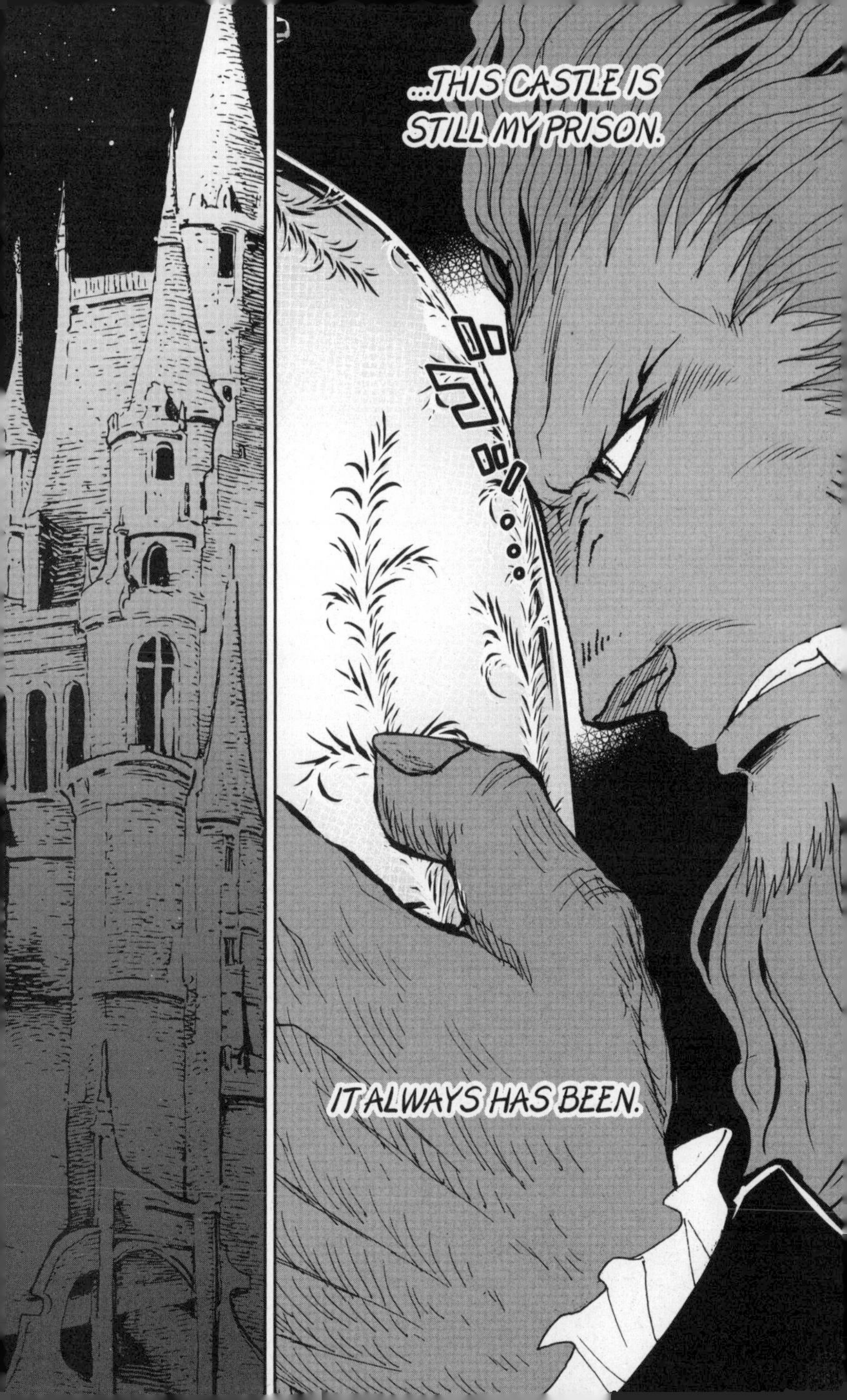
...THIS CASTLE IS STILL MY PRISON.
IT ALWAYS HAS BEEN.

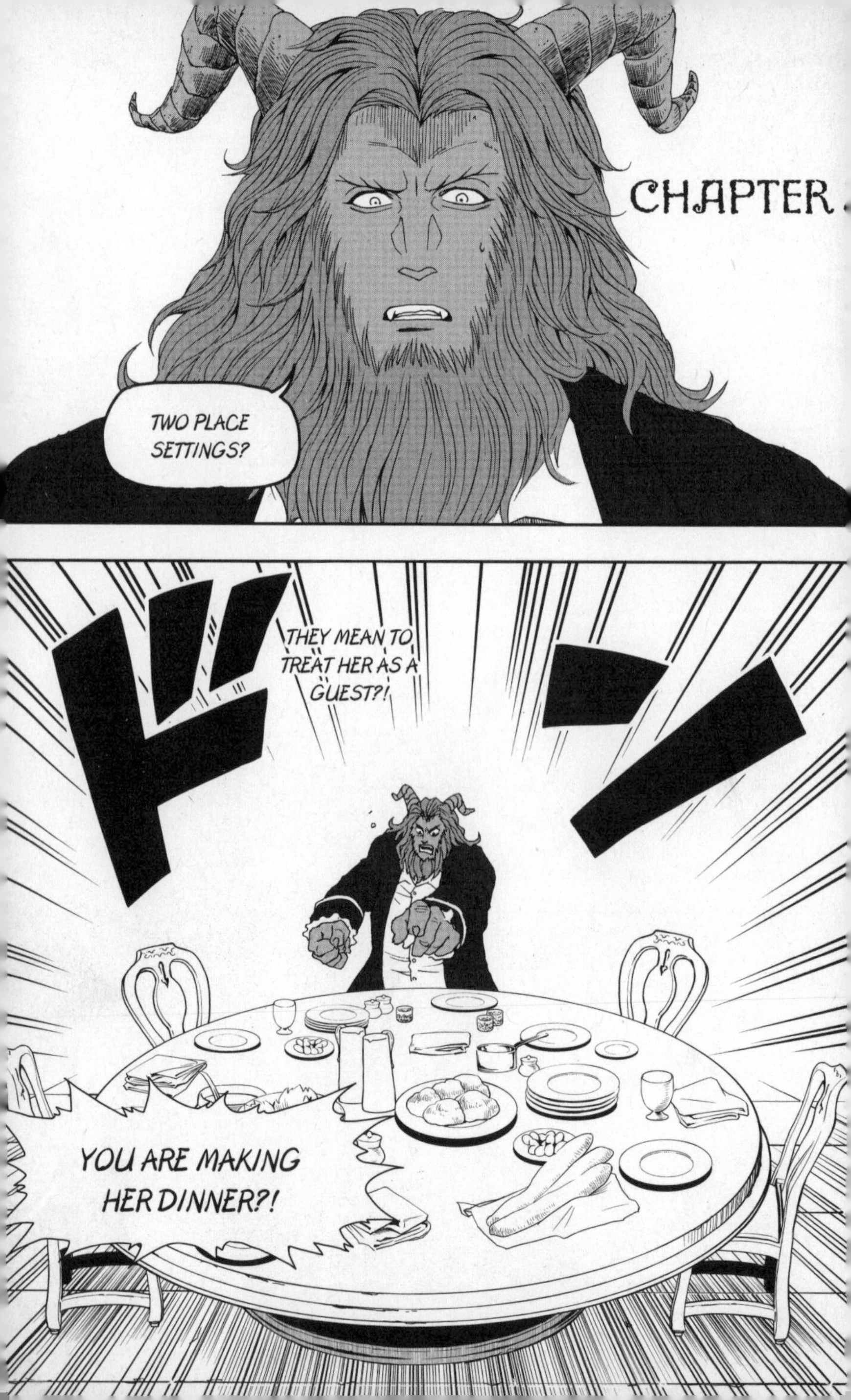
CHAPTER
TWO PLACE SETTINGS?
THEY MEAN TO TREAT HER AS A GUEST?!
ドン
YOU ARE MAKING HER DINNER?!

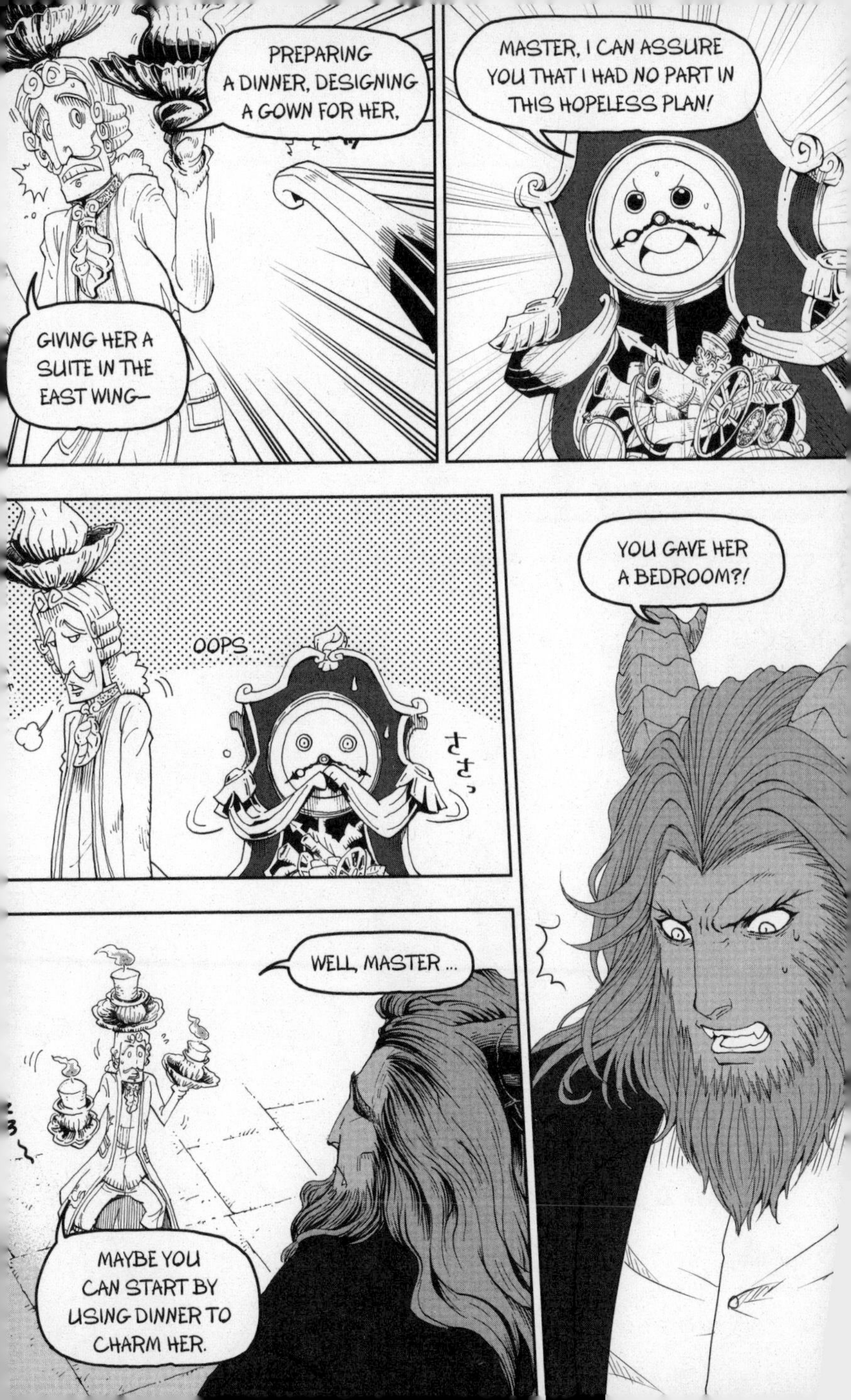
MASTER, I CAN ASSURE YOU THAT I HAD NO PART IN THIS HOPELESS PLAN!
PREPARING A DINNER, DESIGNING A GOWN FOR HER,
GIVING HER A SUITE IN THE EAST WING—
YOU GAVE HER A BEDROOM?!
OOPS
ささっ
WELL, MASTER ...
MAYBE YOU CAN START BY USING DINNER TO CHARM HER.

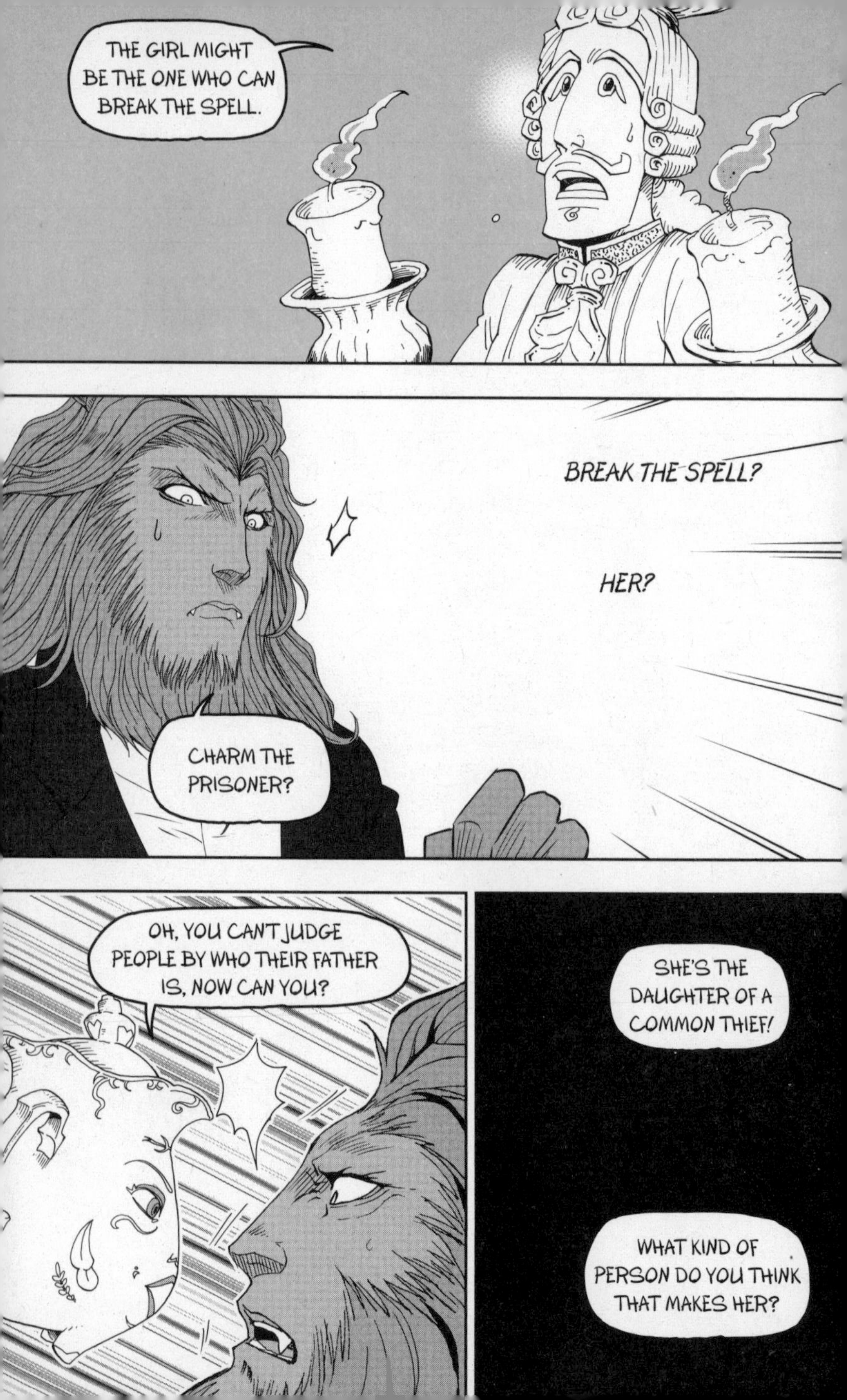
THE GIRL MIGHT BE THE ONE WHO CAN BREAK THE SPELL.
BREAK THE SPELL?
HER?
CHARM THE PRISONER?
SHE'S THE DAUGHTER OF A COMMON THIEF!
WHAT KIND OF PERSON DO YOU THINK THAT MAKES HER?
OH, YOU CAN'T JUDGE PEOPLE BY WHO THEIR FATHER IS, NOW CAN YOU?

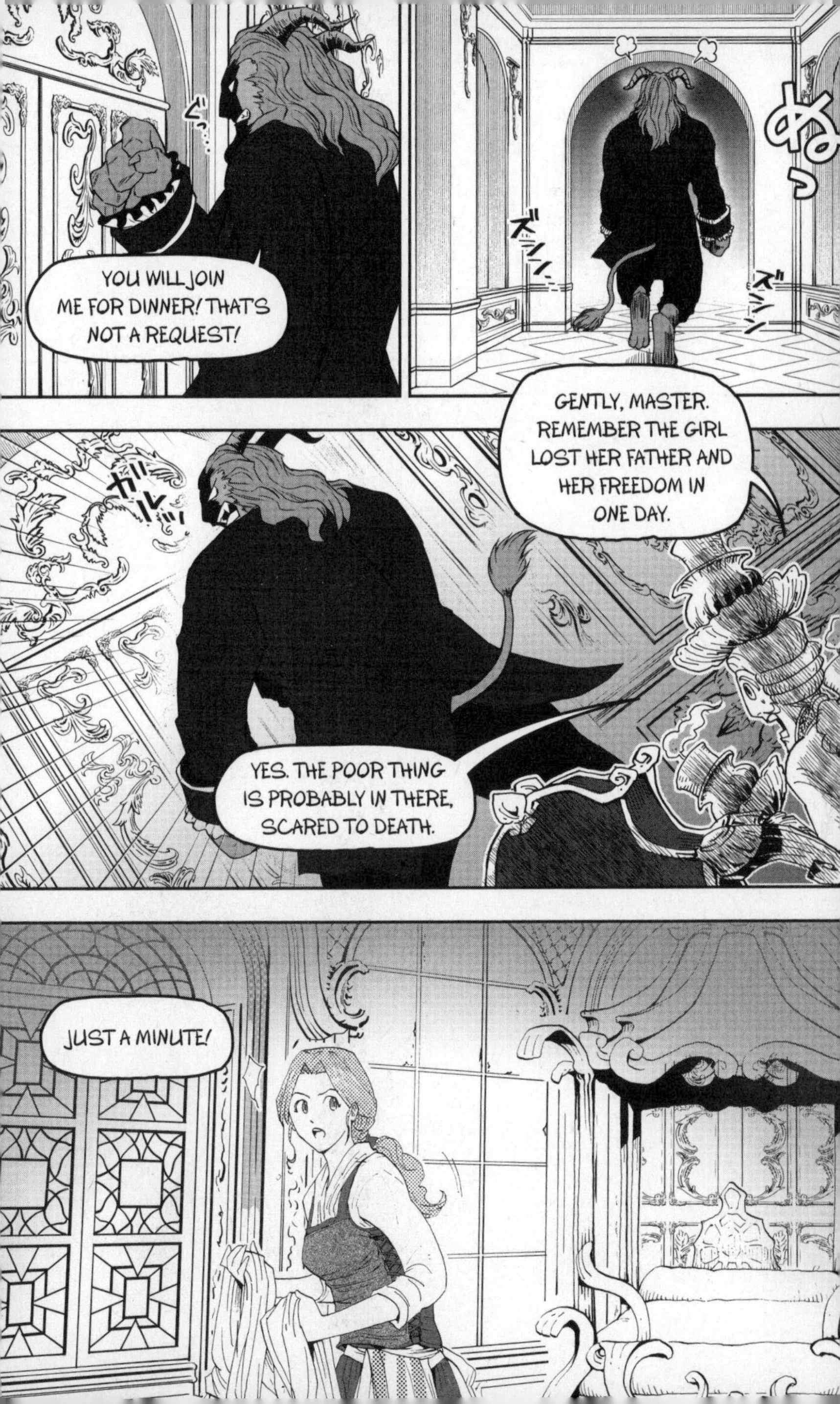

ぬっ
YOU WILL JOIN ME FOR DINNER! THAT'S NOT A REQUEST!
GENTLY, MASTER. REMEMBER THE GIRL LOST HER FATHER AND HER FREEDOM IN ONE DAY.
YES. THE POOR THING IS PROBABLY IN THERE, SCARED TO DEATH.
JUST A MINUTE!

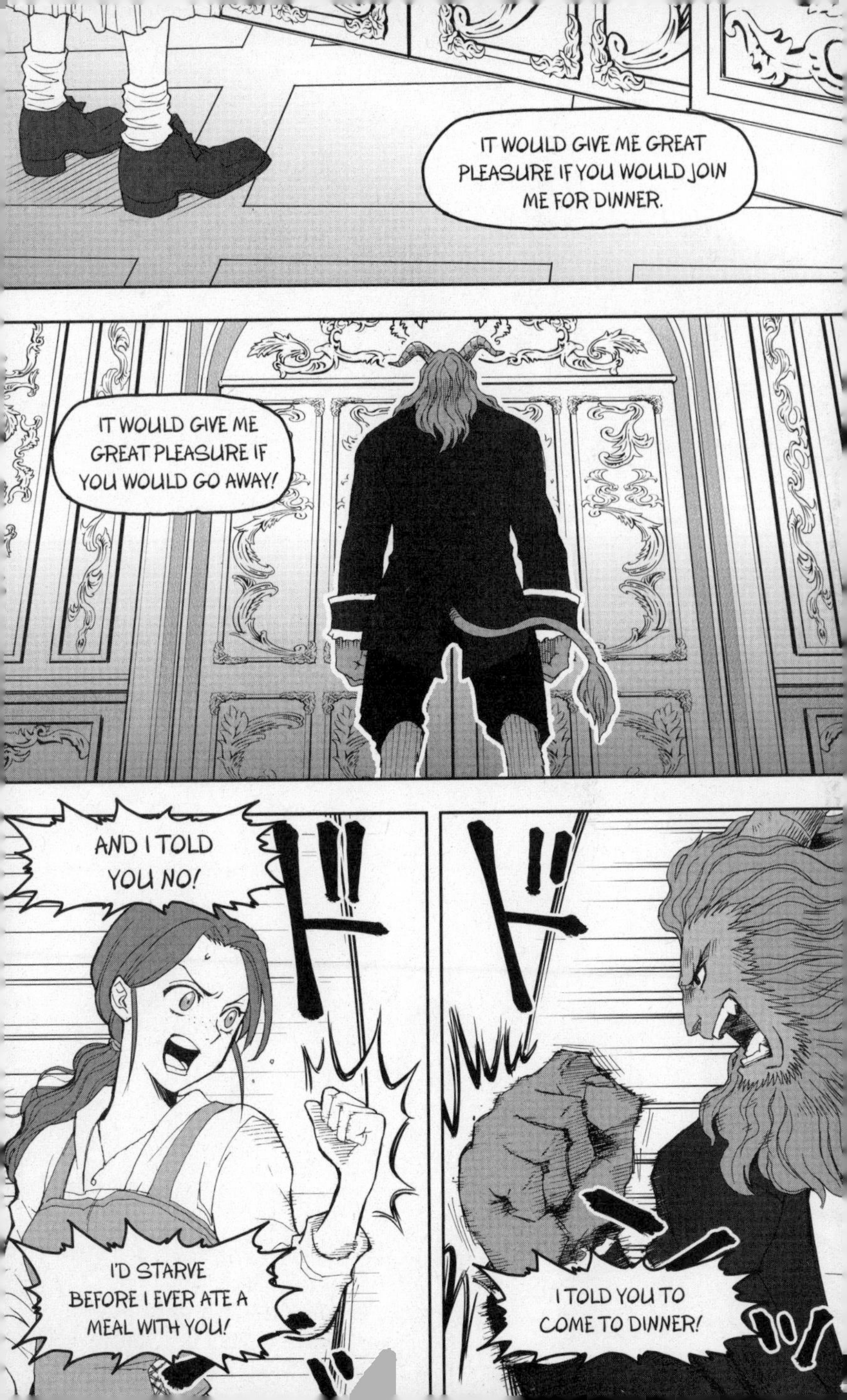
IT WOULD GIVE ME GREAT PLEASURE IF YOU WOULD JOIN ME FOR DINNER.
IT WOULD GIVE ME GREAT PLEASURE IF YOU WOULD GO AWAY!
ド
I TOLD YOU TO COME TO DINNER!
AND I TOLD YOU NO!
ド
I'D STARVE BEFORE I EVER ATE A MEAL WITH YOU!

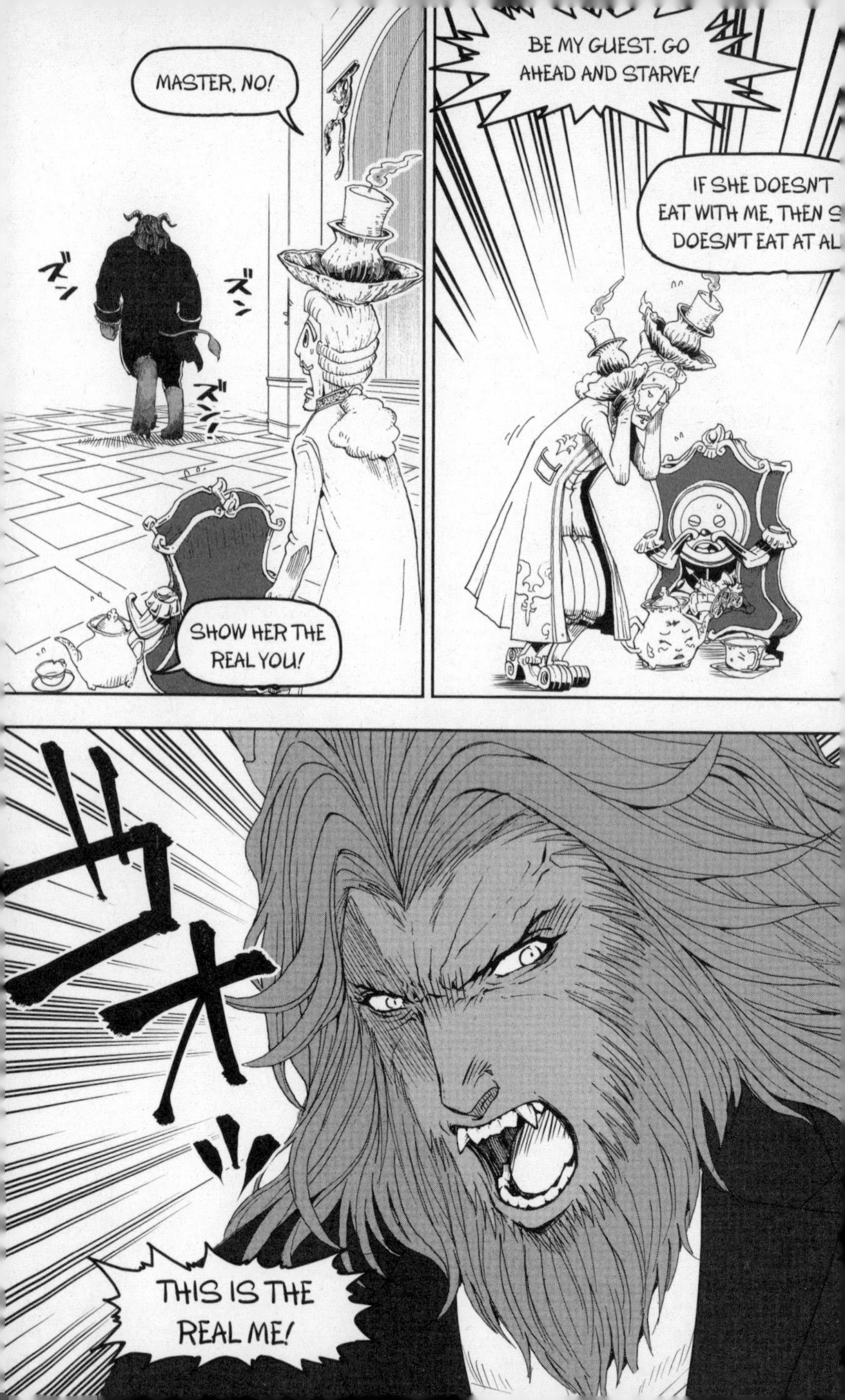
BE MY GUEST. GO AHEAD AND STARVE!
IF SHE DOESN'T EAT WITH ME, THEN S DOESN'T EAT AT AL
MASTER, NO!
ズン ズン ズン!
SHOW HER THE REAL YOU!
THIS IS THE REAL ME!

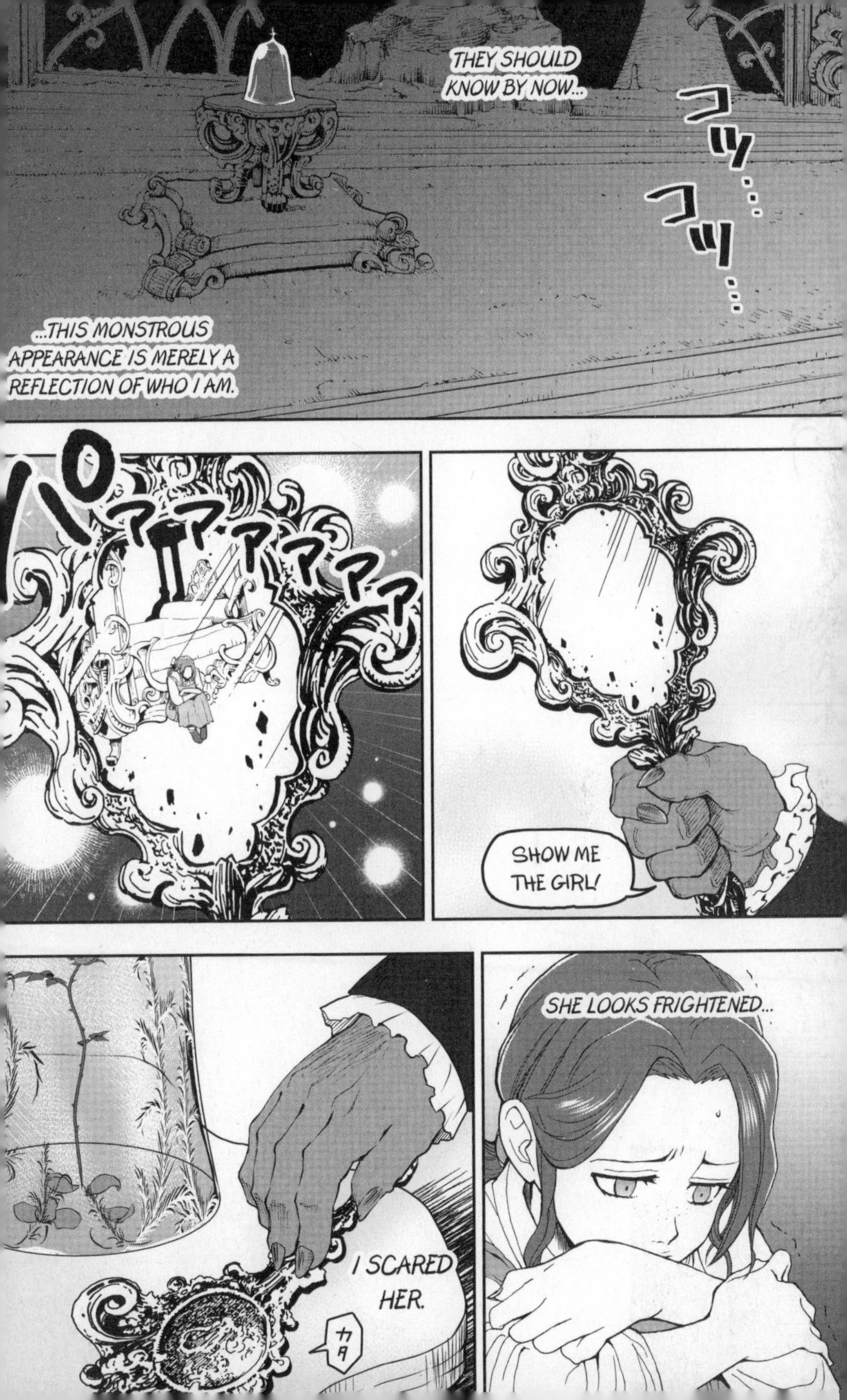
コツ...
コツ...
THEY SHOULD KNOW BY NOW...
...THIS MONSTROUS APPEARANCE IS MERELY A REFLECTION OF WHO I AM.
SHOW ME THE GIRL!
パアアアアアア
SHE LOOKS FRIGHTENED...
I SCARED HER.
カタ

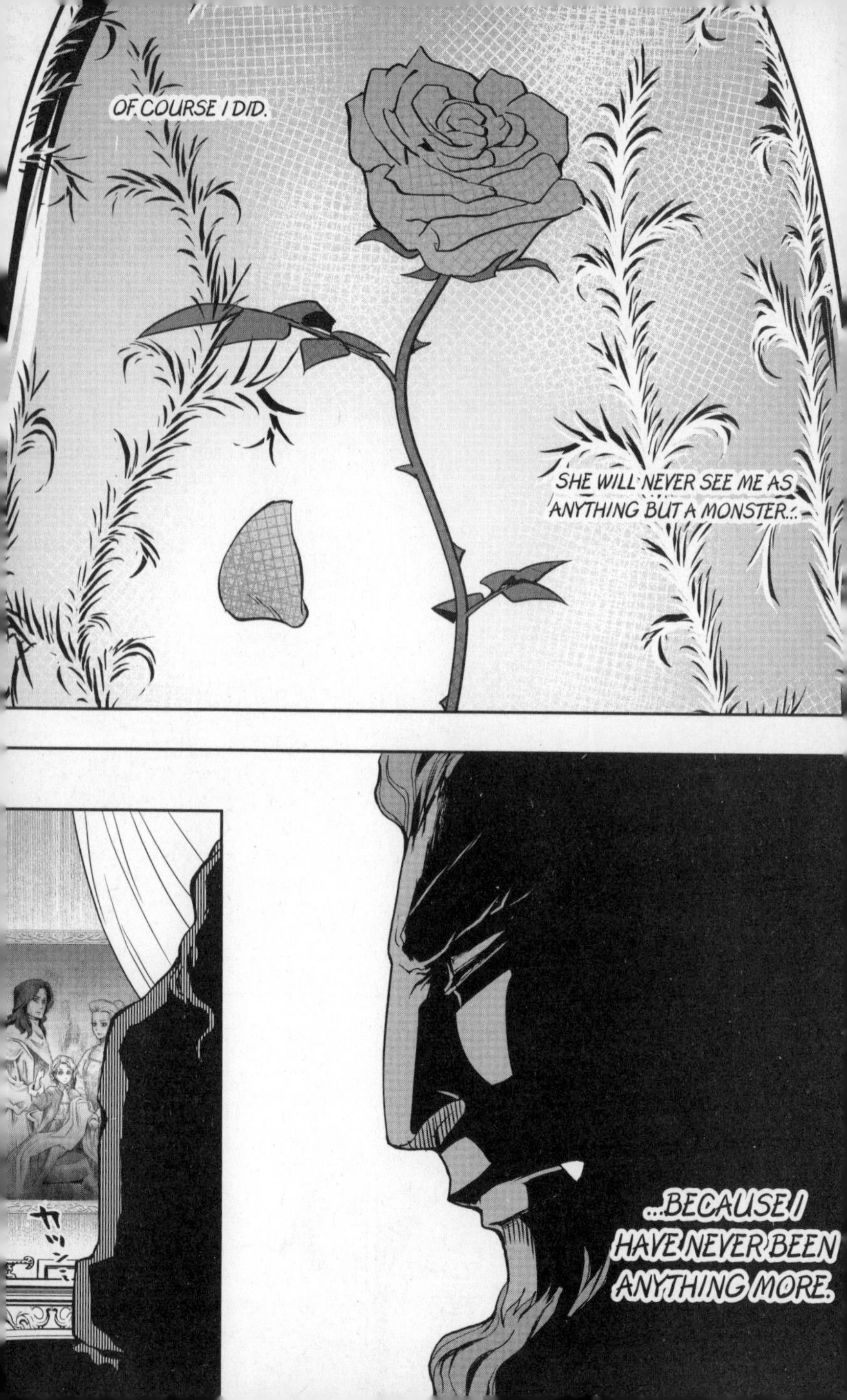
OF COURSE I DID.
SHE WILL NEVER SEE ME AS ANYTHING BUT A MONSTER...
...BECAUSE I HAVE NEVER BEEN ANYTHING MORE.

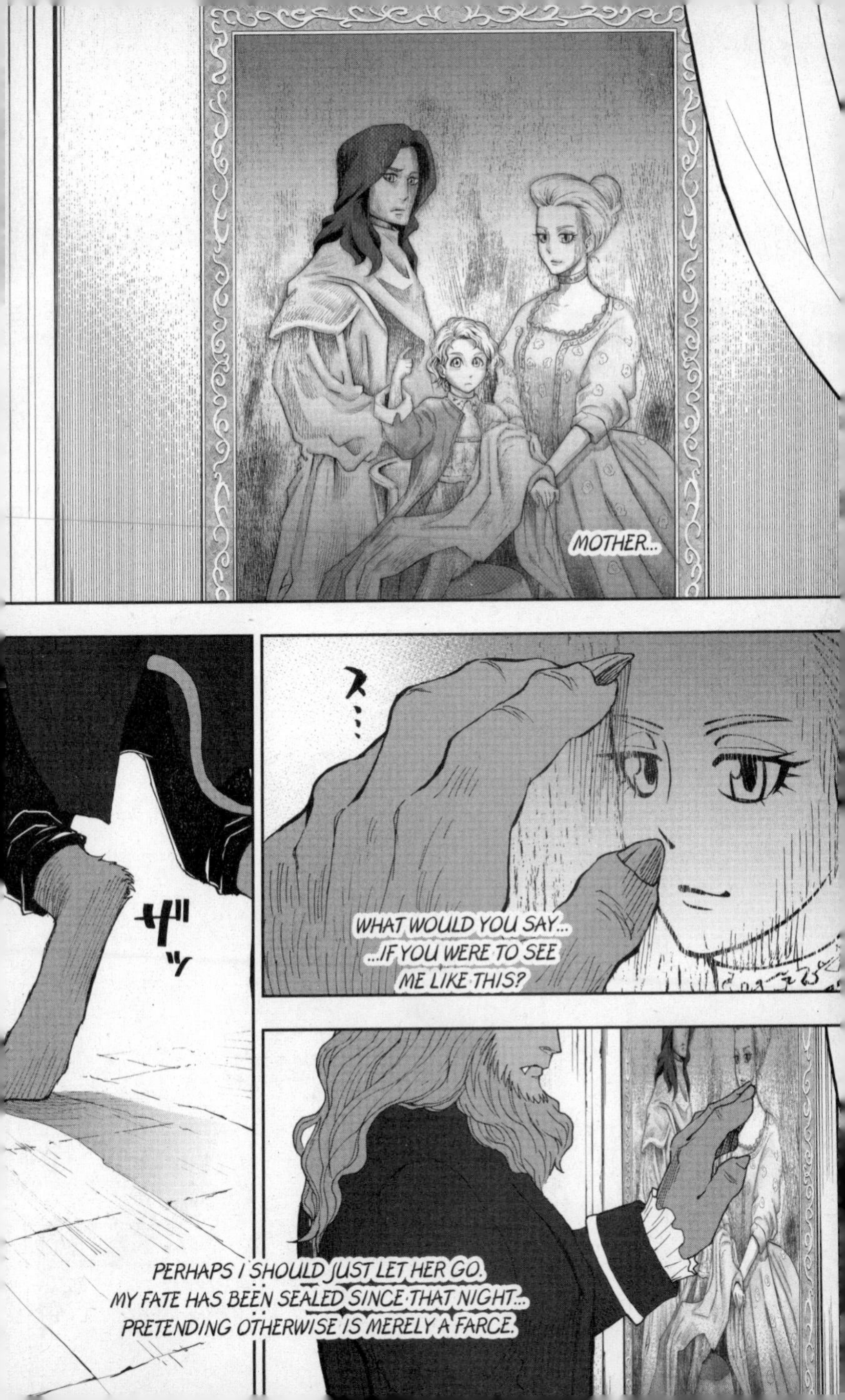

MOTHER...
ス...
WHAT WOULD YOU SAY... ...IF YOU WERE TO SEE ME LIKE THIS?
PERHAPS I SHOULD JUST LET HER GO. MY FATE HAS BEEN SEALED SINCE THAT NIGHT... PRETENDING OTHERWISE IS MERELY A FARCE.
ザッ

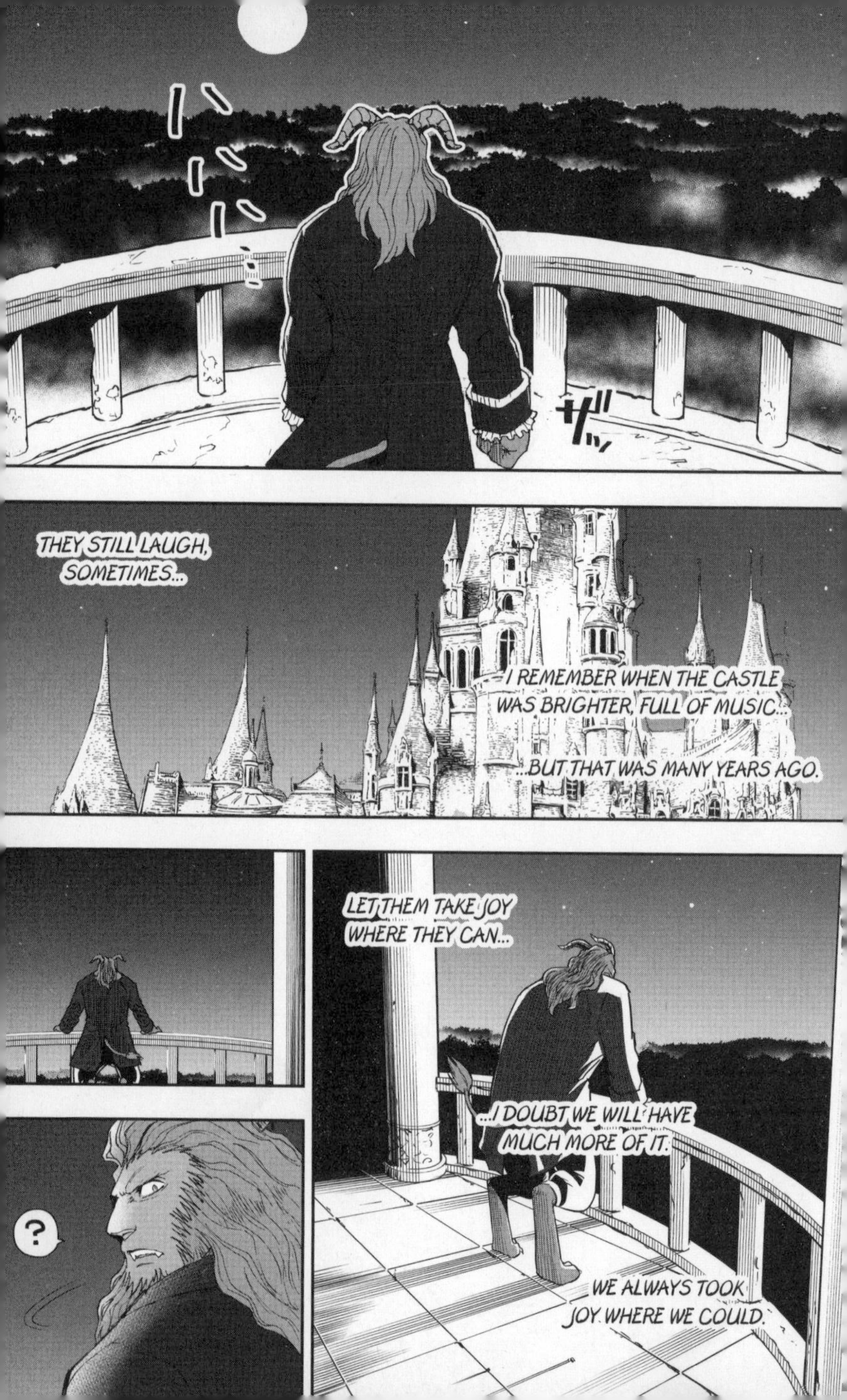
THEY STILL LAUGH, SOMETIMES...
I REMEMBER WHEN THE CASTLE WAS BRIGHTER, FULL OF MUSIC...
...BUT THAT WAS MANY YEARS AGO.
LET THEM TAKE JOY WHERE THEY CAN...
...I DOUBT WE WILL HAVE MUCH MORE OF IT.
WE ALWAYS TOOK JOY WHERE WE COULD.
?

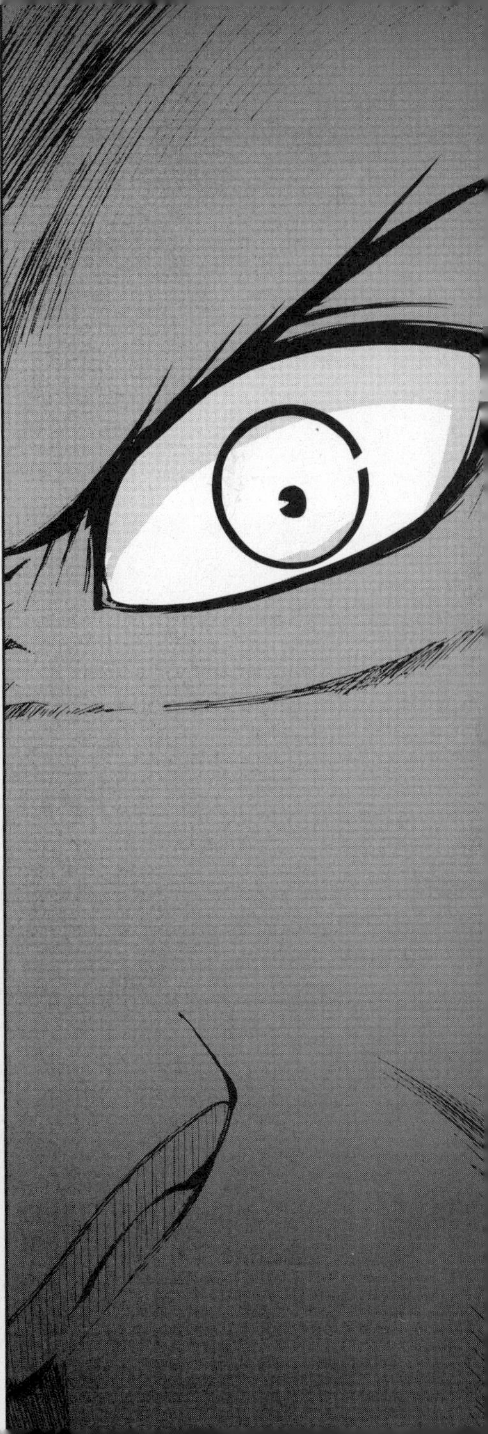
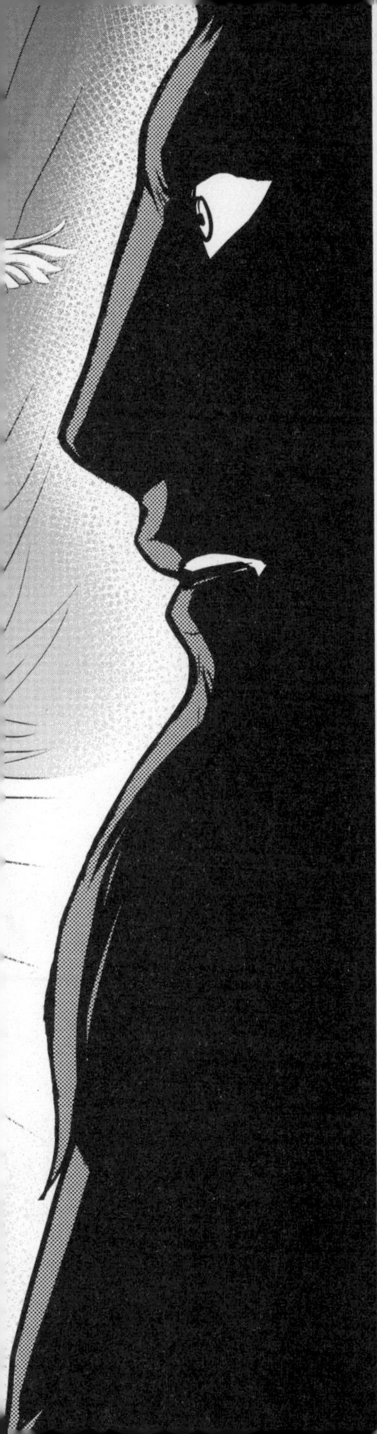

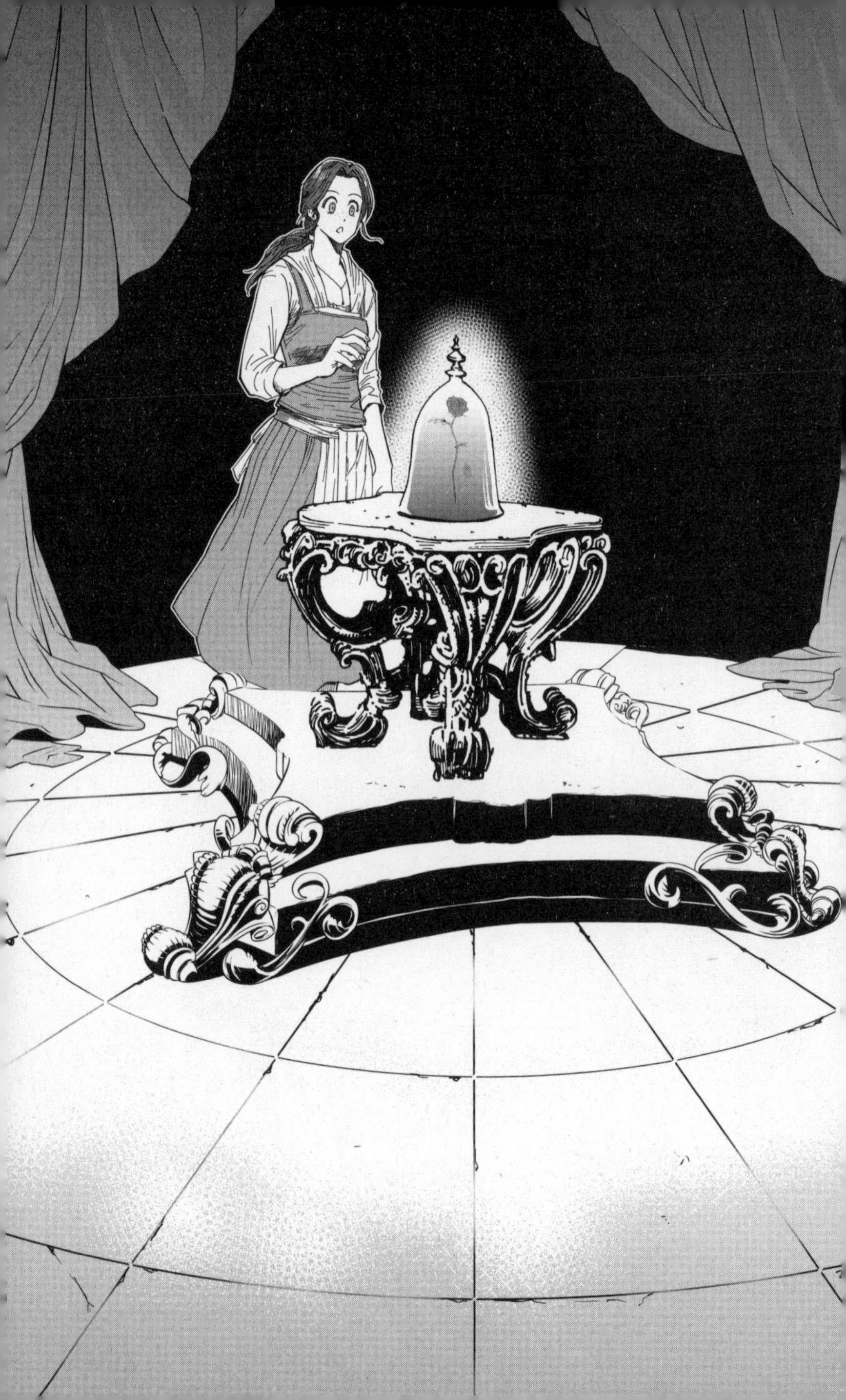

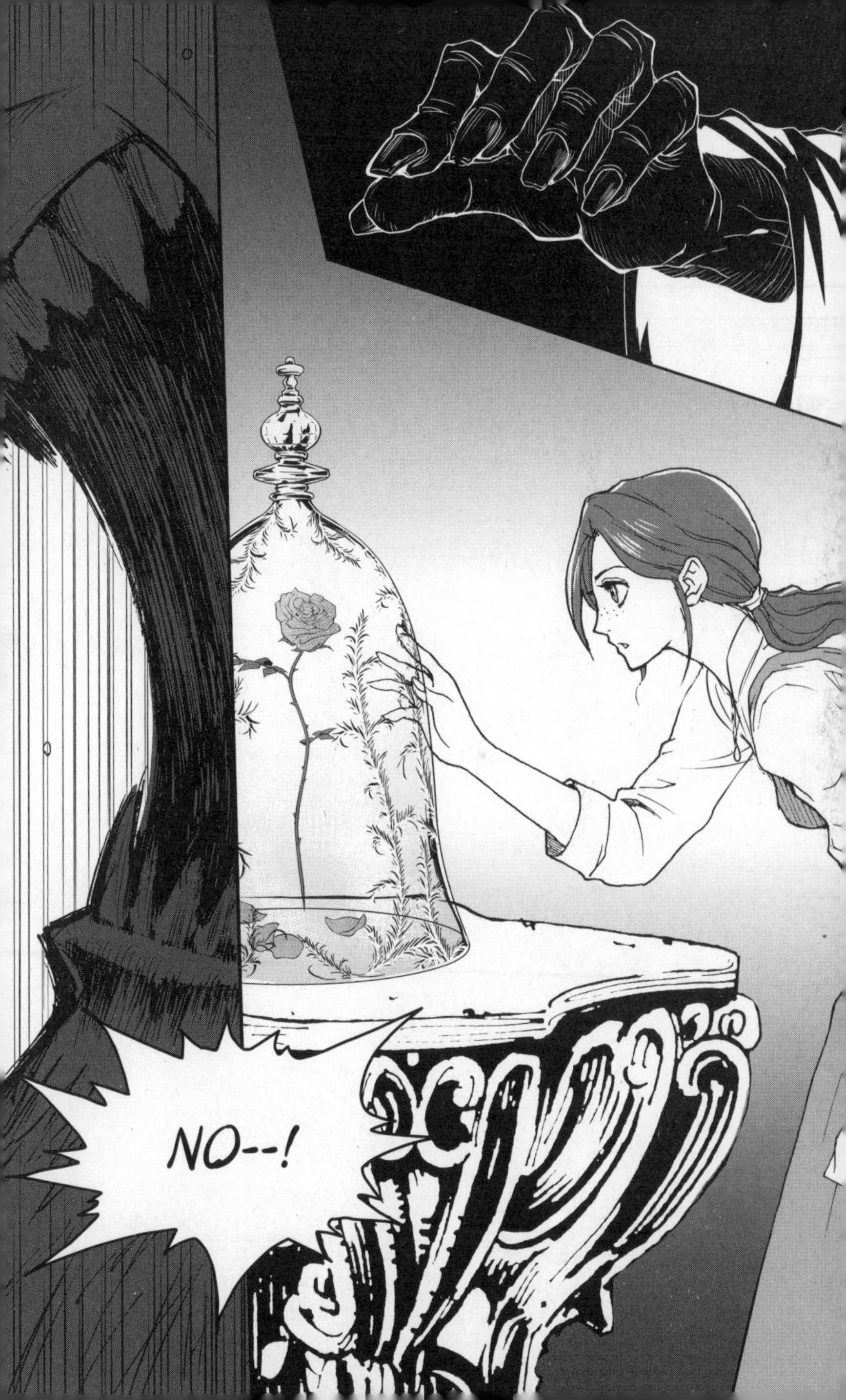
NO--!

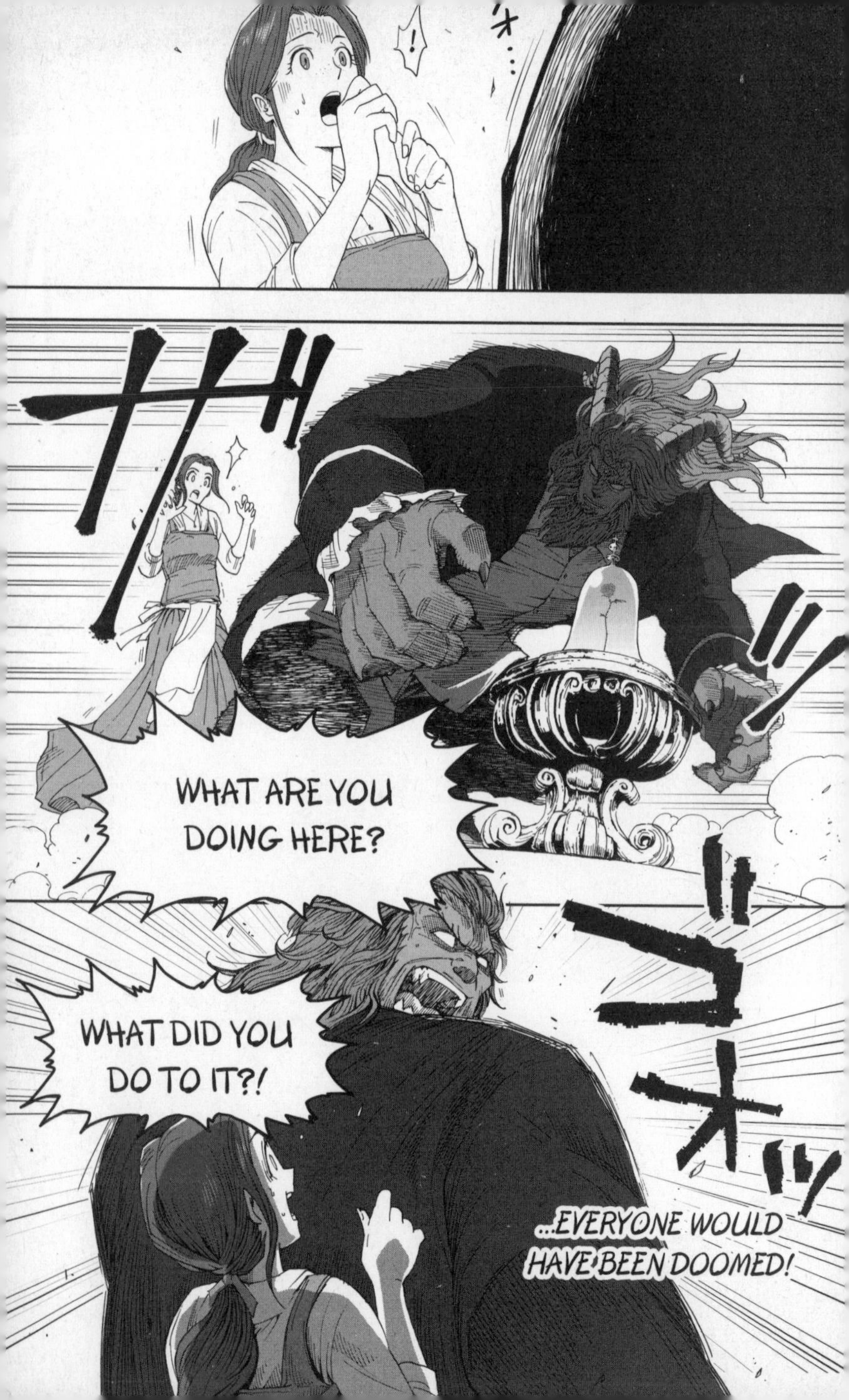
WHAT ARE YOU DOING HERE?
WHAT DID YOU DO TO IT?!
...EVERYONE WOULD HAVE BEEN DOOMED!

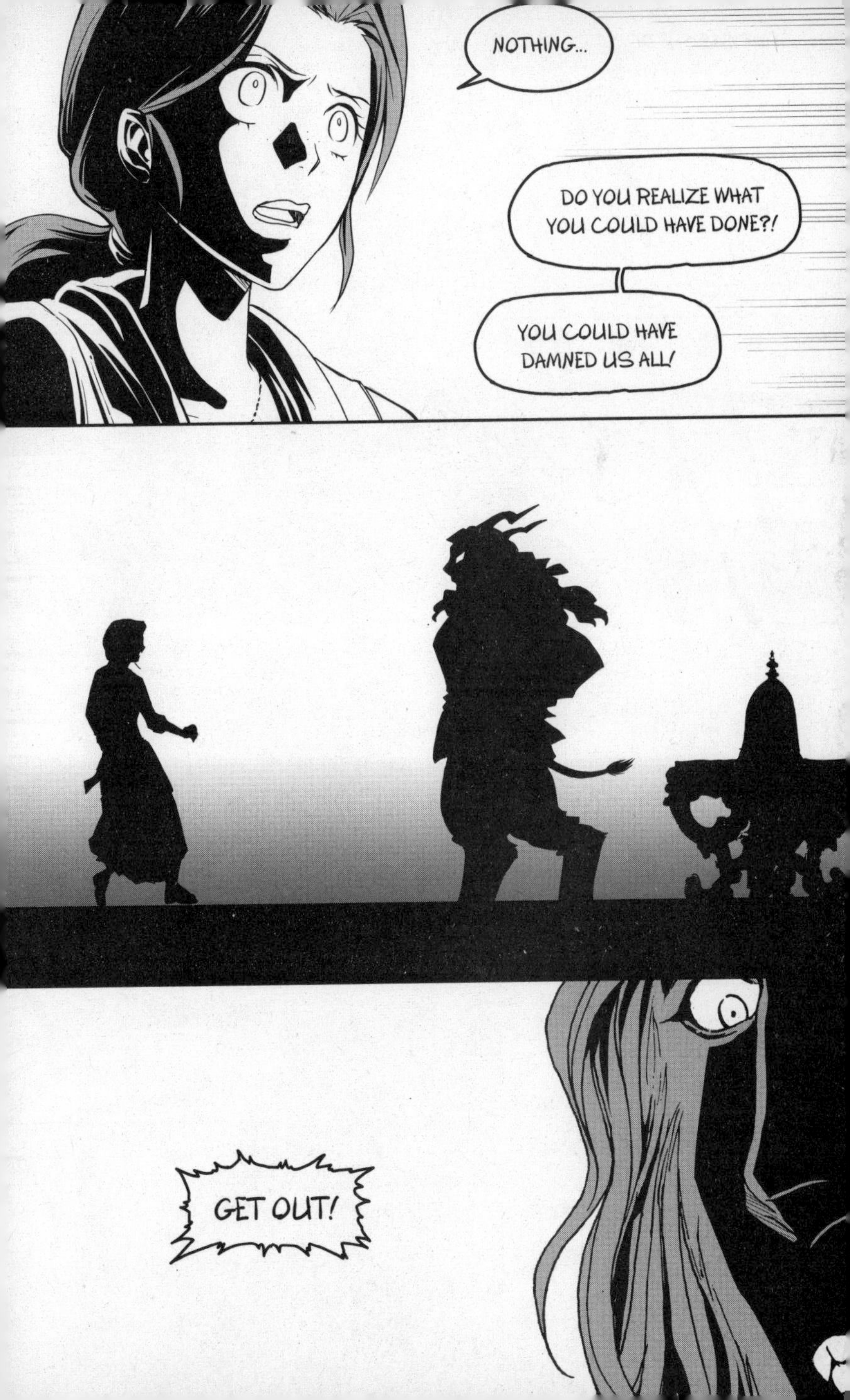
NOTHING...
DO YOU REALIZE WHAT YOU COULD HAVE DONE?!
YOU COULD HAVE DAMNED US ALL!
GET OUT!

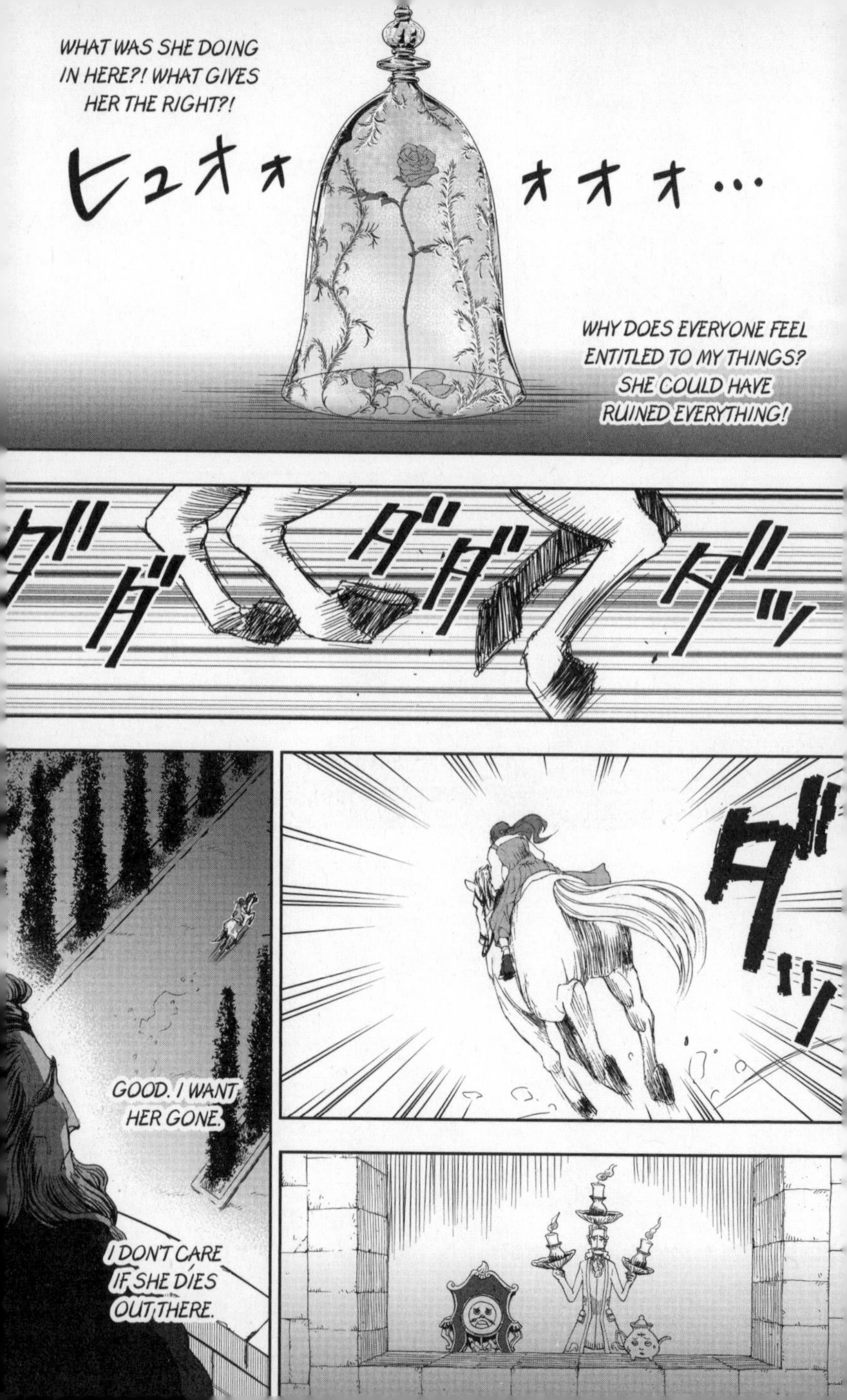
WHAT WAS SHE DOING IN HERE?! WHAT GIVES HER THE RIGHT?!
ヒュオォ
オオオ…
WHY DOES EVERYONE FEEL ENTITLED TO MY THINGS? SHE COULD HAVE RUINED EVERYTHING!
ダダダダッ
ダッ
GOOD. I WANT HER GONE.
I DON'T CARE IF SHE DIES OUT THERE.

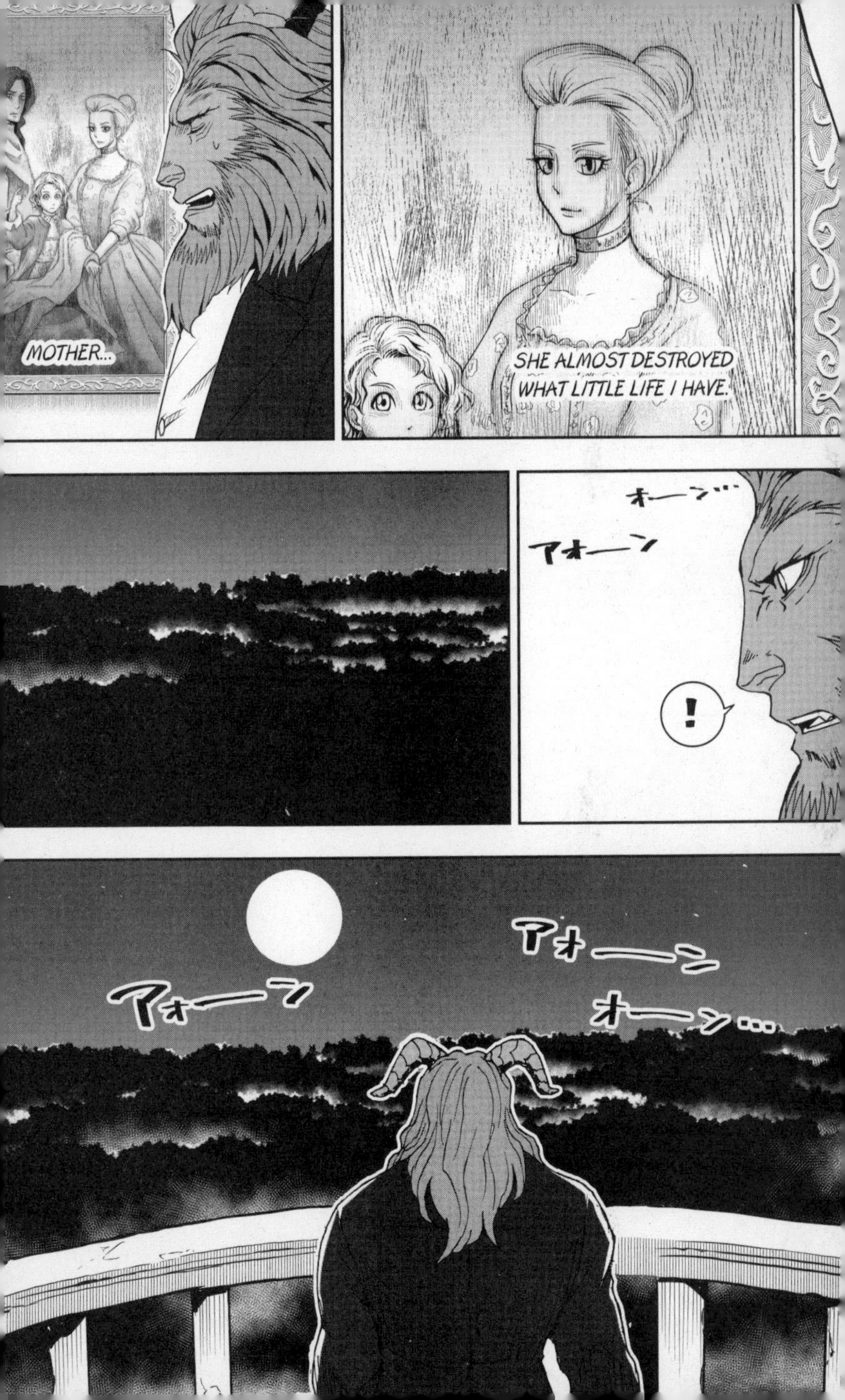
SHE ALMOST DESTROYED WHAT LITTLE LIFE I HAVE.
MOTHER...
オーン
アオーン
!
アオーーン
オーーン…
アォーン

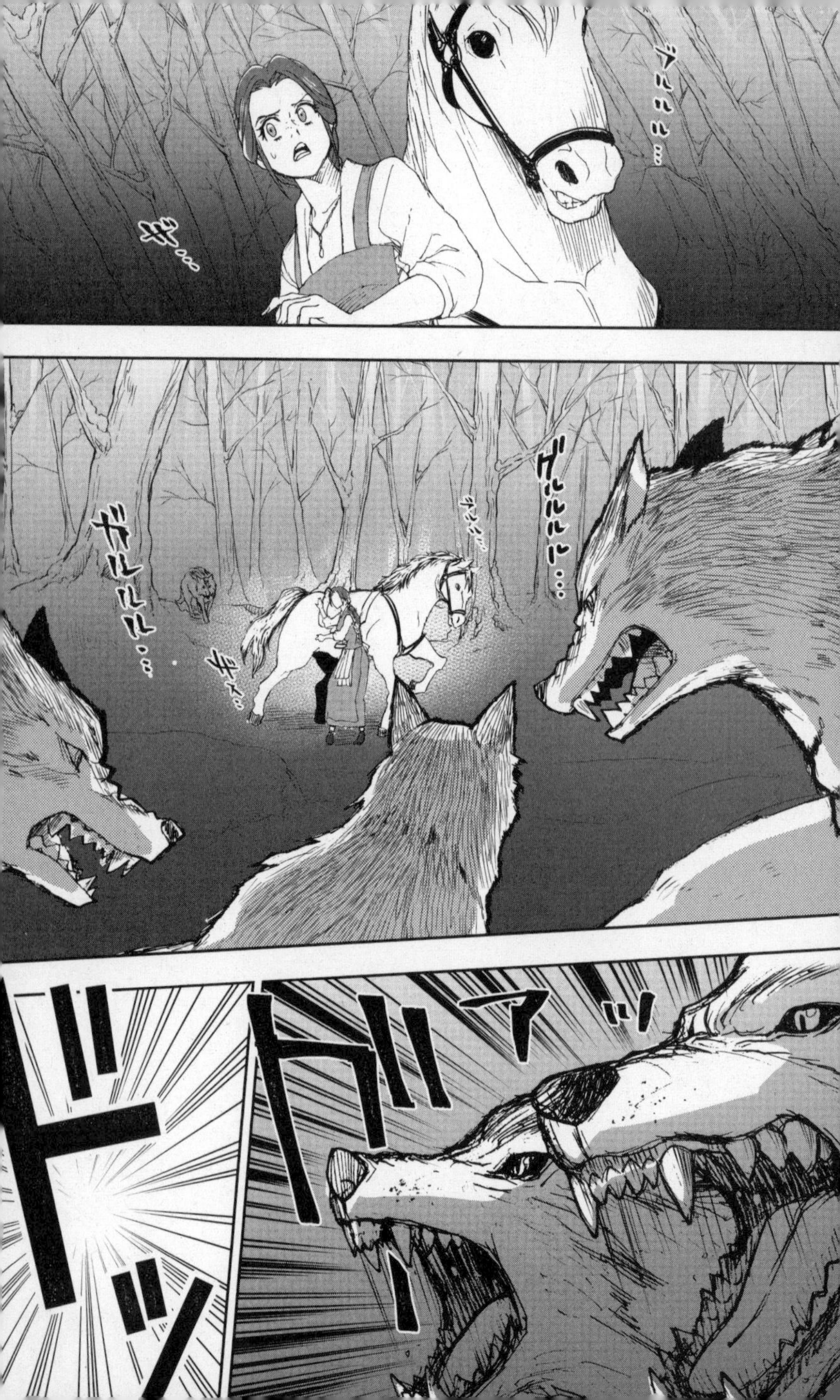
ブルルル…
ザ…
ガルルルル…
ブルル…
ガルルルル…
ザ…
ドバァッ
ドッ

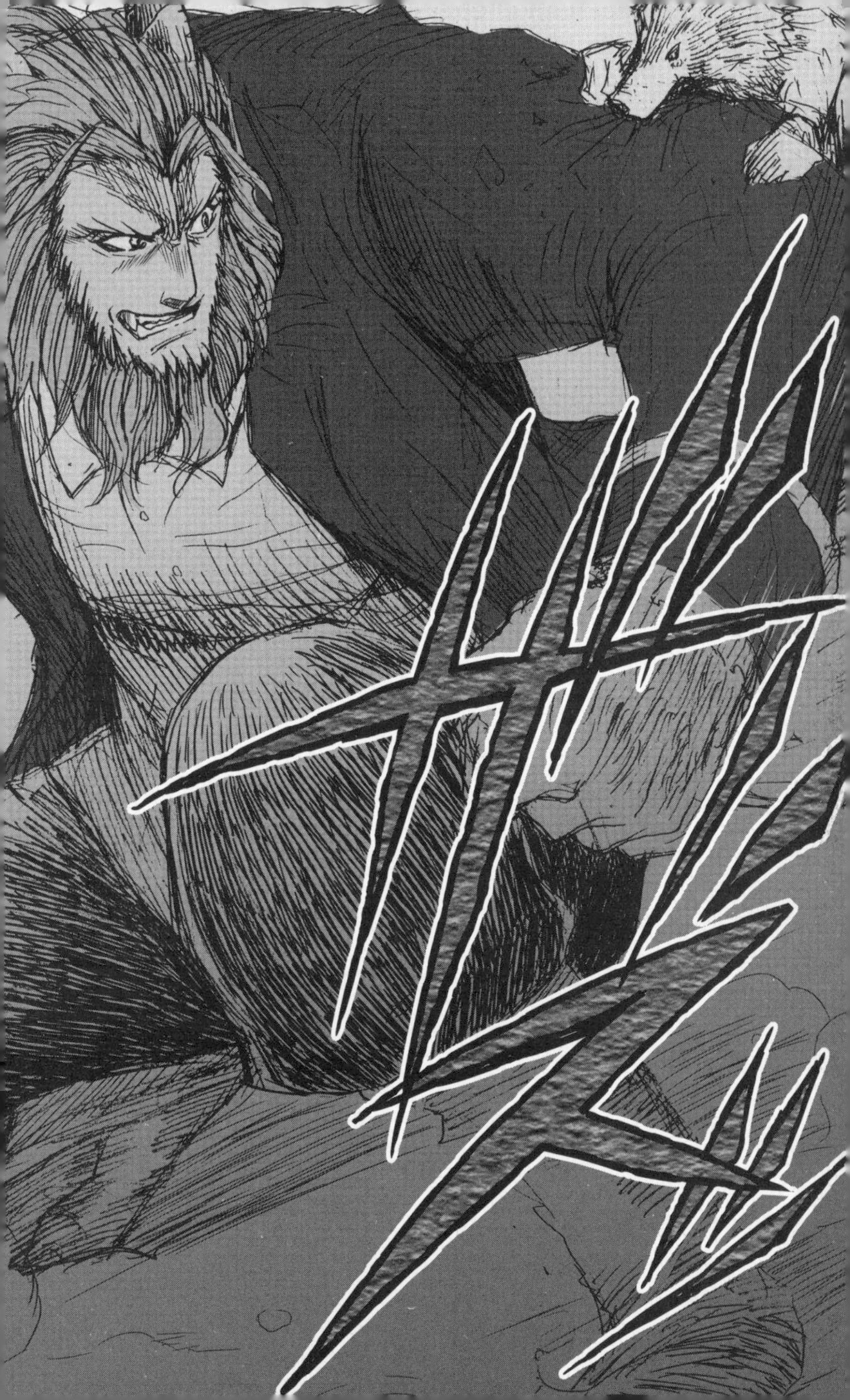

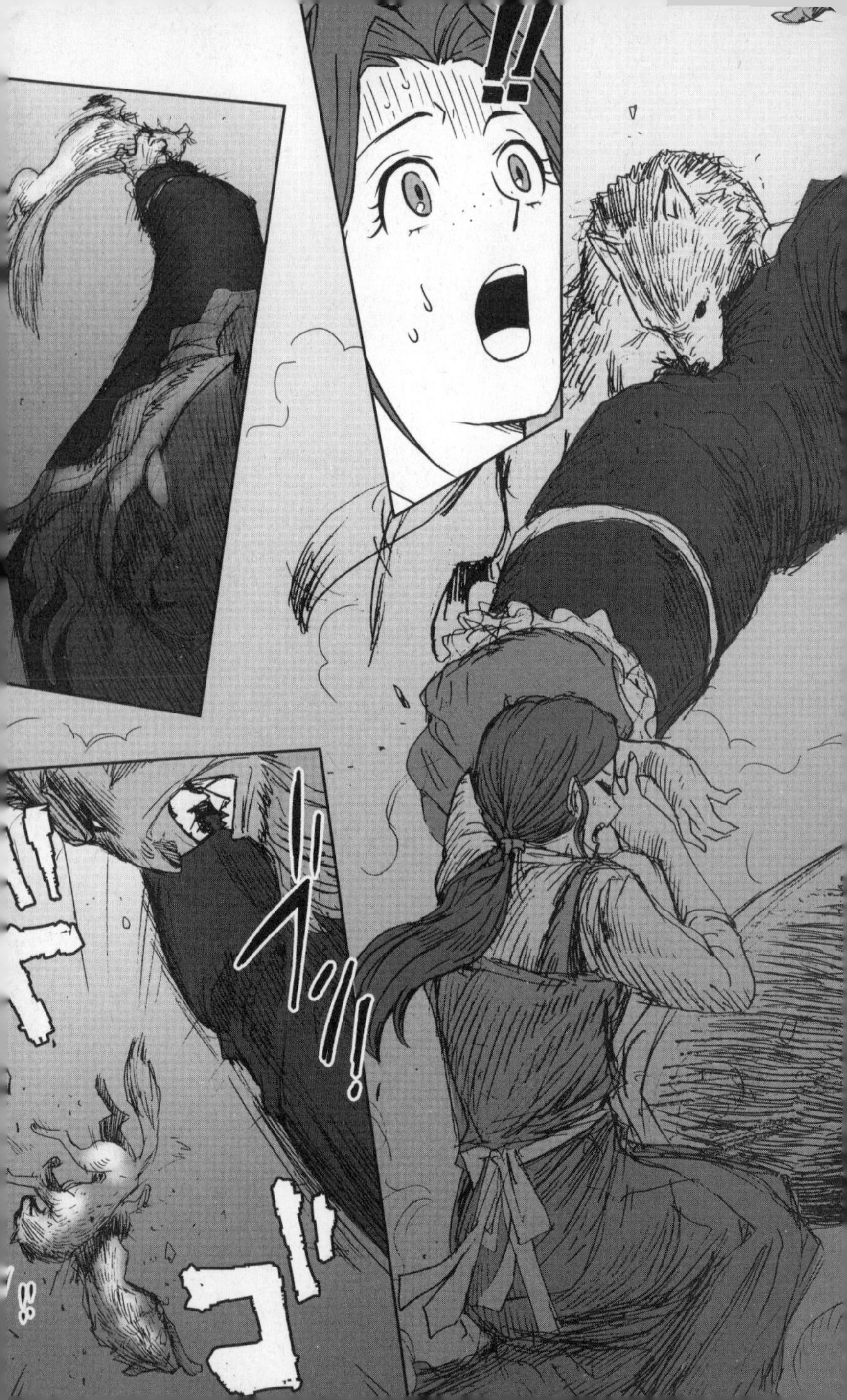
!!
ベッ!!
ゴ

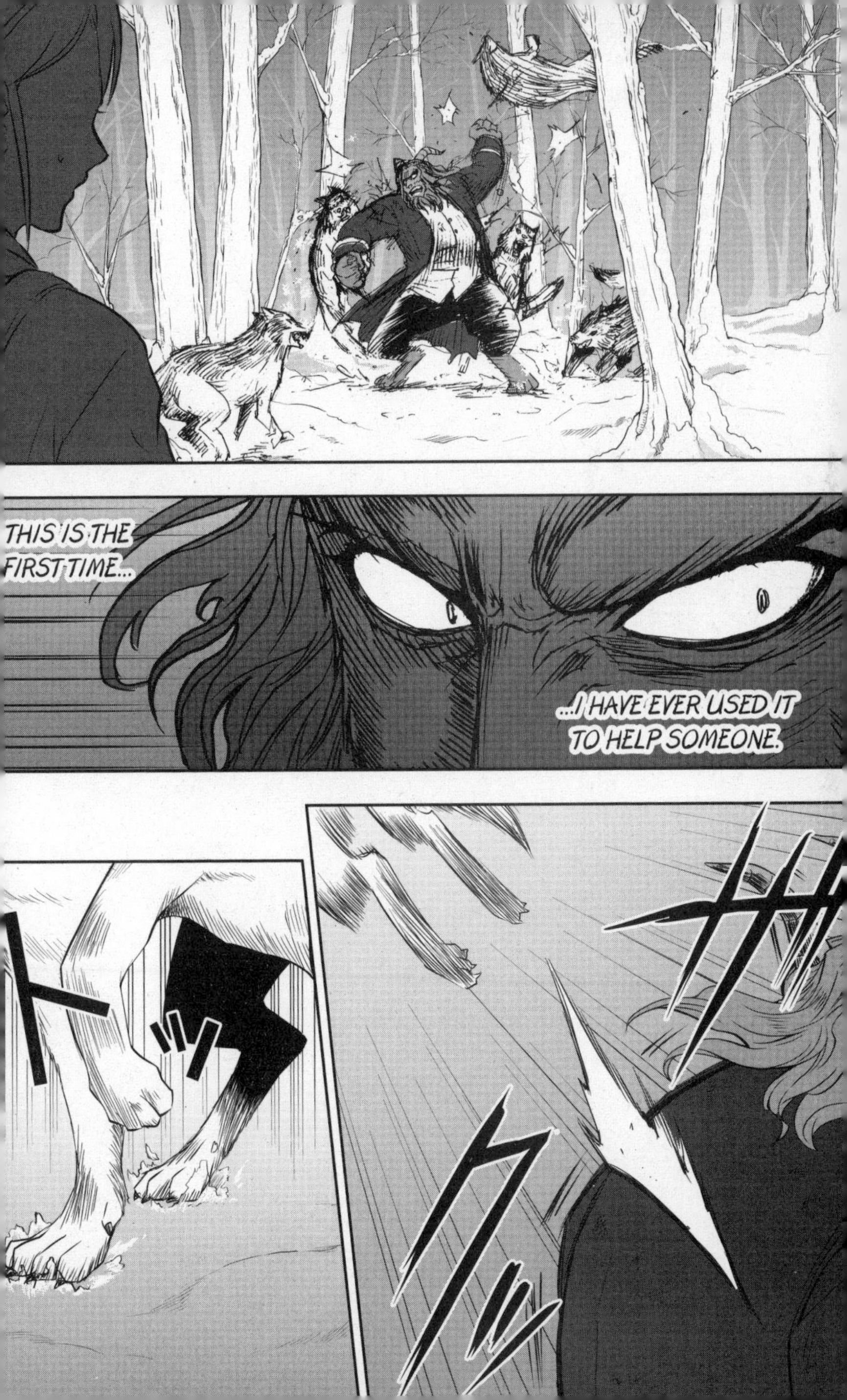
THIS IS THE FIRST TIME...
...I HAVE EVER USED IT TO HELP SOMEONE.

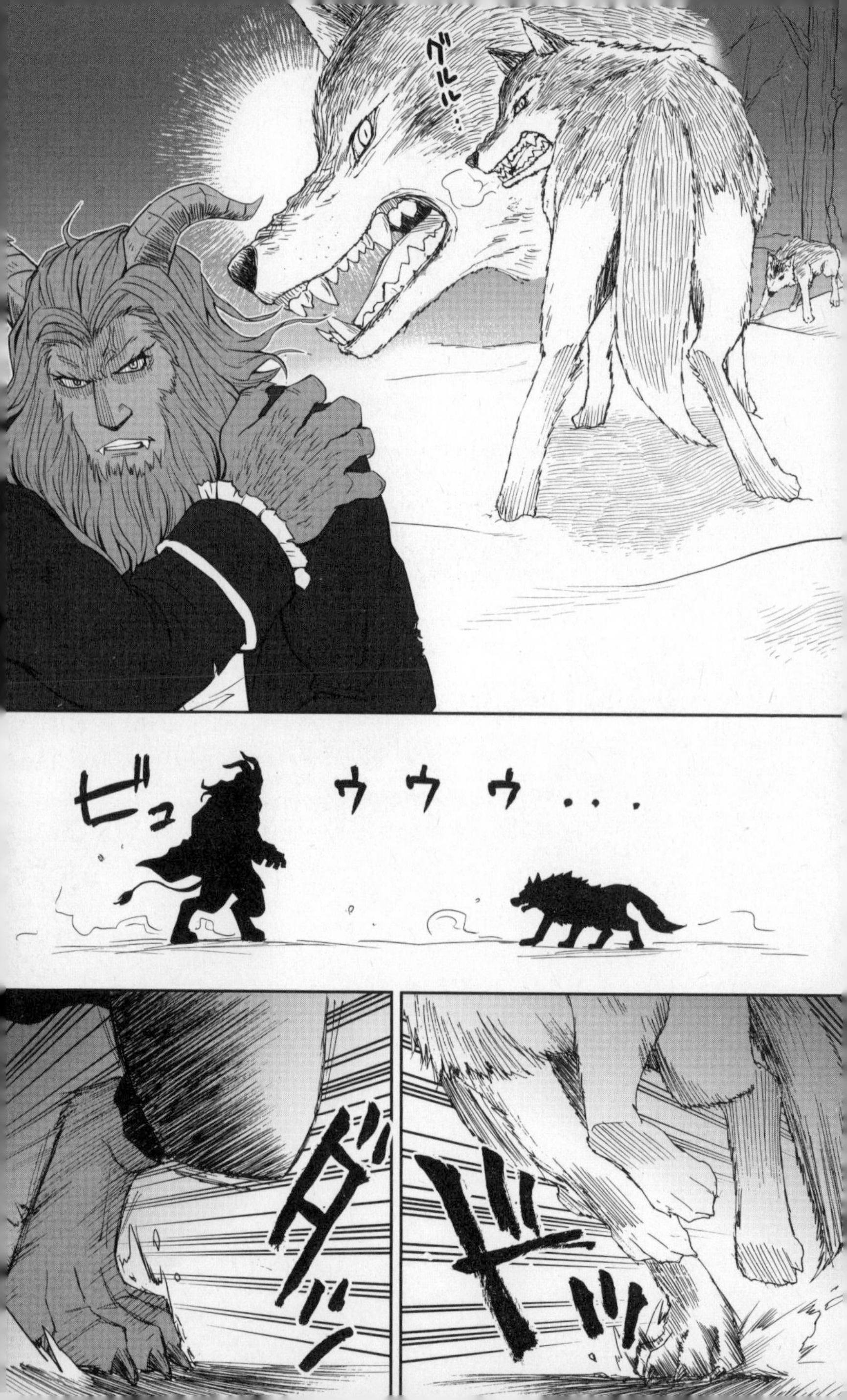
グルル…
ウウウ…
ビュ
ダッ

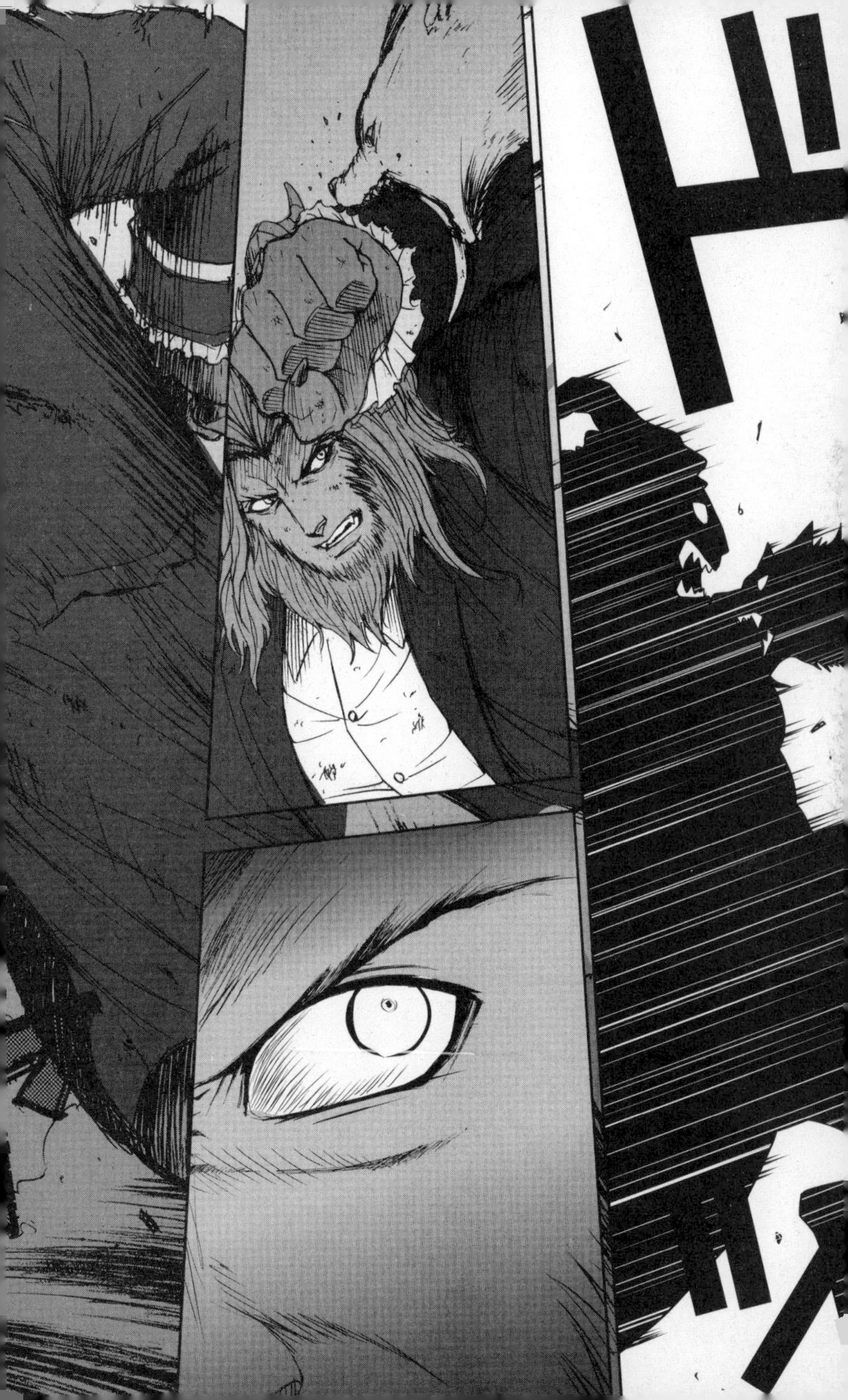
ド

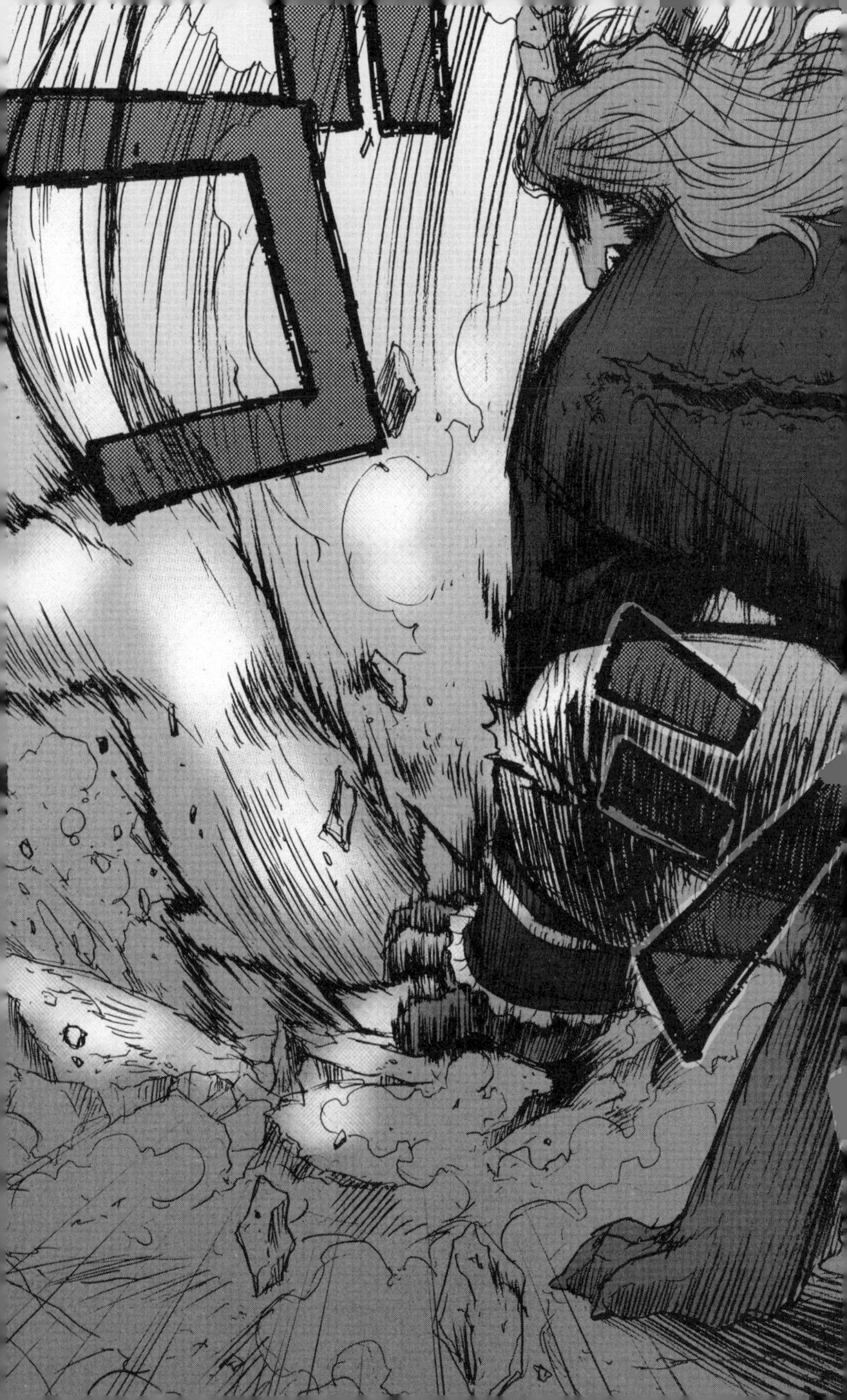

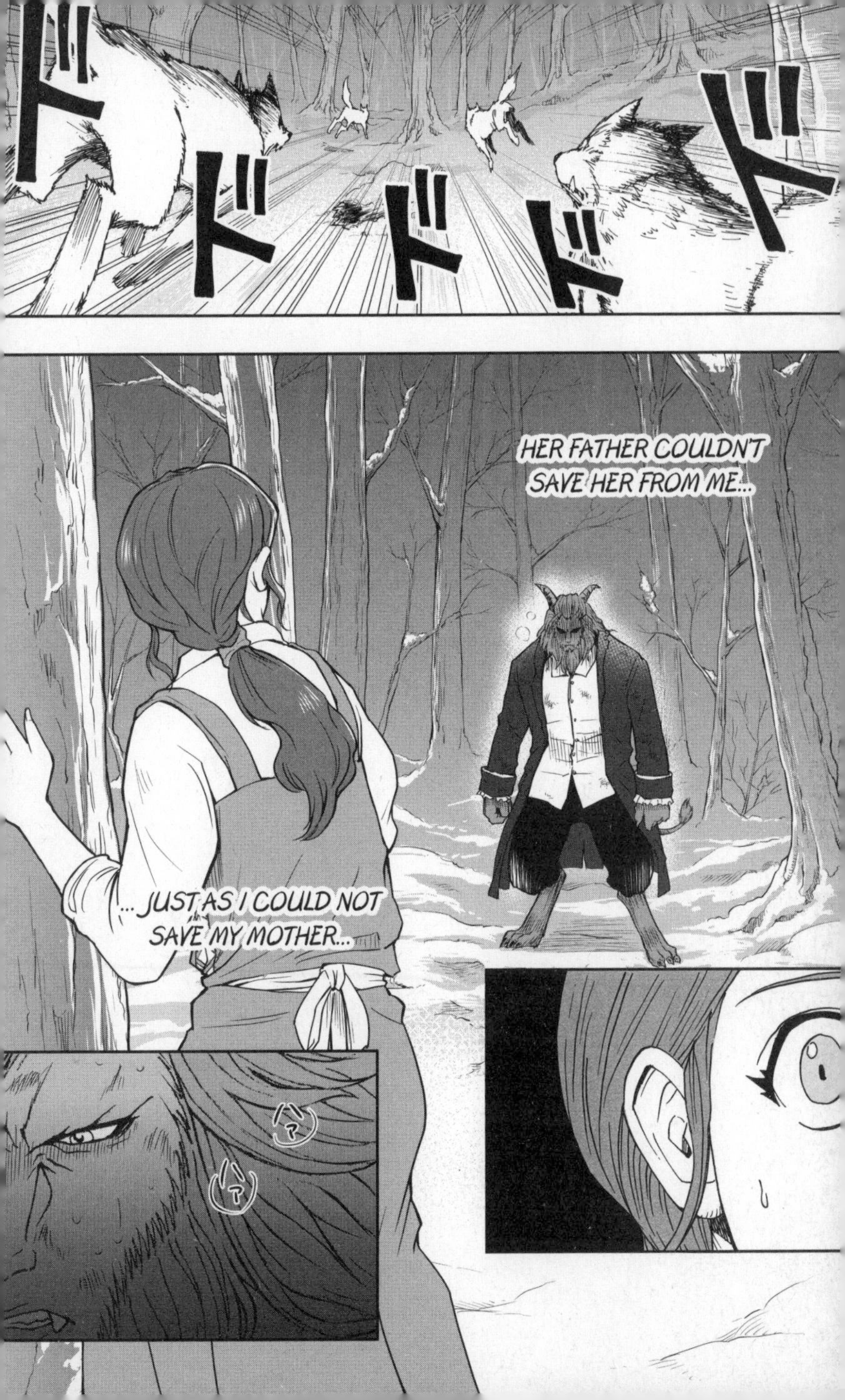
ドドドドド
HER FATHER COULDN'T SAVE HER FROM ME...
...JUST AS I COULD NOT SAVE MY MOTHER...
ハァ
ハァ

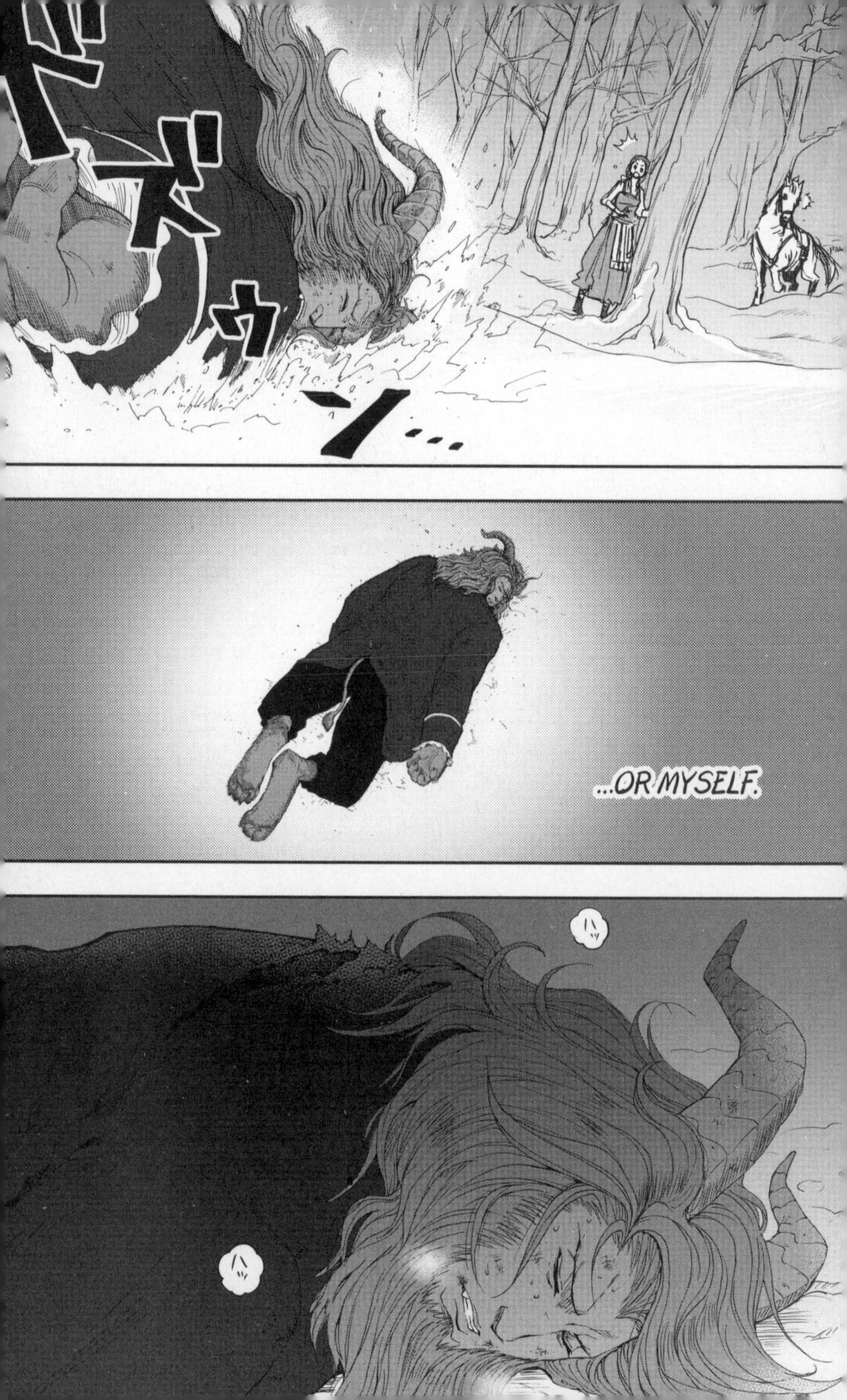
ドズゥーン…
...OR MYSELF.
ハッ
ハッ

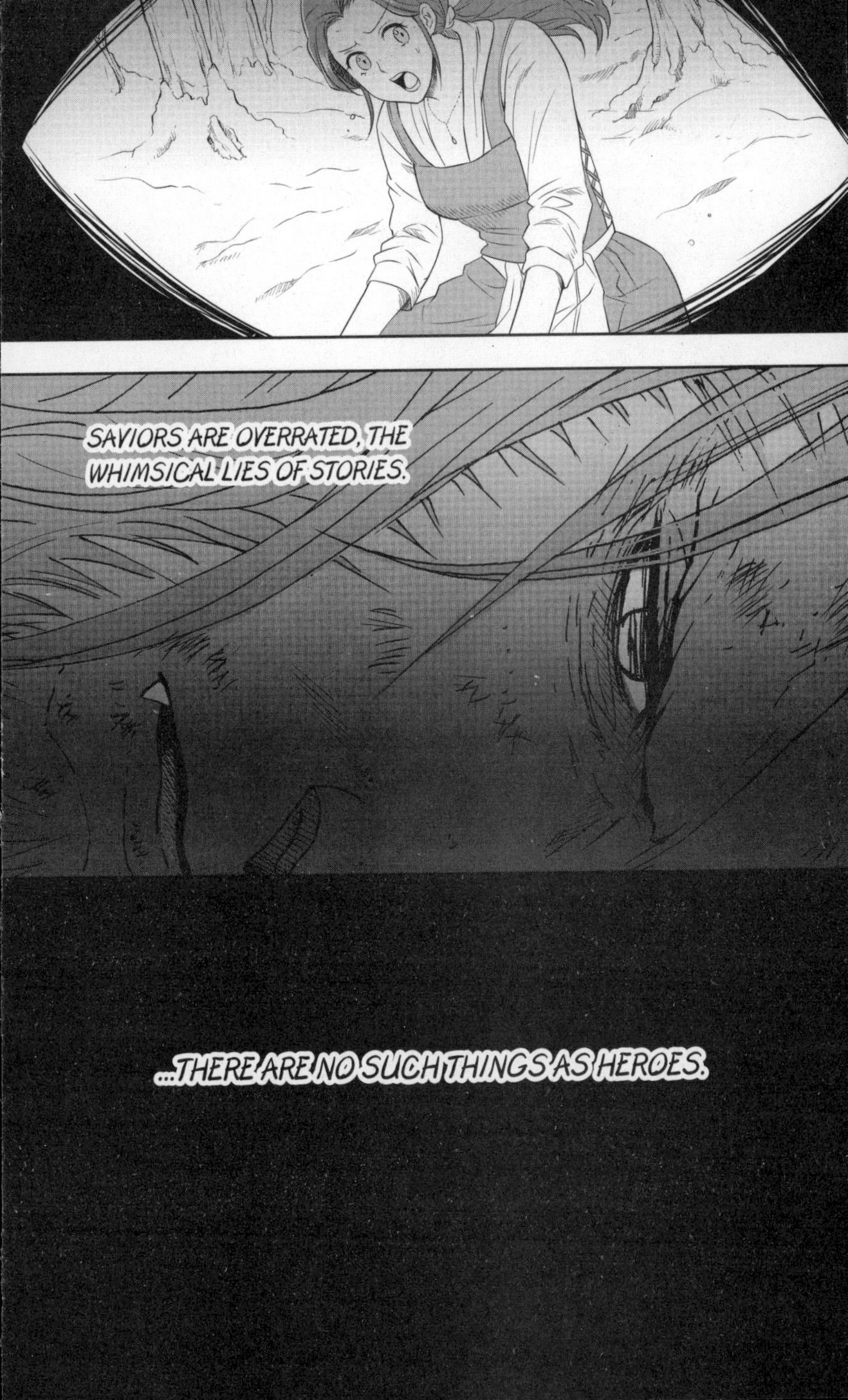
SAVIORS ARE OVERRATED, THE WHIMSICAL LIES OF STORIES.
...THERE ARE NO SUCH THINGS AS HEROES.

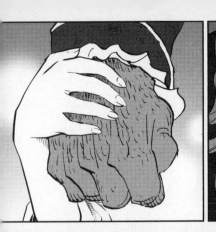

SHE...

...DIDN'T LEAVE...?

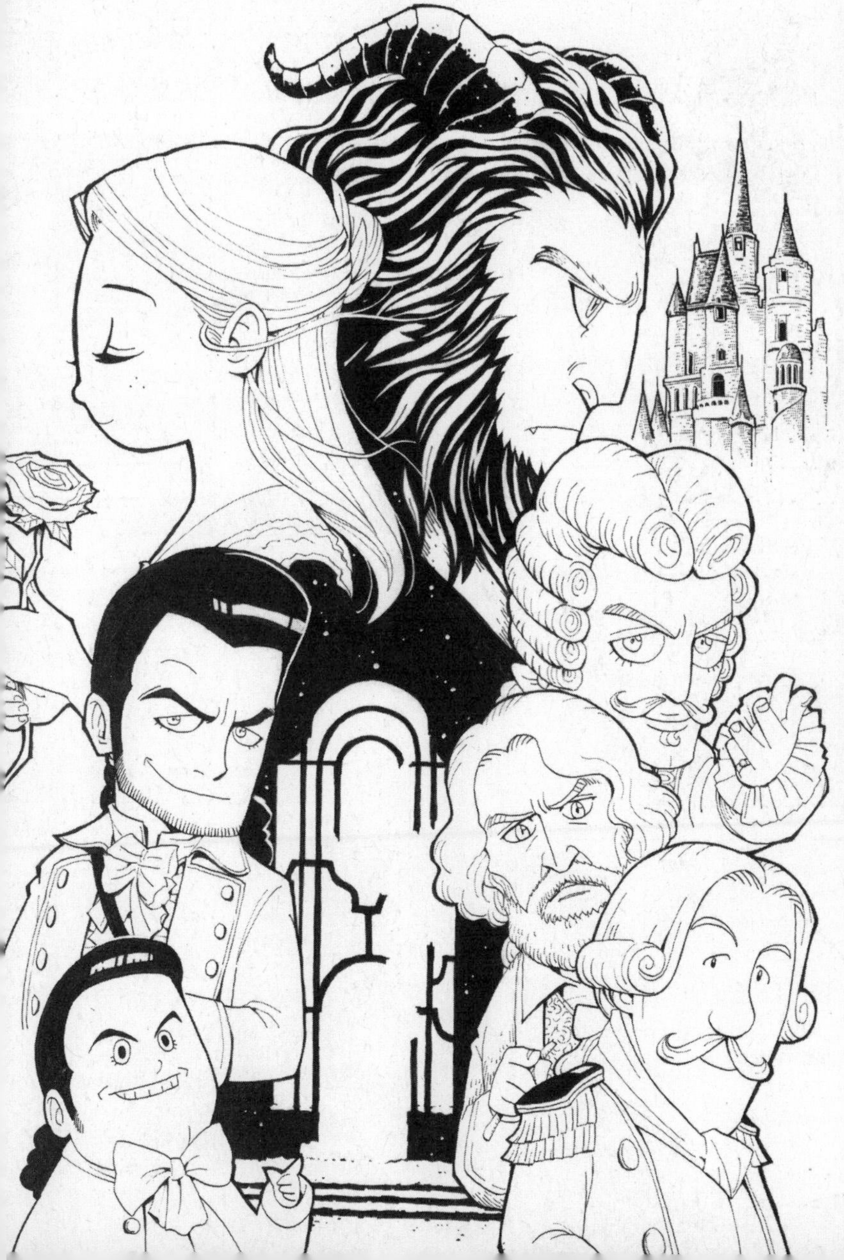

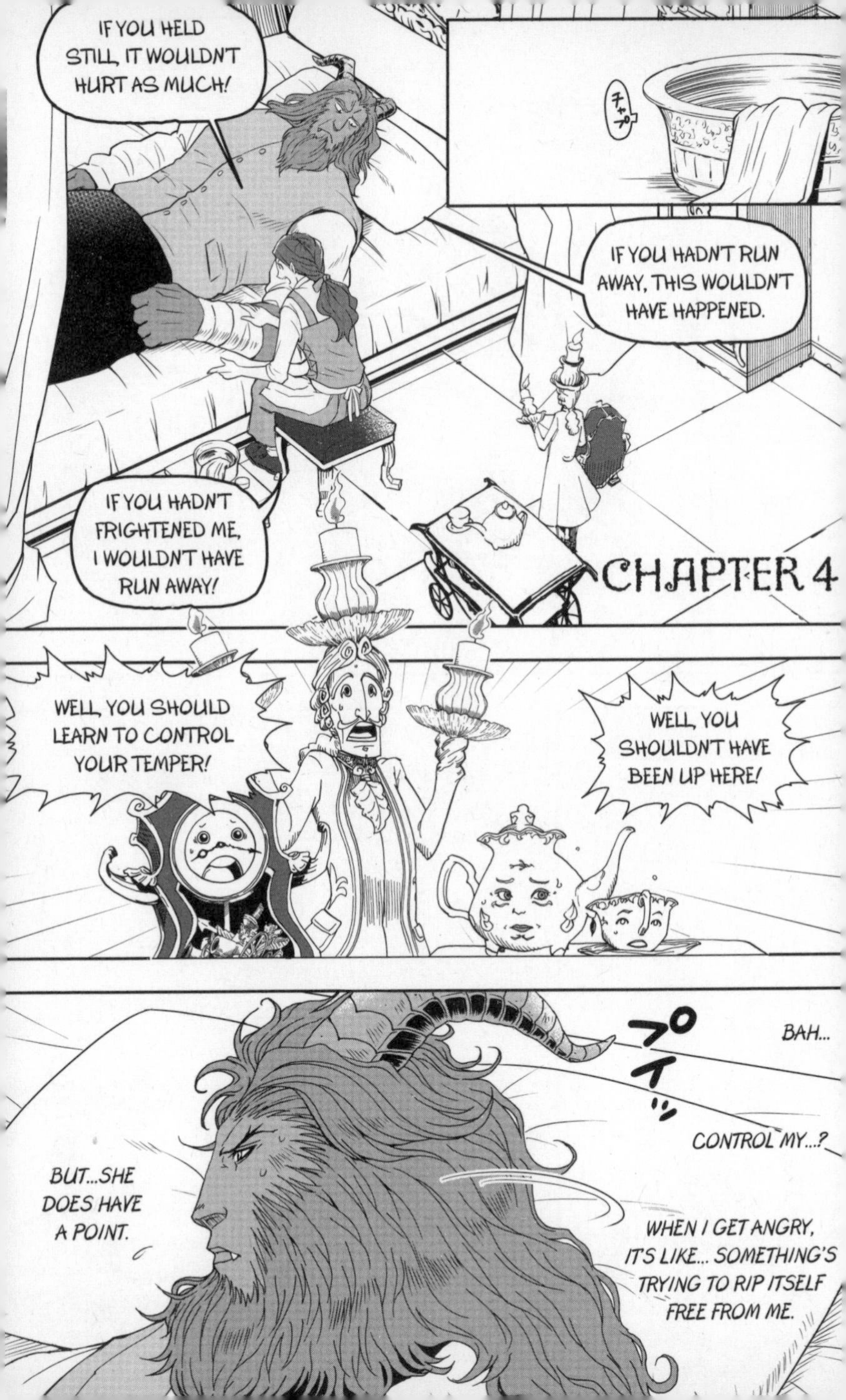
チャプ
IF YOU HELD STILL, IT WOULDN'T HURT AS MUCH!
IF YOU HADN'T RUN AWAY, THIS WOULDN'T HAVE HAPPENED.
IF YOU HADN'T FRIGHTENED ME, I WOULDN'T HAVE RUN AWAY!
CHAPTER 4
WELL, YOU SHOULDN'T HAVE BEEN UP HERE!
WELL, YOU SHOULD LEARN TO CONTROL YOUR TEMPER!
BAH...
プイッ
CONTROL MY...?
WHEN I GET ANGRY, IT'S LIKE... SOMETHING'S TRYING TO RIP ITSELF FREE FROM ME.
BUT...SHE DOES HAVE A POINT.

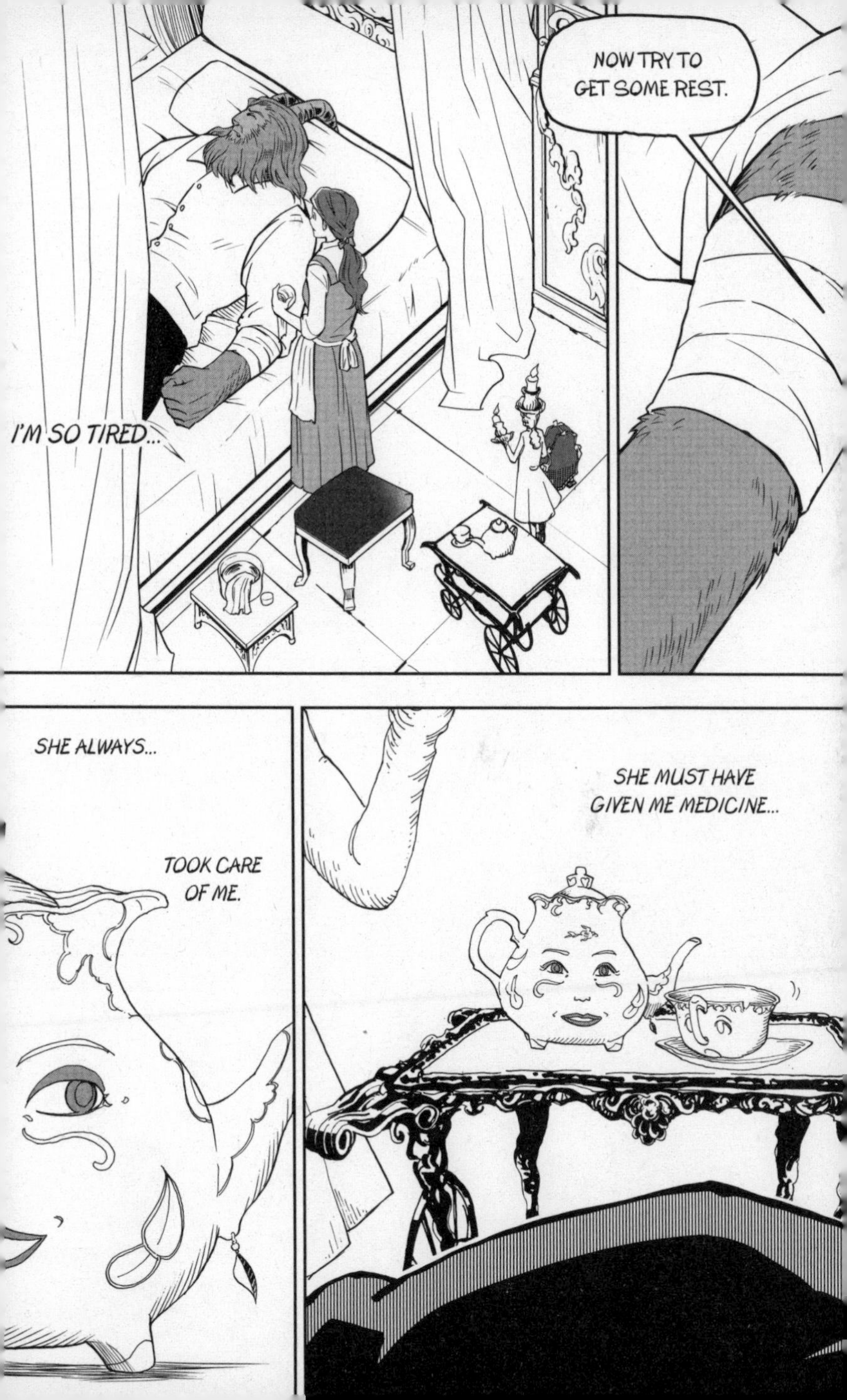
NOW TRY TO GET SOME REST.
I'M SO TIRED...
SHE MUST HAVE GIVEN ME MEDICINE...
SHE ALWAYS...
TOOK CARE OF ME.

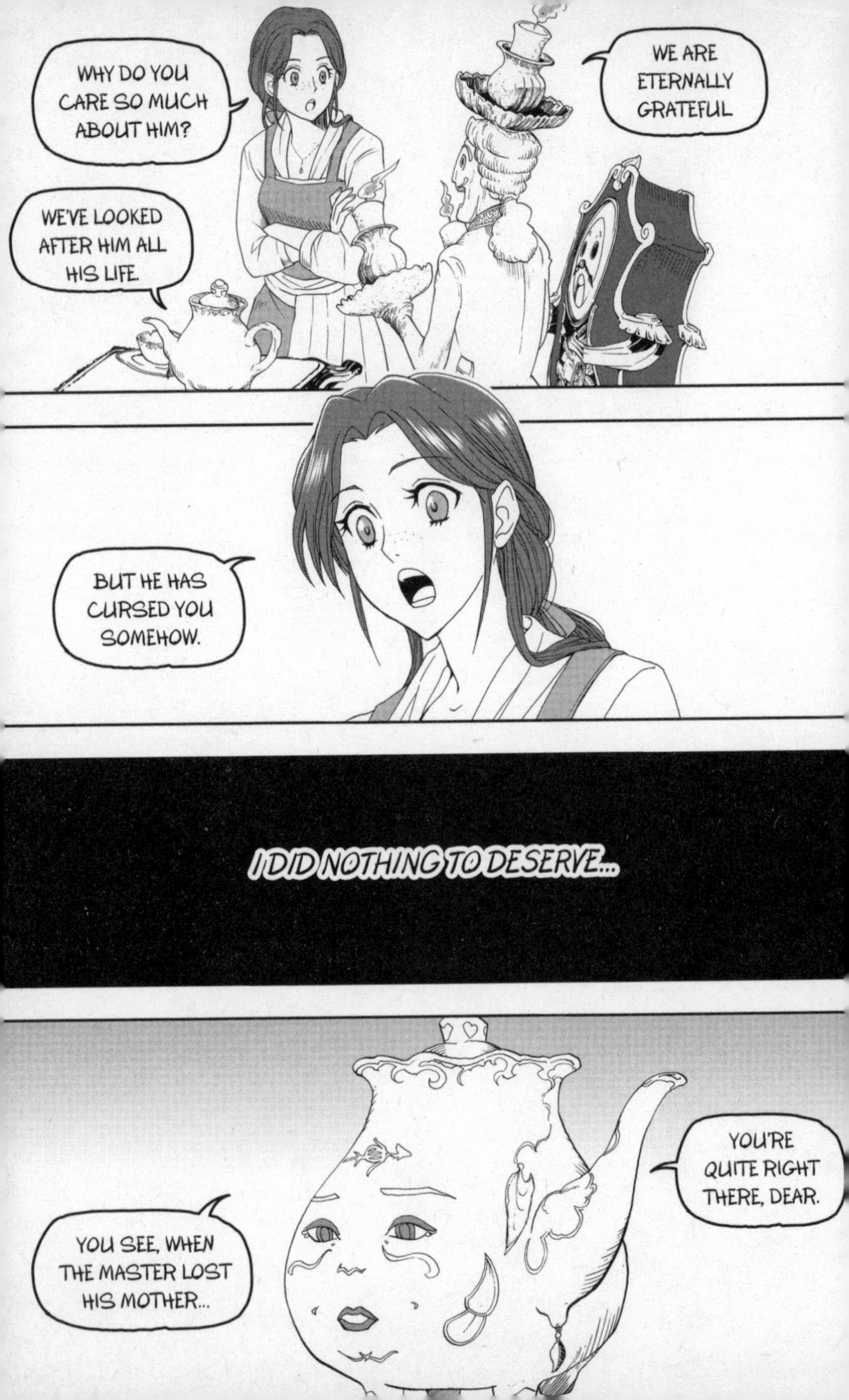
WE ARE ETERNALLY GRATEFUL
WHY DO YOU CARE SO MUCH ABOUT HIM?
WE'VE LOOKED AFTER HIM ALL HIS LIFE.
BUT HE HAS CURSED YOU SOMEHOW.
I DID NOTHING TO DESERVE...
YOU'RE QUITE RIGHT THERE, DEAR.
YOU SEE, WHEN THE MASTER LOST HIS MOTHER...

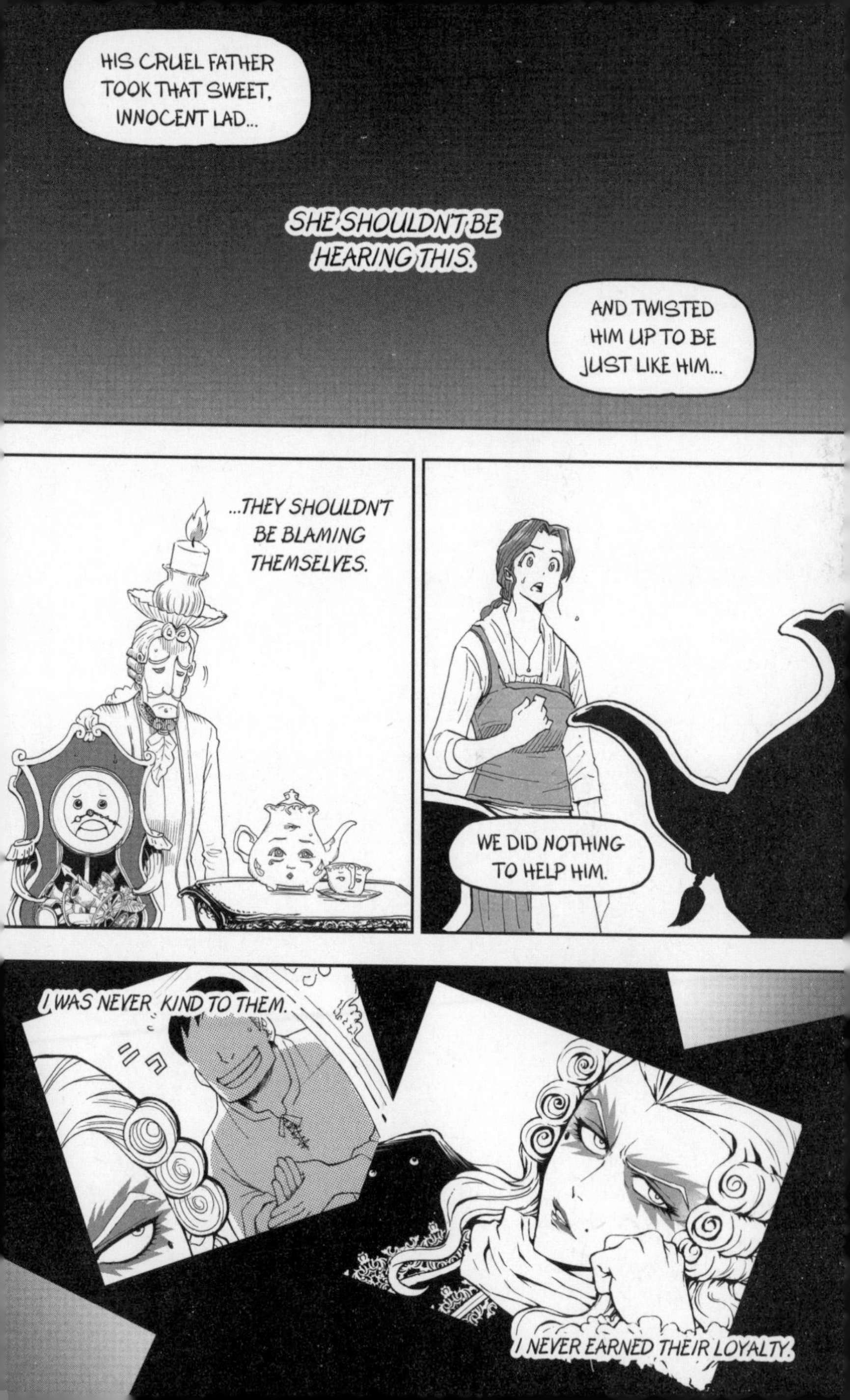
HIS CRUEL FATHER TOOK THAT SWEET, INNOCENT LAD...
SHE SHOULDN'T BE HEARING THIS.
AND TWISTED HIM UP TO BE JUST LIKE HIM...
WE DID NOTHING TO HELP HIM.
...THEY SHOULDN'T BE BLAMING THEMSELVES.
I NEVER EARNED THEIR LOYALTY.
I WAS NEVER KIND TO THEM.

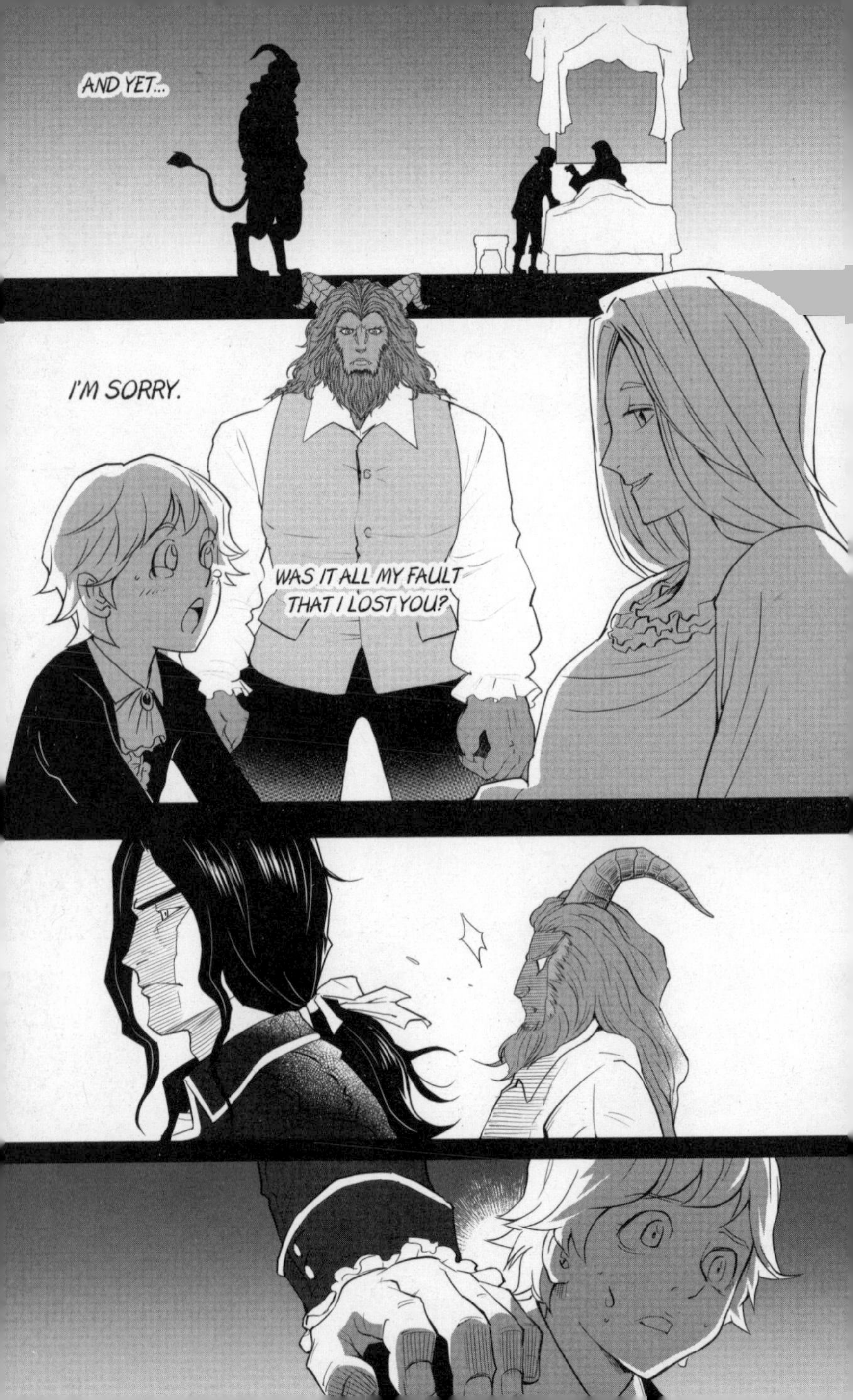
AND YET...
I'M SORRY.
WAS IT ALL MY FAULT THAT I LOST YOU?

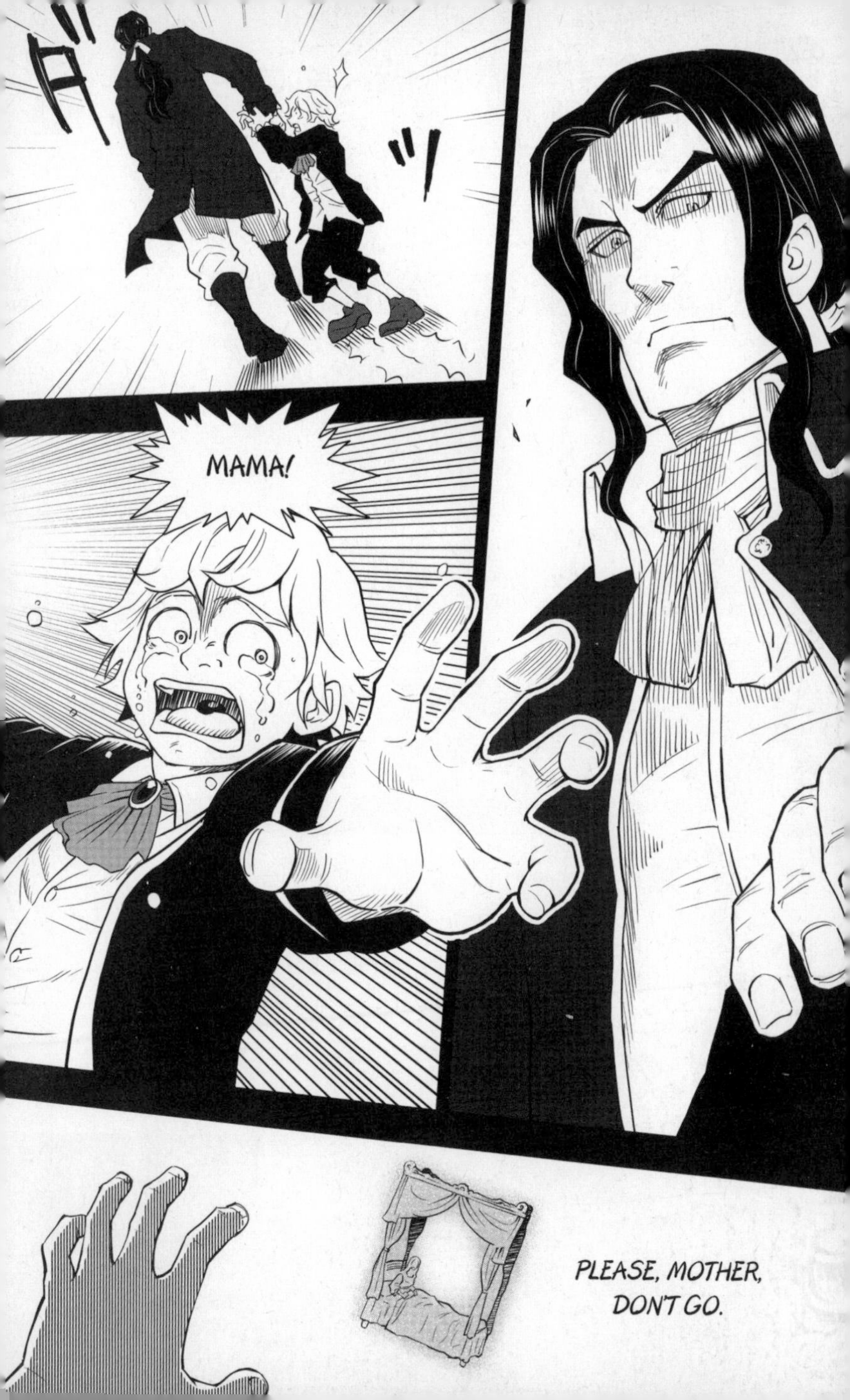
MAMA!
PLEASE, MOTHER, DON'T GO.

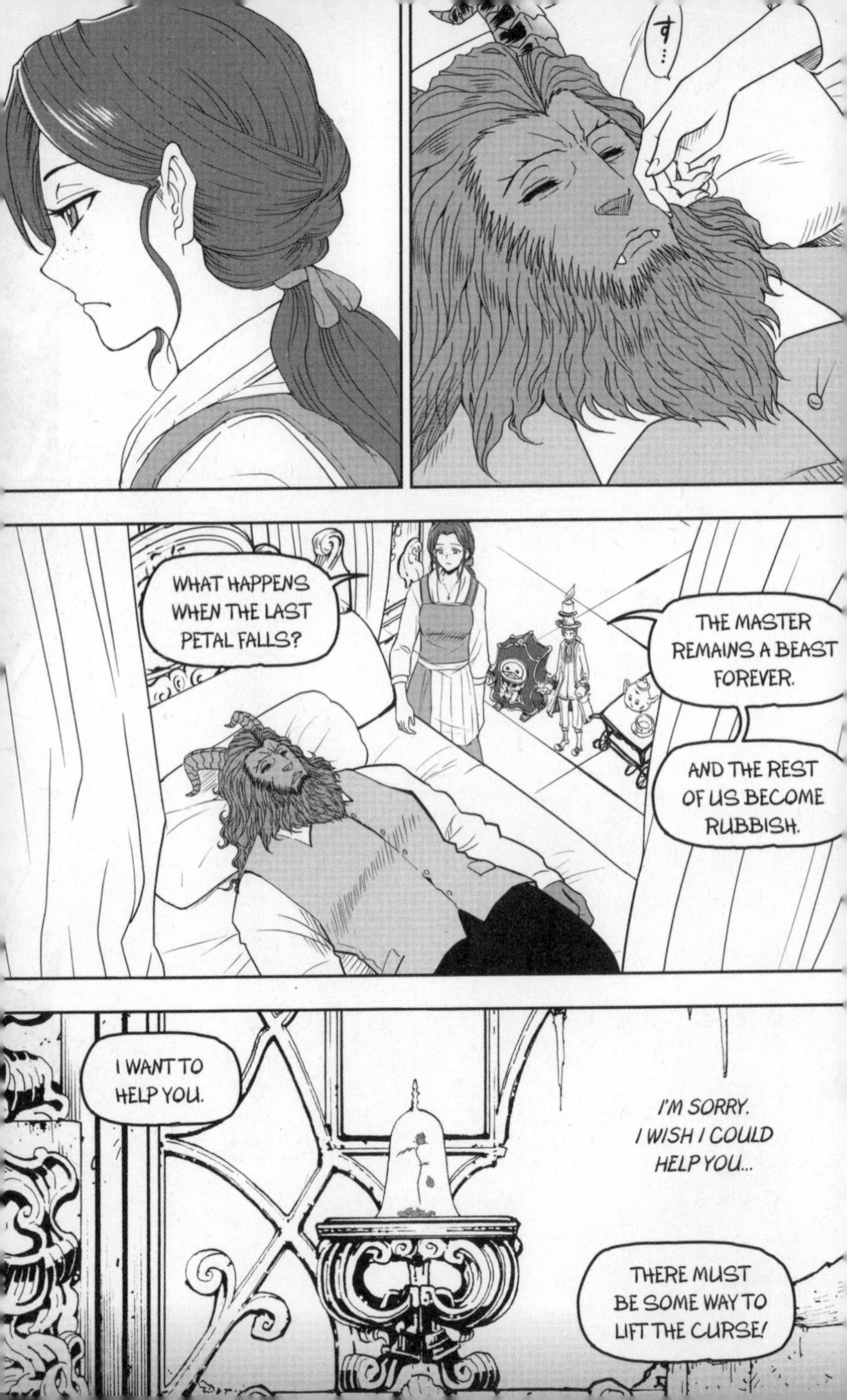
す…
WHAT HAPPENS WHEN THE LAST PETAL FALLS?
THE MASTER REMAINS A BEAST FOREVER.
AND THE REST OF US BECOME RUBBISH.
I WANT TO HELP YOU.
I'M SORRY. I WISH I COULD HELP YOU...
THERE MUST BE SOME WAY TO LIFT THE CURSE!

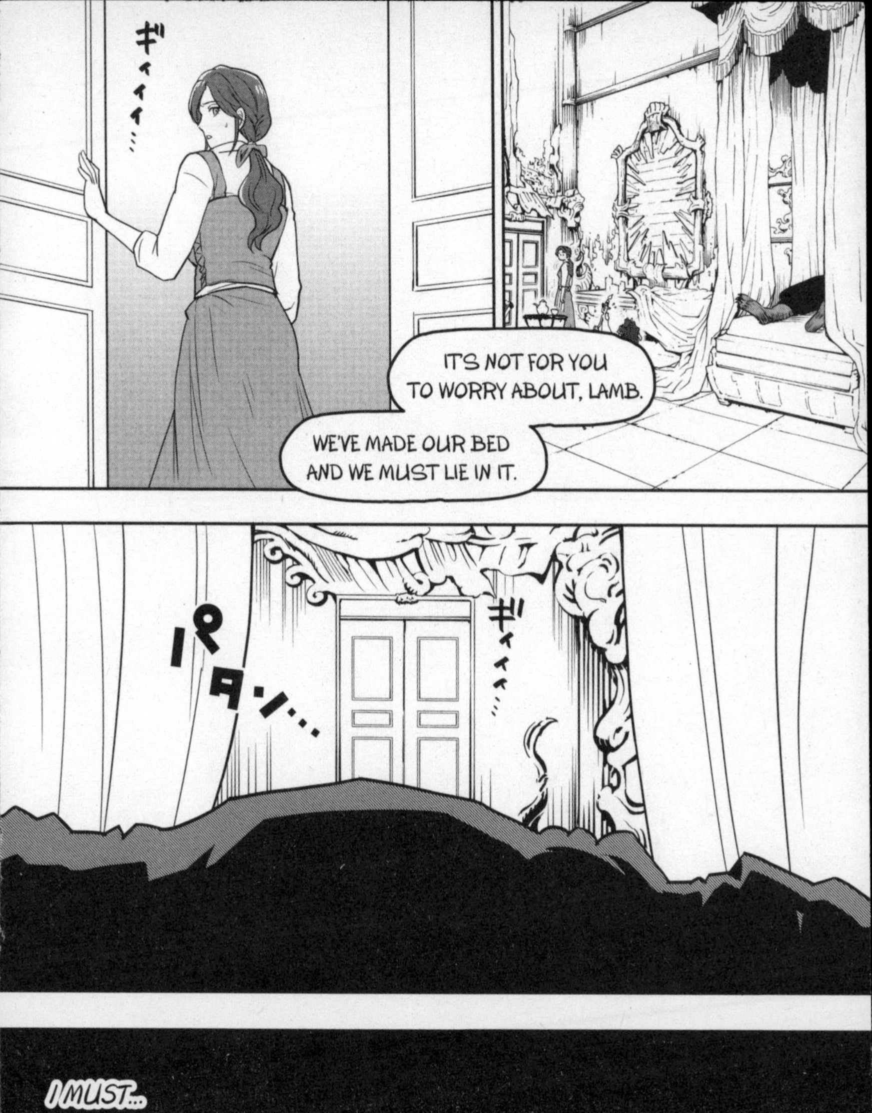
IT'S NOT FOR YOU TO WORRY ABOUT, LAMB.
WE'VE MADE OUR BED AND WE MUST LIE IN IT.
ギィィィ…
ギィィィ…
パタン…
I MUST...

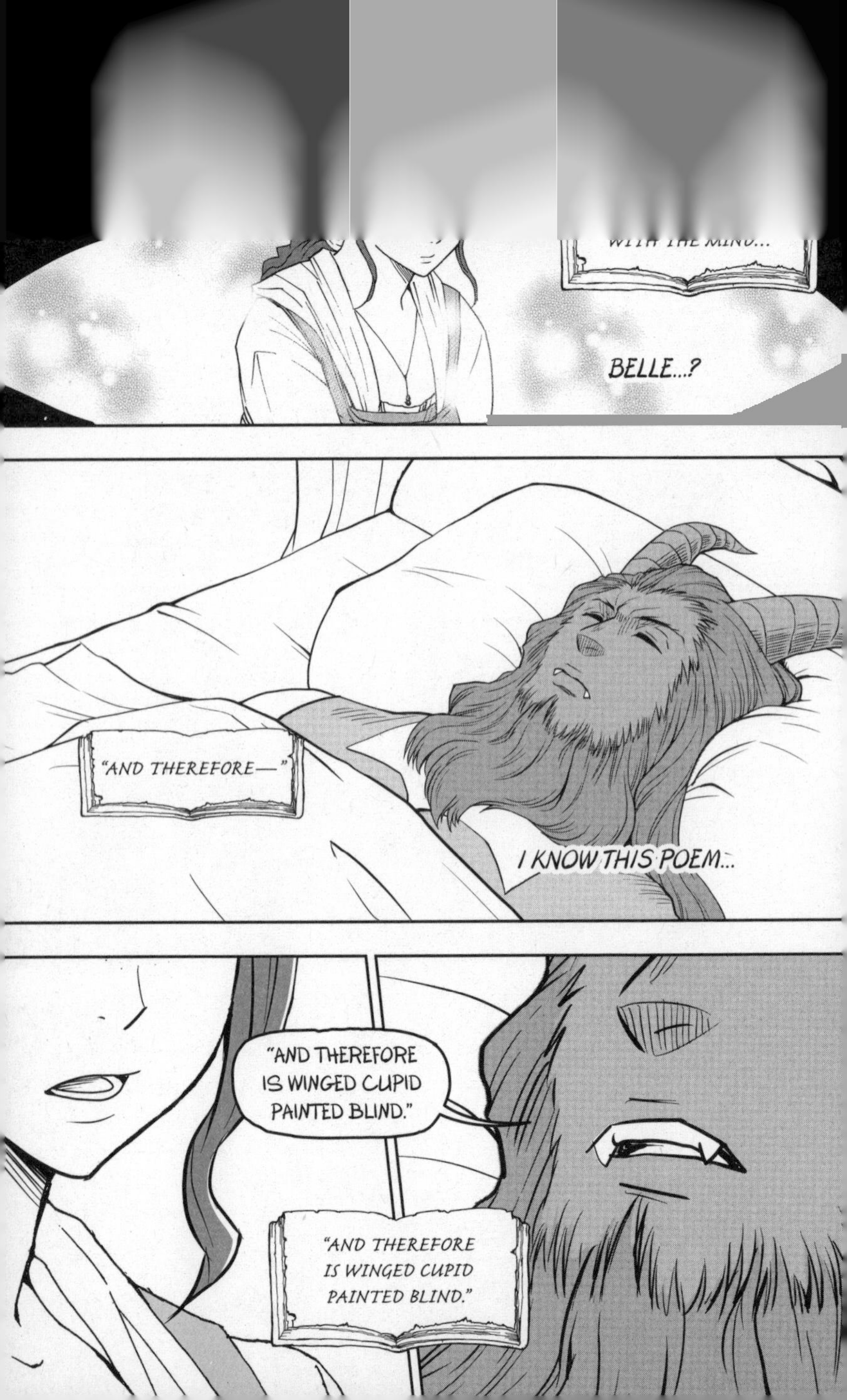
BELLE...?
"AND THEREFORE—"
I KNOW THIS POEM...
"AND THEREFORE IS WINGED CUPID PAINTED BLIND."
"AND THEREFORE IS WINGED CUPID PAINTED BLIND."

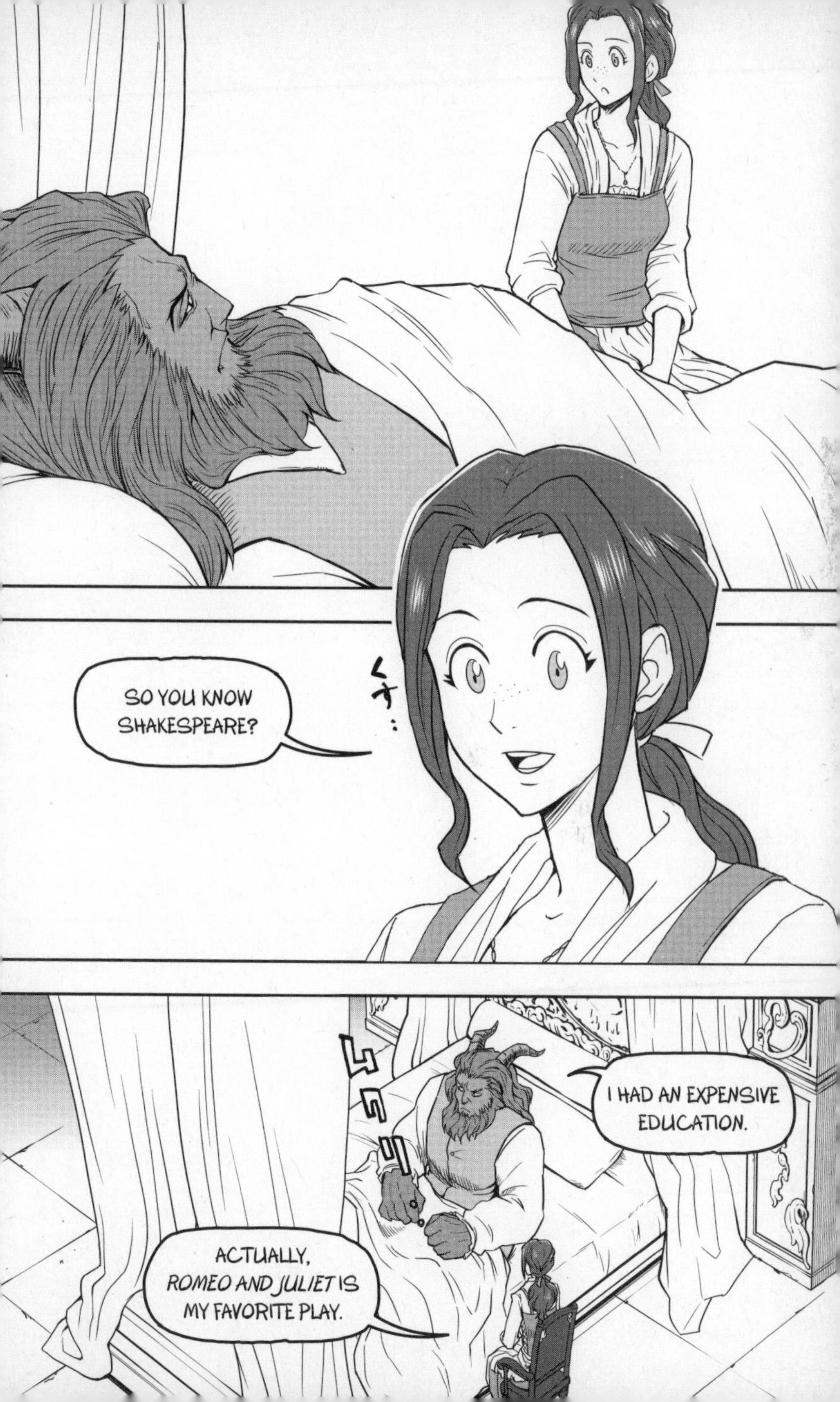
くす…
SO YOU KNOW SHAKESPEARE?
I HAD AN EXPENSIVE EDUCATION.
ACTUALLY, *ROMEO AND JULIET* IS MY FAVORITE PLAY.

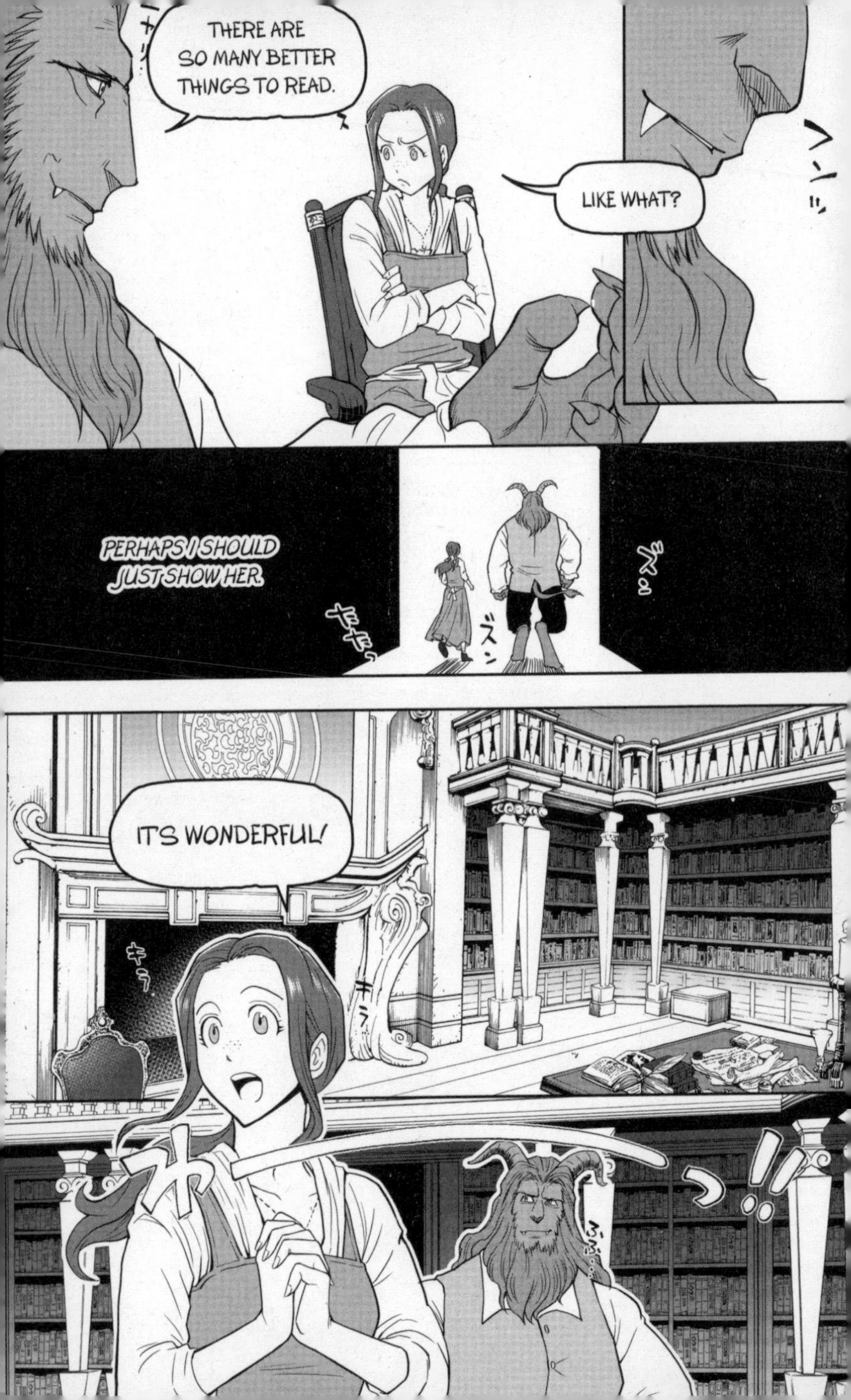
THERE ARE SO MANY BETTER THINGS TO READ.
LIKE WHAT?
PERHAPS I SHOULD JUST SHOW HER.
IT'S WONDERFUL!

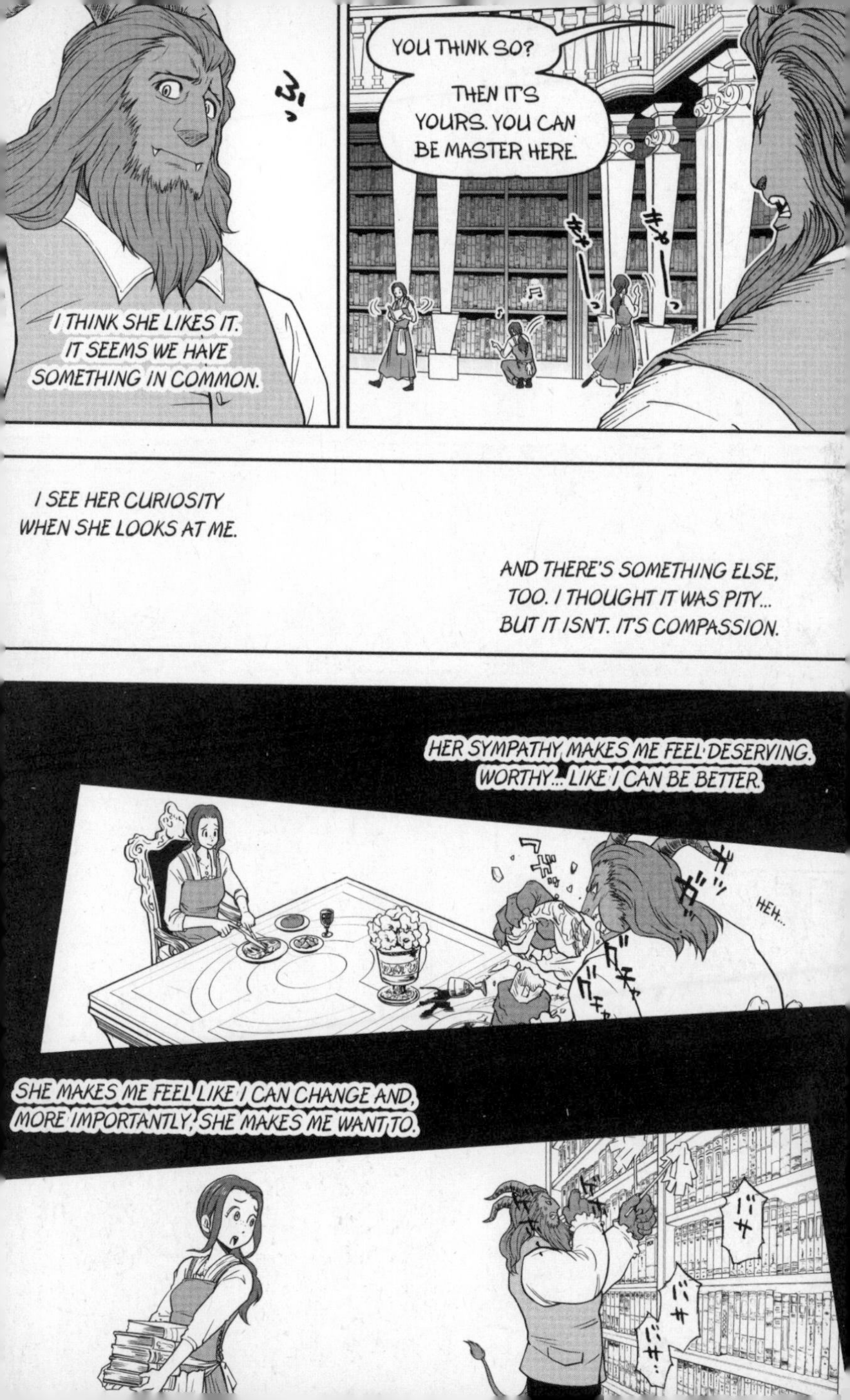
YOU THINK SO?
THEN IT'S YOURS. YOU CAN BE MASTER HERE.
I THINK SHE LIKES IT. IT SEEMS WE HAVE SOMETHING IN COMMON.
I SEE HER CURIOSITY WHEN SHE LOOKS AT ME.
AND THERE'S SOMETHING ELSE, TOO. I THOUGHT IT WAS PITY... BUT IT ISN'T. IT'S COMPASSION.
HER SYMPATHY MAKES ME FEEL DESERVING. WORTHY... LIKE I CAN BE BETTER.
HEH...
SHE MAKES ME FEEL LIKE I CAN CHANGE AND, MORE IMPORTANTLY, SHE MAKES ME WANT TO.

HER COMPASSION AND SELFLESSNESS ARE HER STRENGTHS...

ONES I HAVE BEEN TOO AFRAID TO OFFER.

TO REACH OUT MEANS TO RISK BEING HURT...

BUT SHE MAKES ME LESS AFRAID TO TRY.

WHAT ARE YOU READING?

Guinevere and Lancelot.

NOTHING!

BUT STILL... IT'S A ROMANCE

KING ARTHUR AND THE ROUND TABLE. SWORDS, FIGHTING...

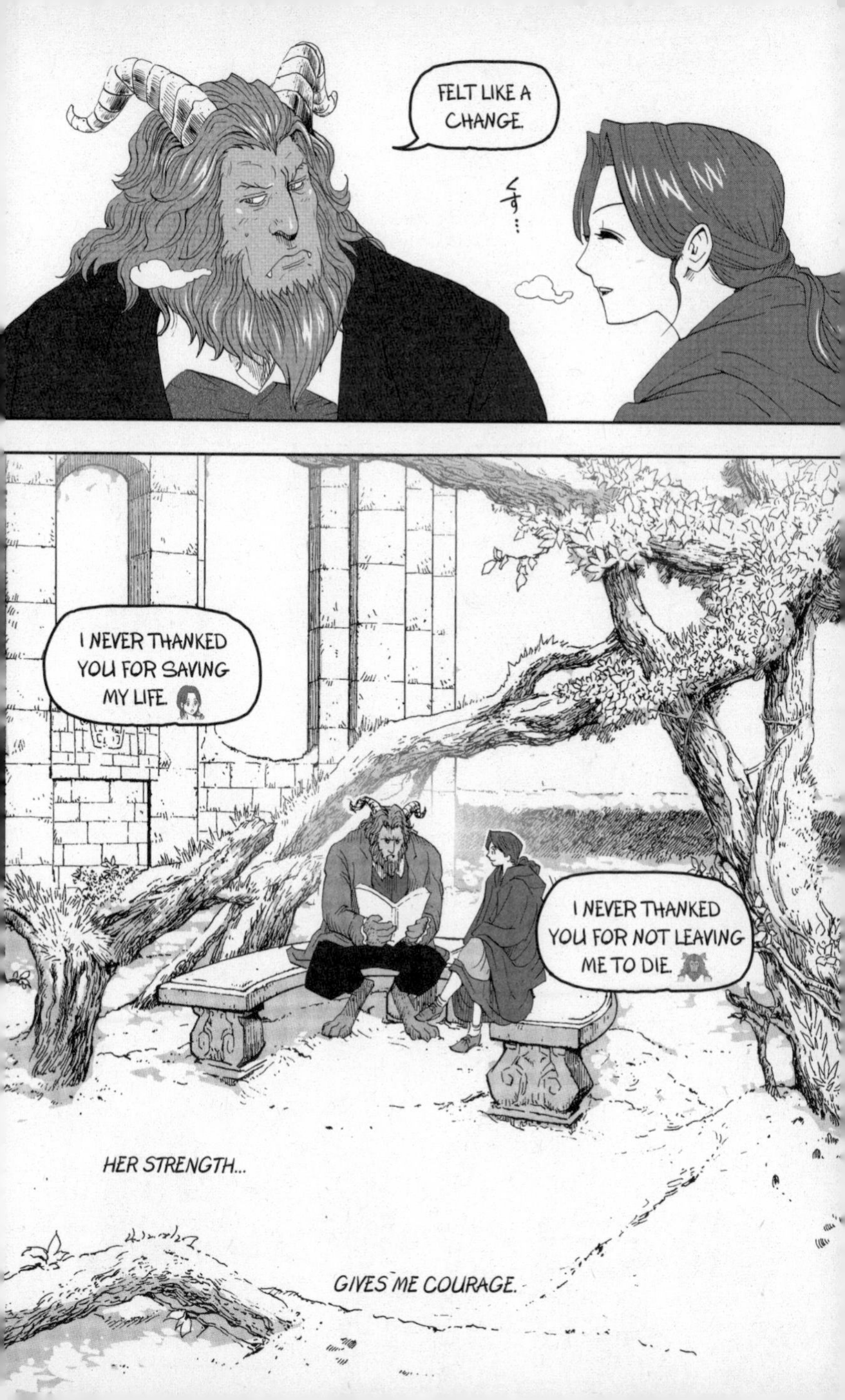
FELT LIKE A CHANGE.
くす…
I NEVER THANKED YOU FOR SAVING MY LIFE.
I NEVER THANKED YOU FOR NOT LEAVING ME TO DIE.
HER STRENGTH...
GIVES ME COURAGE.

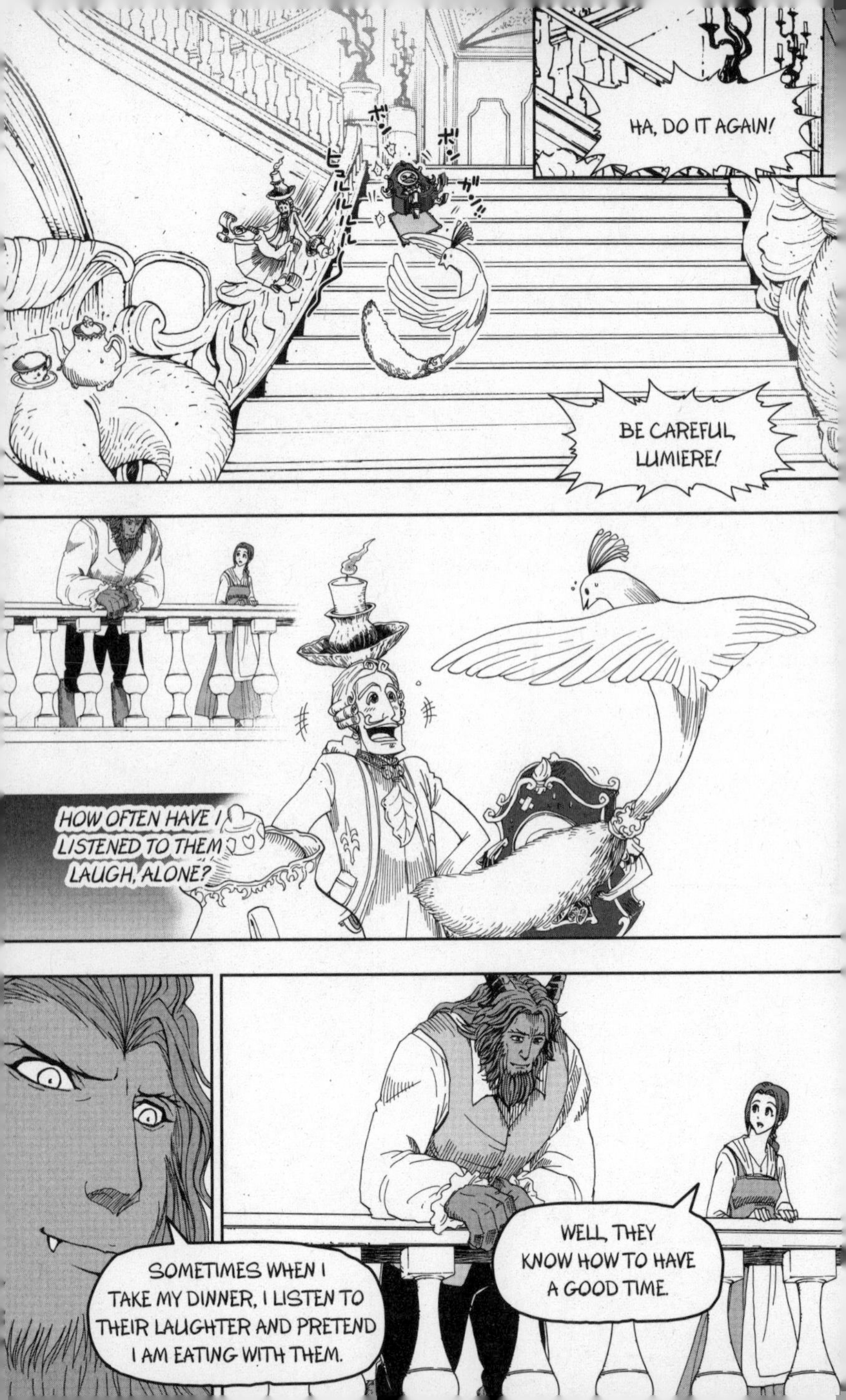
HA, DO IT AGAIN!
ボン
ボン
ガン!!
ヒュルルルル
BE CAREFUL, LUMIERE!
HOW OFTEN HAVE I LISTENED TO THEM LAUGH, ALONE?
WELL, THEY KNOW HOW TO HAVE A GOOD TIME.
SOMETIMES WHEN I TAKE MY DINNER, I LISTEN TO THEIR LAUGHTER AND PRETEND I AM EATING WITH THEM.

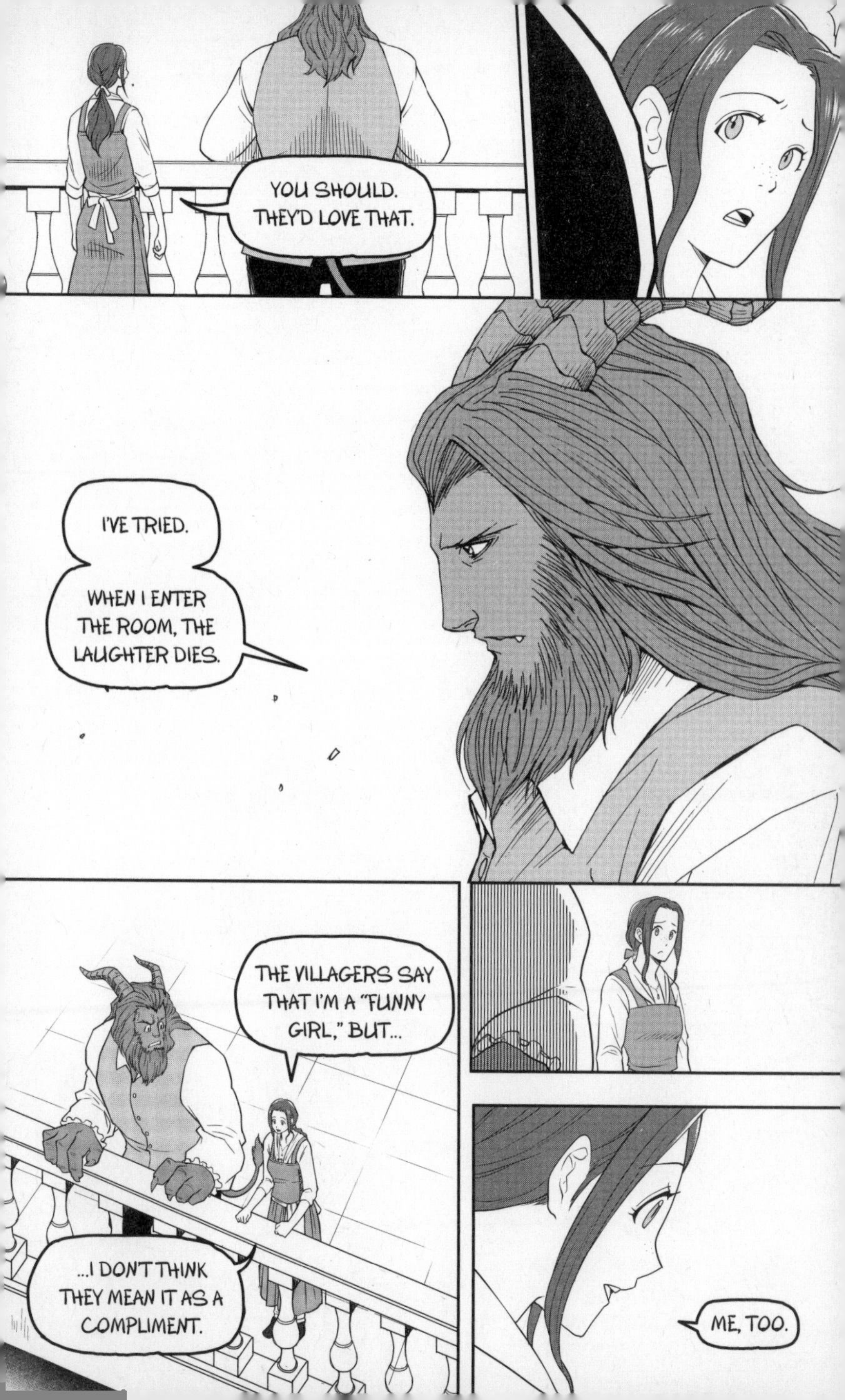
YOU SHOULD. THEY'D LOVE THAT.
I'VE TRIED.
WHEN I ENTER THE ROOM, THE LAUGHTER DIES.
THE VILLAGERS SAY THAT I'M A "FUNNY GIRL," BUT...
...I DON'T THINK THEY MEAN IT AS A COMPLIMENT.
ME, TOO.

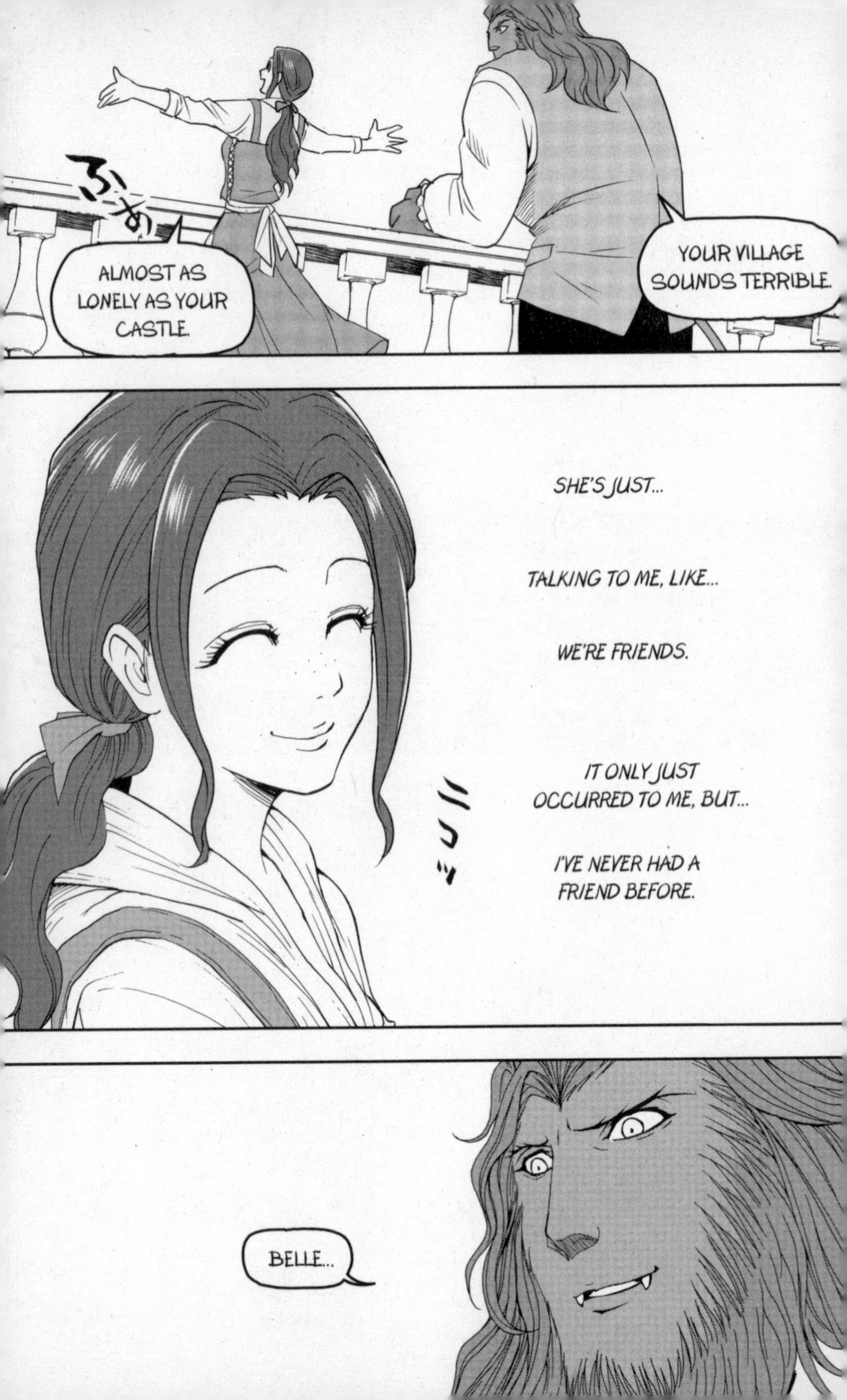
YOUR VILLAGE SOUNDS TERRIBLE.
ALMOST AS LONELY AS YOUR CASTLE.
ふぁ
SHE'S JUST...
TALKING TO ME, LIKE...
WE'RE FRIENDS.
IT ONLY JUST OCCURRED TO ME, BUT...
I'VE NEVER HAD A FRIEND BEFORE.
ニコッ
BELLE...

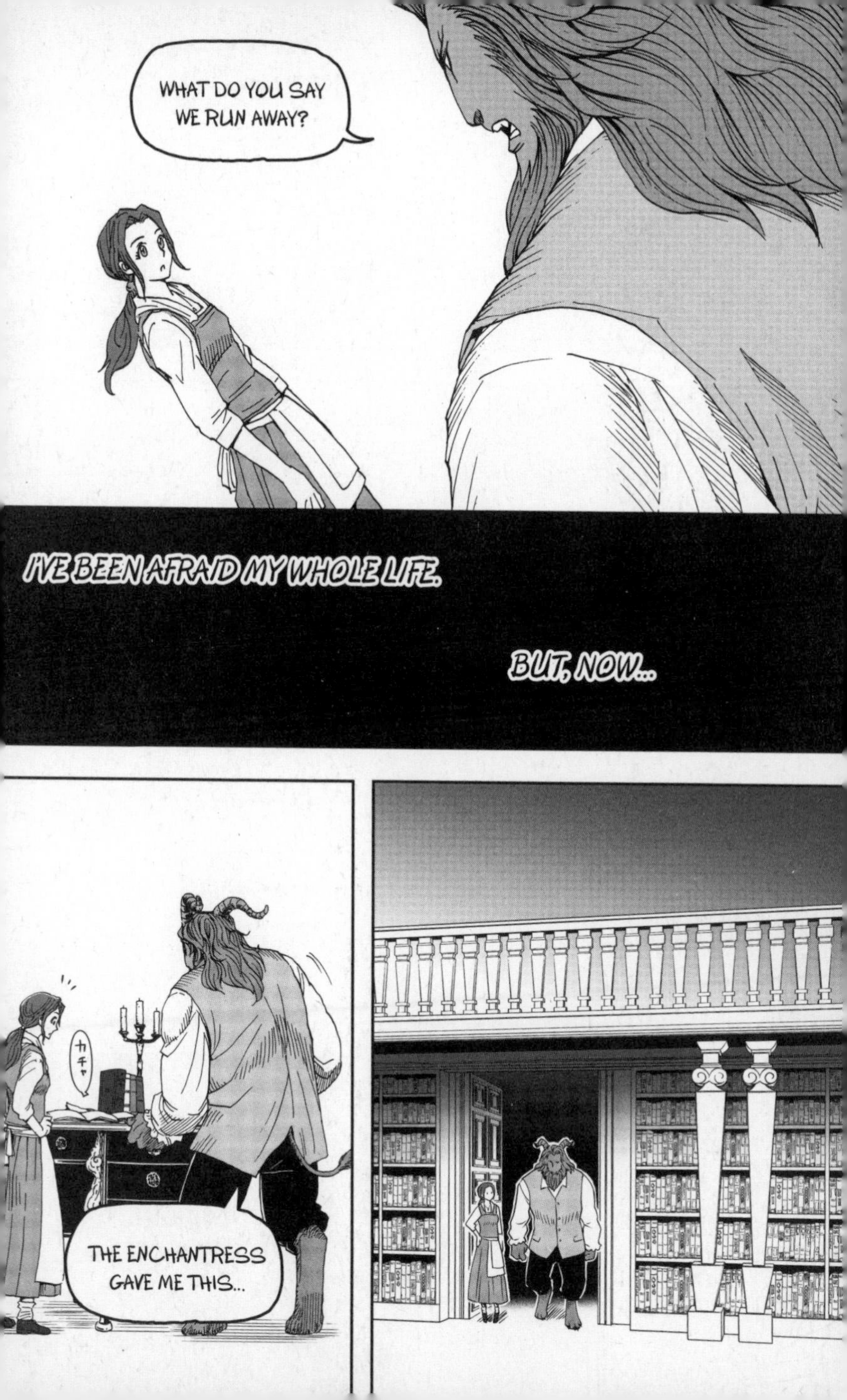
WHAT DO YOU SAY WE RUN AWAY?
I'VE BEEN AFRAID MY WHOLE LIFE.
BUT, NOW...
カチャ
THE ENCHANTRESS GAVE ME THIS...

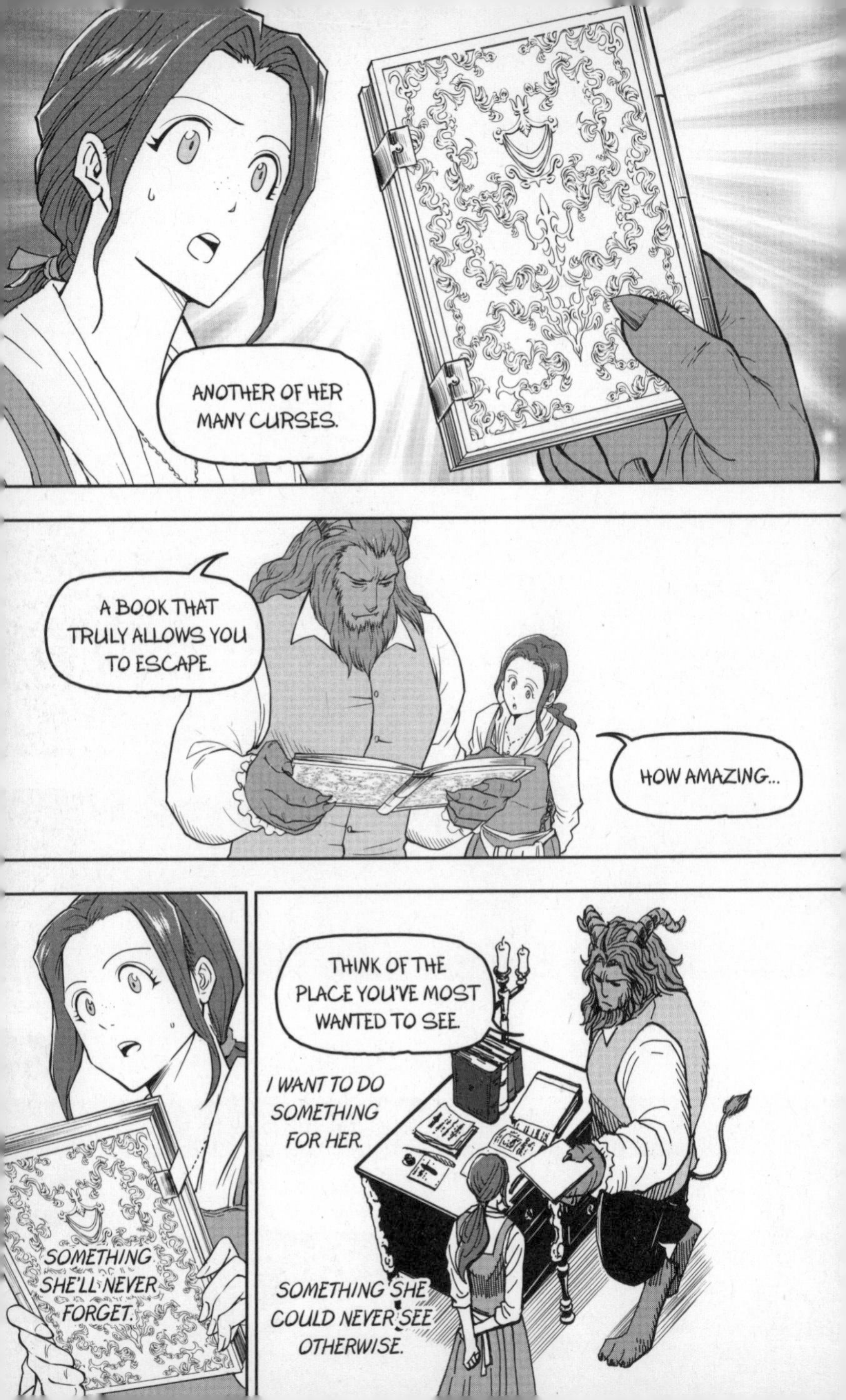
ANOTHER OF HER MANY CURSES.
A BOOK THAT TRULY ALLOWS YOU TO ESCAPE.
HOW AMAZING...
THINK OF THE PLACE YOU'VE MOST WANTED TO SEE.
I WANT TO DO SOMETHING FOR HER.
SOMETHING SHE COULD NEVER SEE OTHERWISE.
SOMETHING SHE'LL NEVER FORGET.

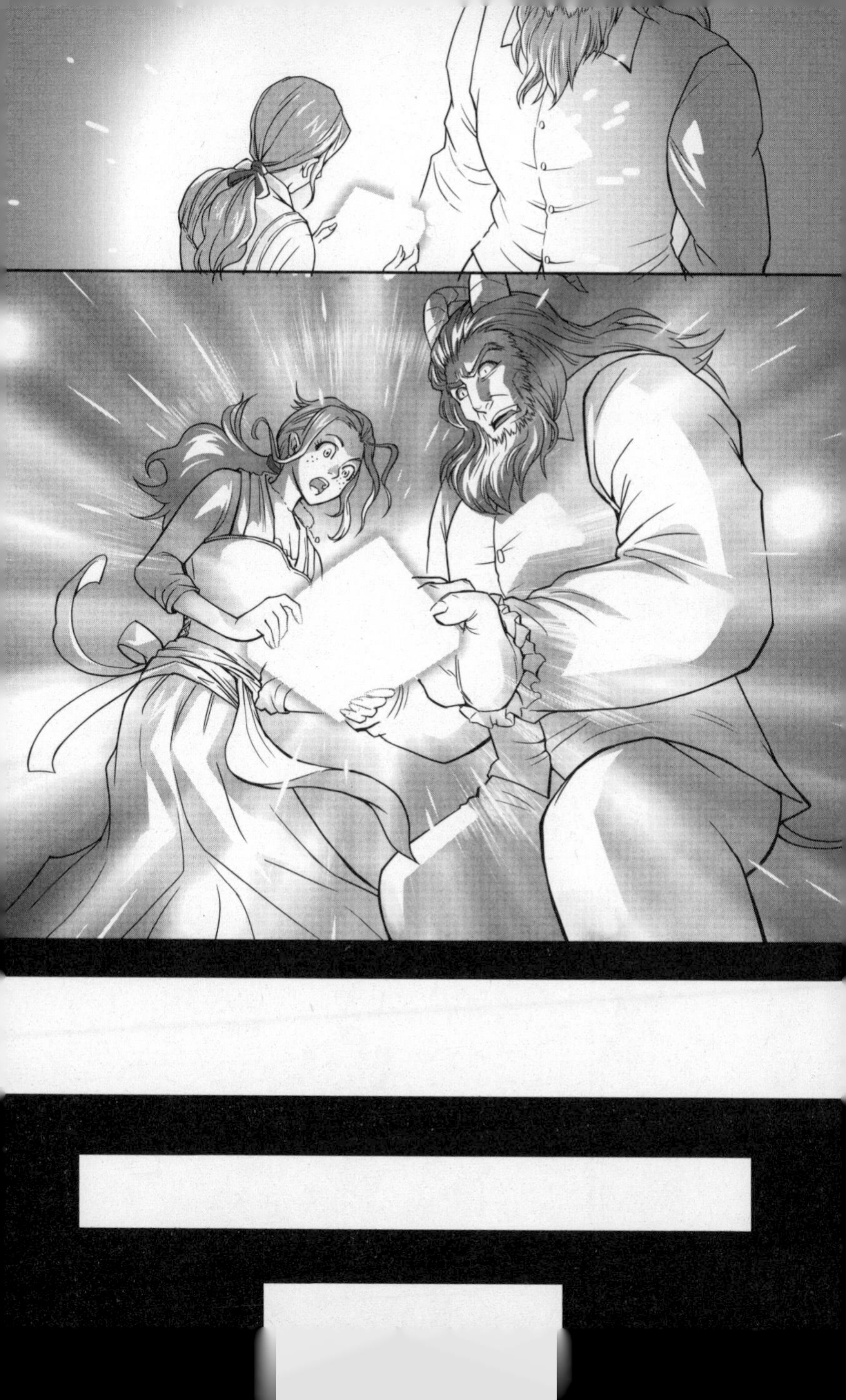

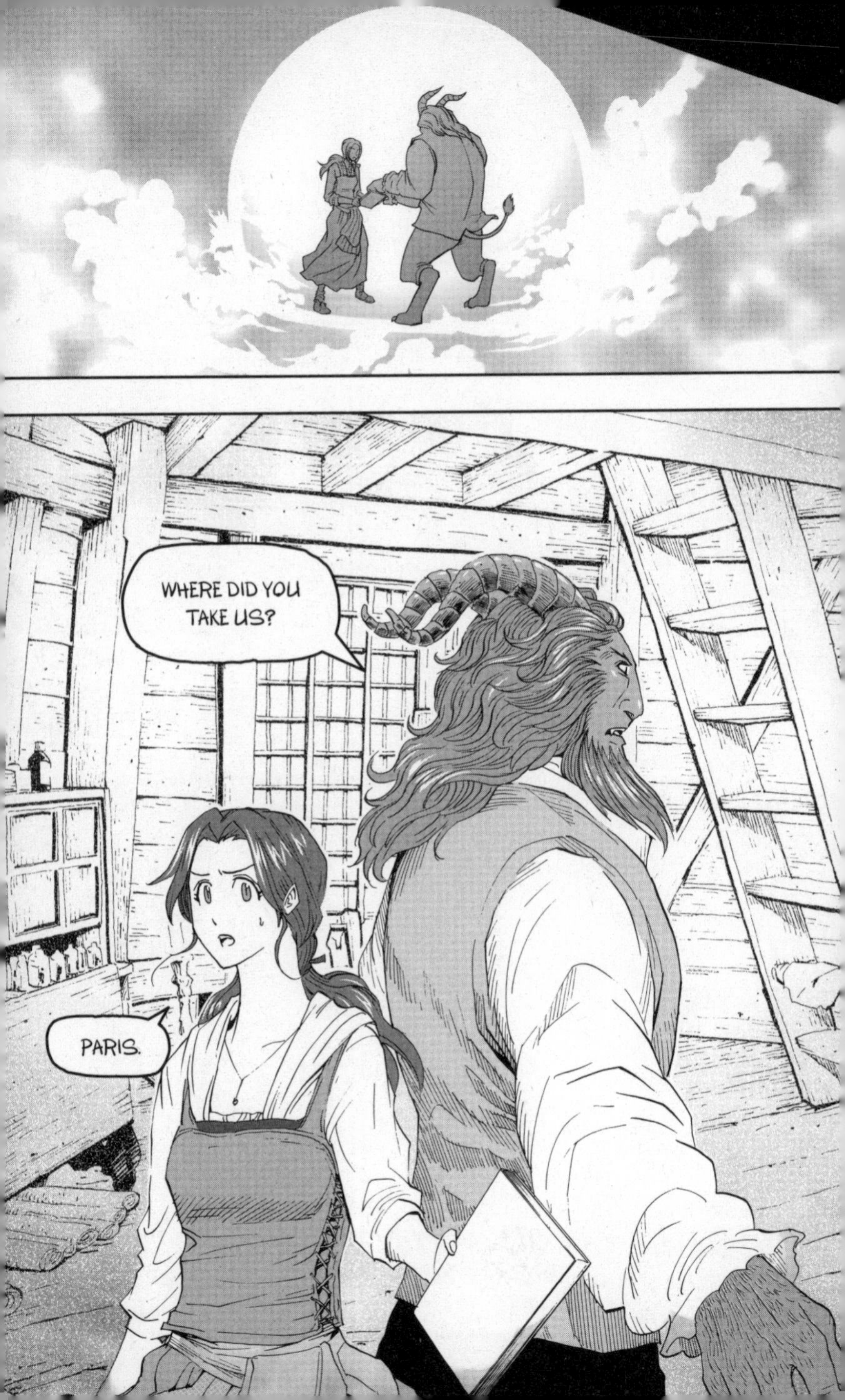
WHERE DID YOU TAKE US?
PARIS.

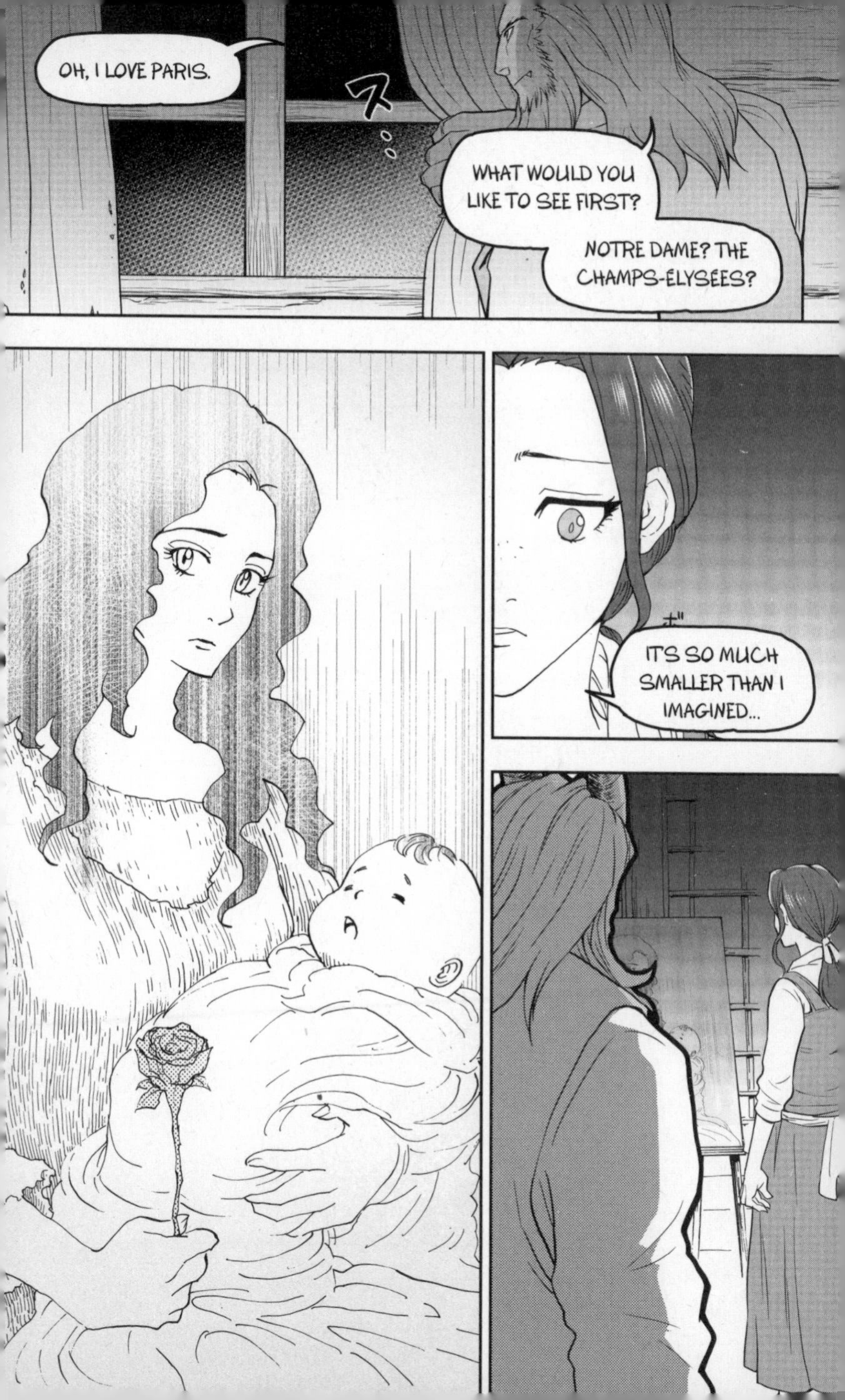
WHAT WOULD YOU LIKE TO SEE FIRST?
NOTRE DAME? THE CHAMPS-ELYSEES?
OH, I LOVE PARIS.
IT'S SO MUCH SMALLER THAN I IMAGINED...

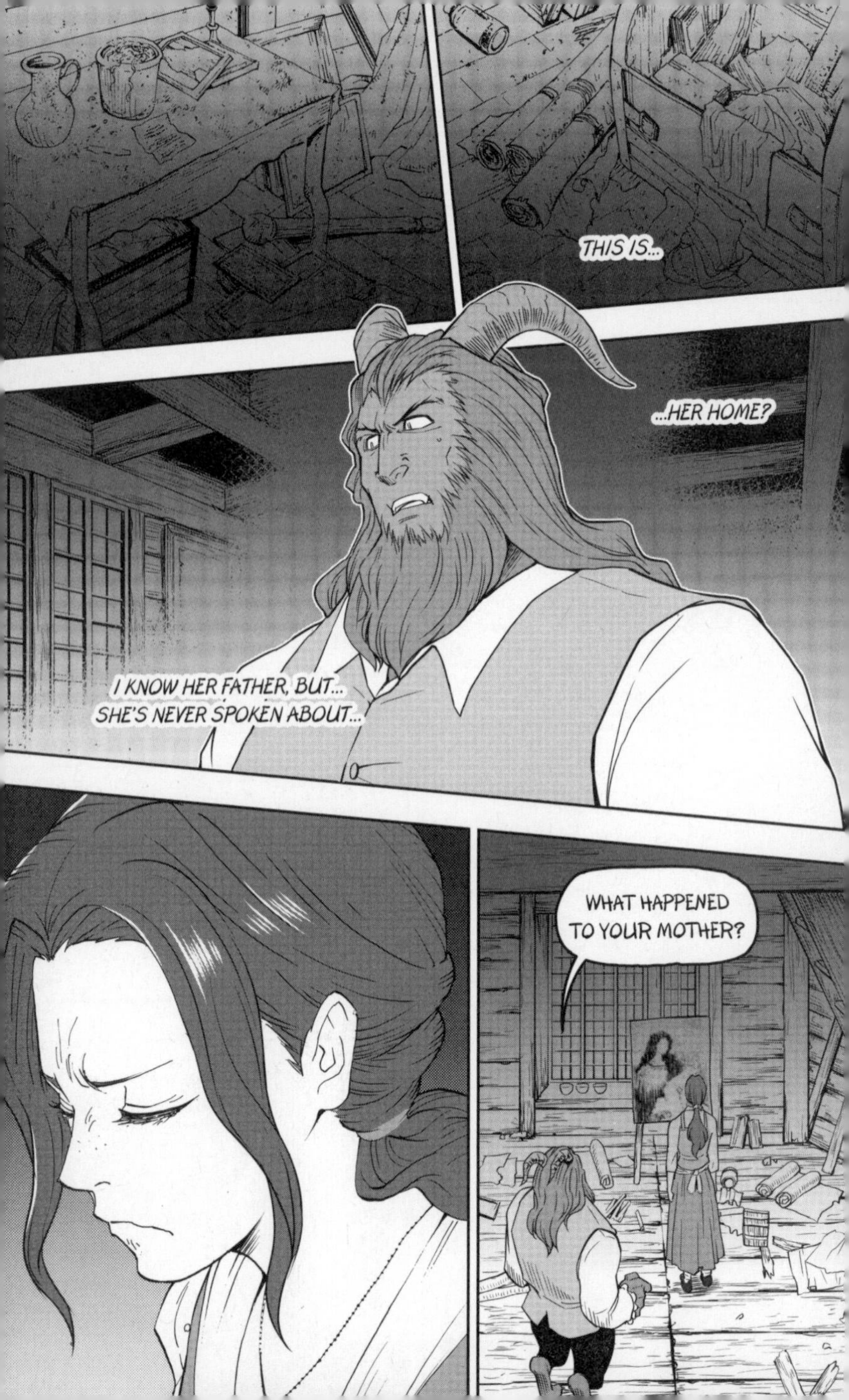
THIS IS...
...HER HOME?
I KNOW HER FATHER, BUT... SHE'S NEVER SPOKEN ABOUT...
WHAT HAPPENED TO YOUR MOTHER?

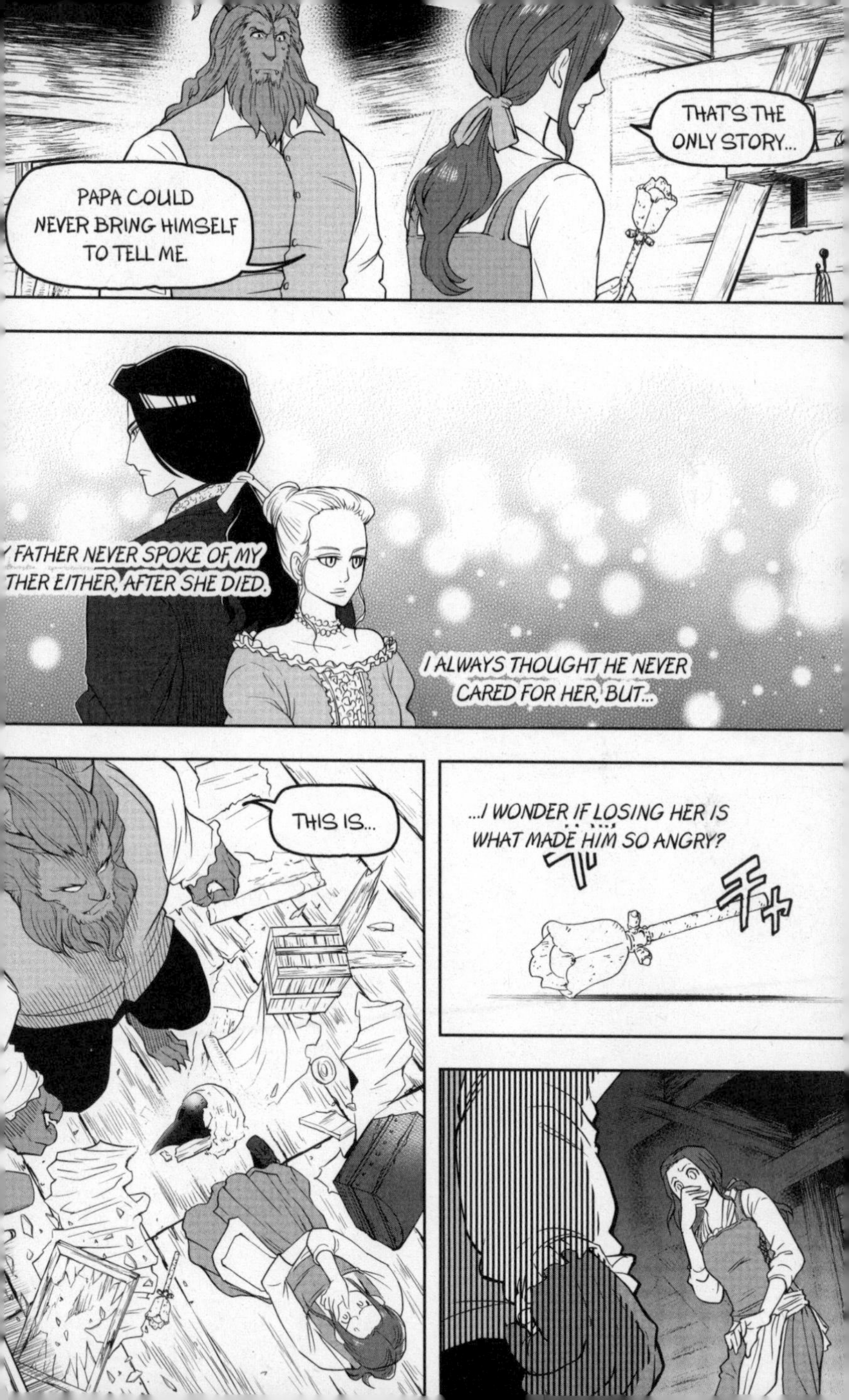
THAT'S THE ONLY STORY...
PAPA COULD NEVER BRING HIMSELF TO TELL ME.
Y FATHER NEVER SPOKE OF MY THER EITHER, AFTER SHE DIED.
I ALWAYS THOUGHT HE NEVER CARED FOR HER, BUT...
...I WONDER IF LOSING HER IS WHAT MADE HIM SO ANGRY?
チャ
THIS IS...

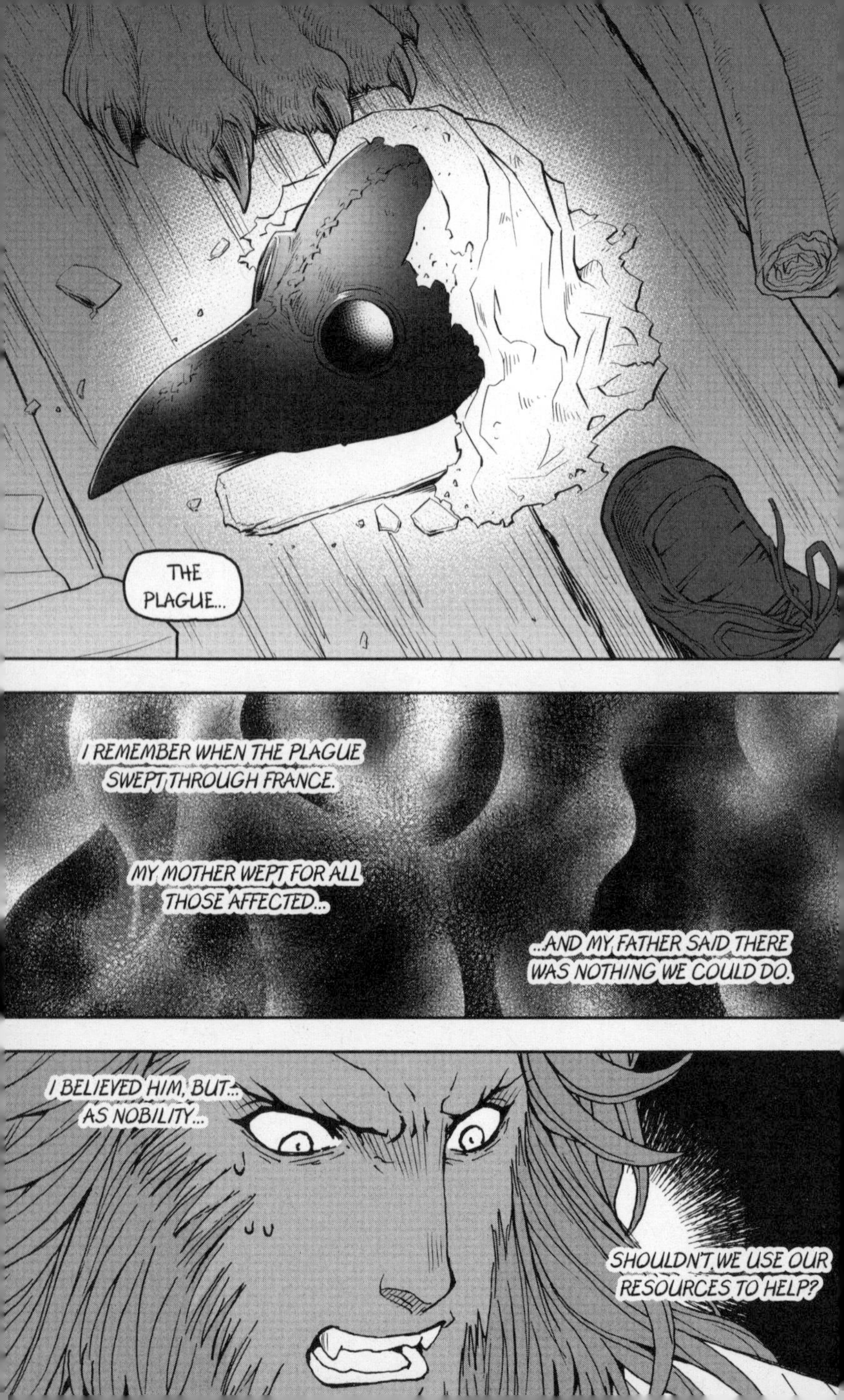
THE PLAGUE...
I REMEMBER WHEN THE PLAGUE SWEPT THROUGH FRANCE.
MY MOTHER WEPT FOR ALL THOSE AFFECTED...
...AND MY FATHER SAID THERE WAS NOTHING WE COULD DO.
I BELIEVED HIM, BUT... AS NOBILITY...
SHOULDN'T WE USE OUR RESOURCES TO HELP?

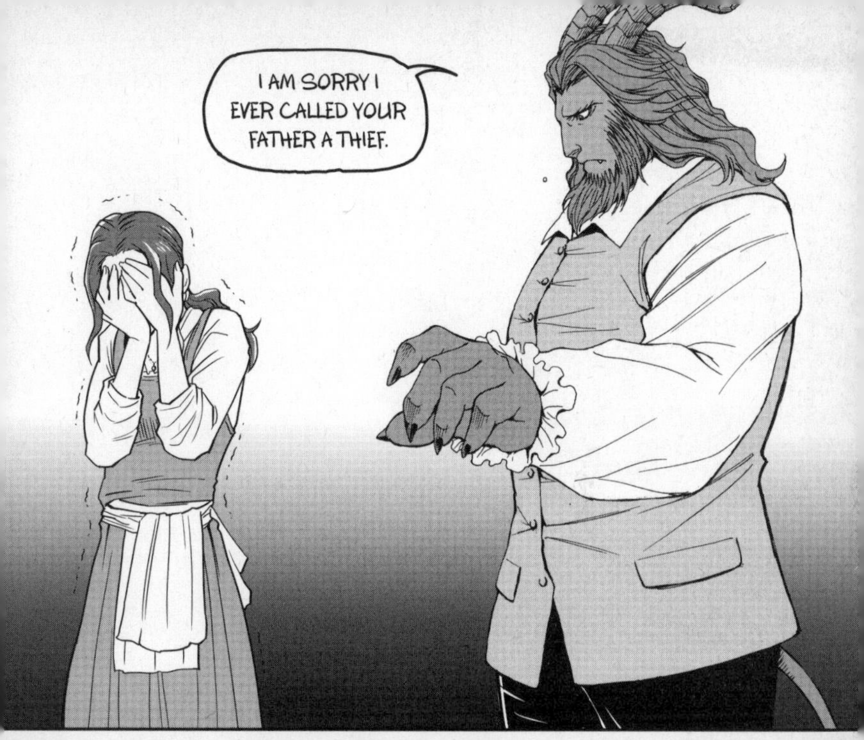
I AM SORRY I EVER CALLED YOUR FATHER A THIEF.
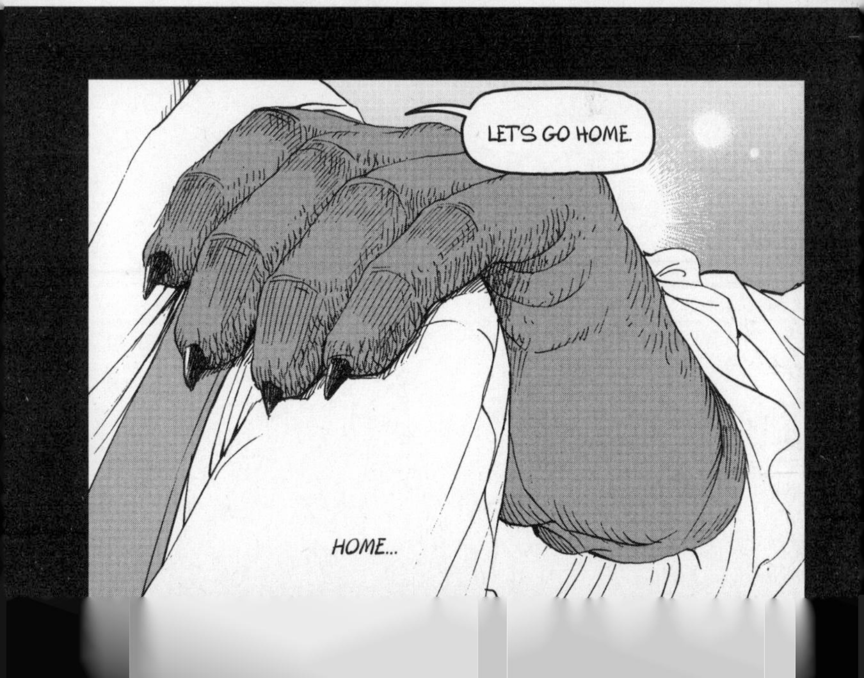
LET'S GO HOME.
HOME...

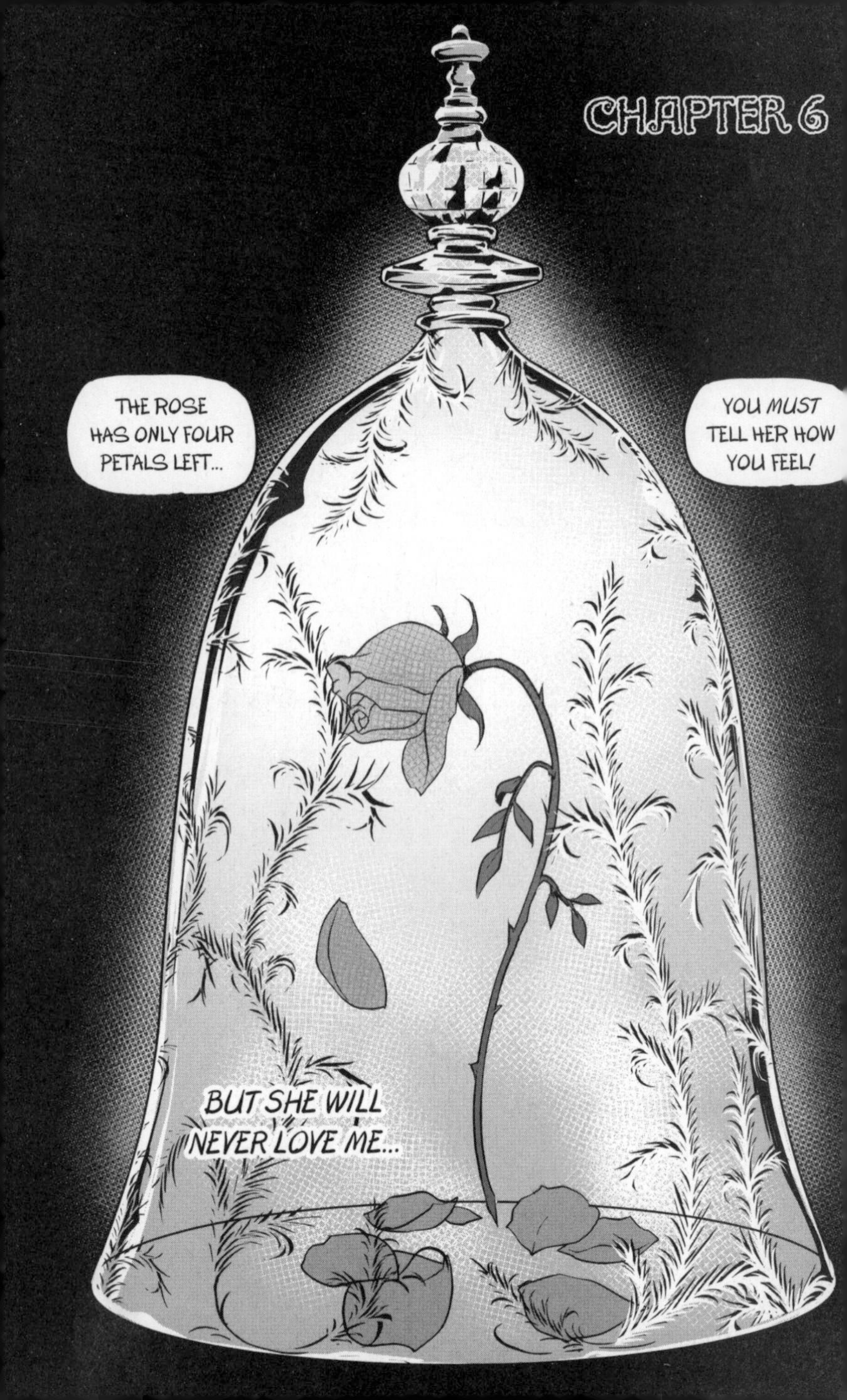
CHAPTER 6
YOU MUST TELL HER HOW YOU FEEL!
THE ROSE HAS ONLY FOUR PETALS LEFT...
BUT SHE WILL NEVER LOVE ME...

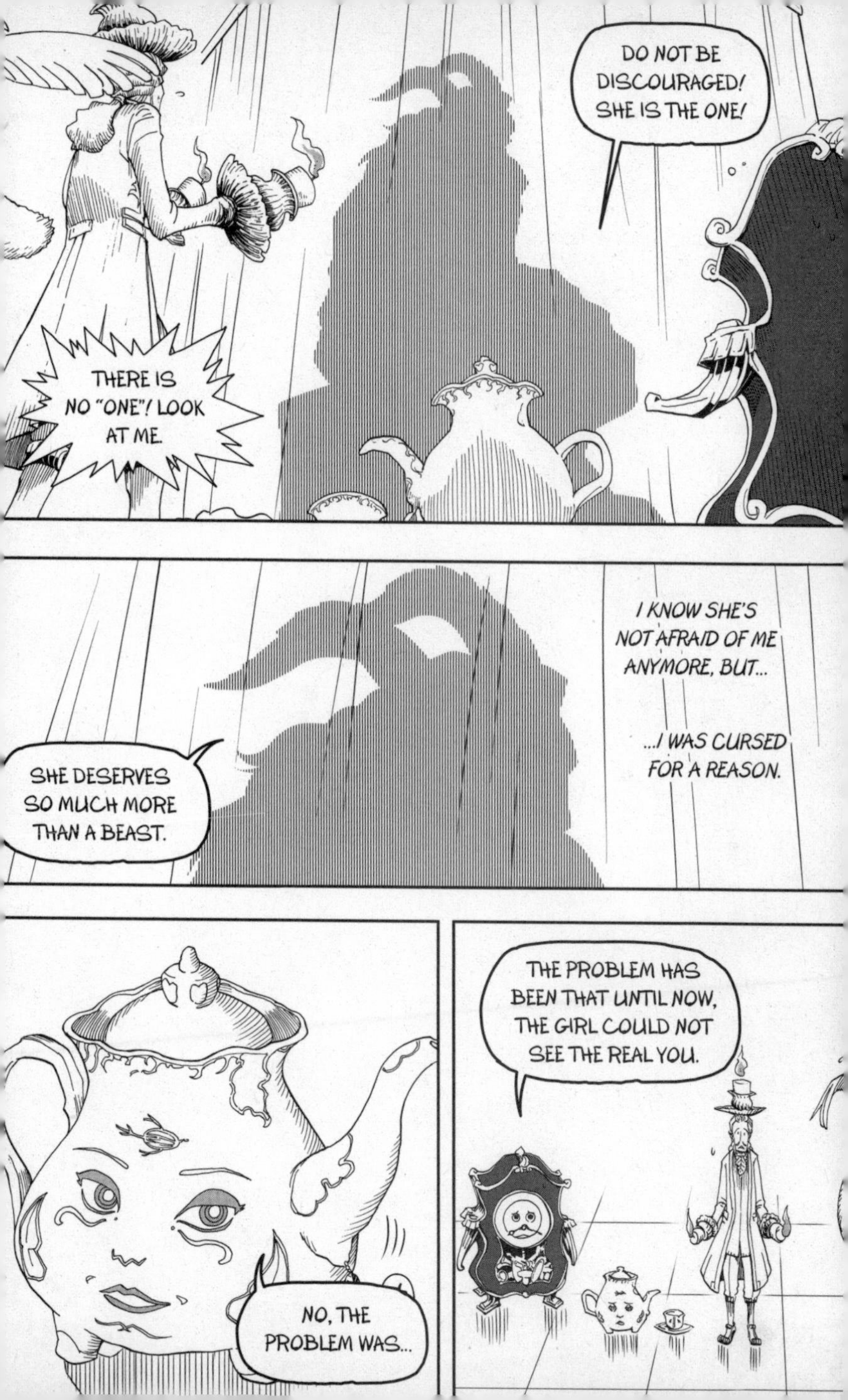
DO NOT BE DISCOURAGED! SHE IS THE ONE!
THERE IS NO "ONE"! LOOK AT ME.
I KNOW SHE'S NOT AFRAID OF ME ANYMORE, BUT...
...I WAS CURSED FOR A REASON.
SHE DESERVES SO MUCH MORE THAN A BEAST.
THE PROBLEM HAS BEEN THAT UNTIL NOW, THE GIRL COULD NOT SEE THE REAL YOU.
NO, THE PROBLEM WAS...

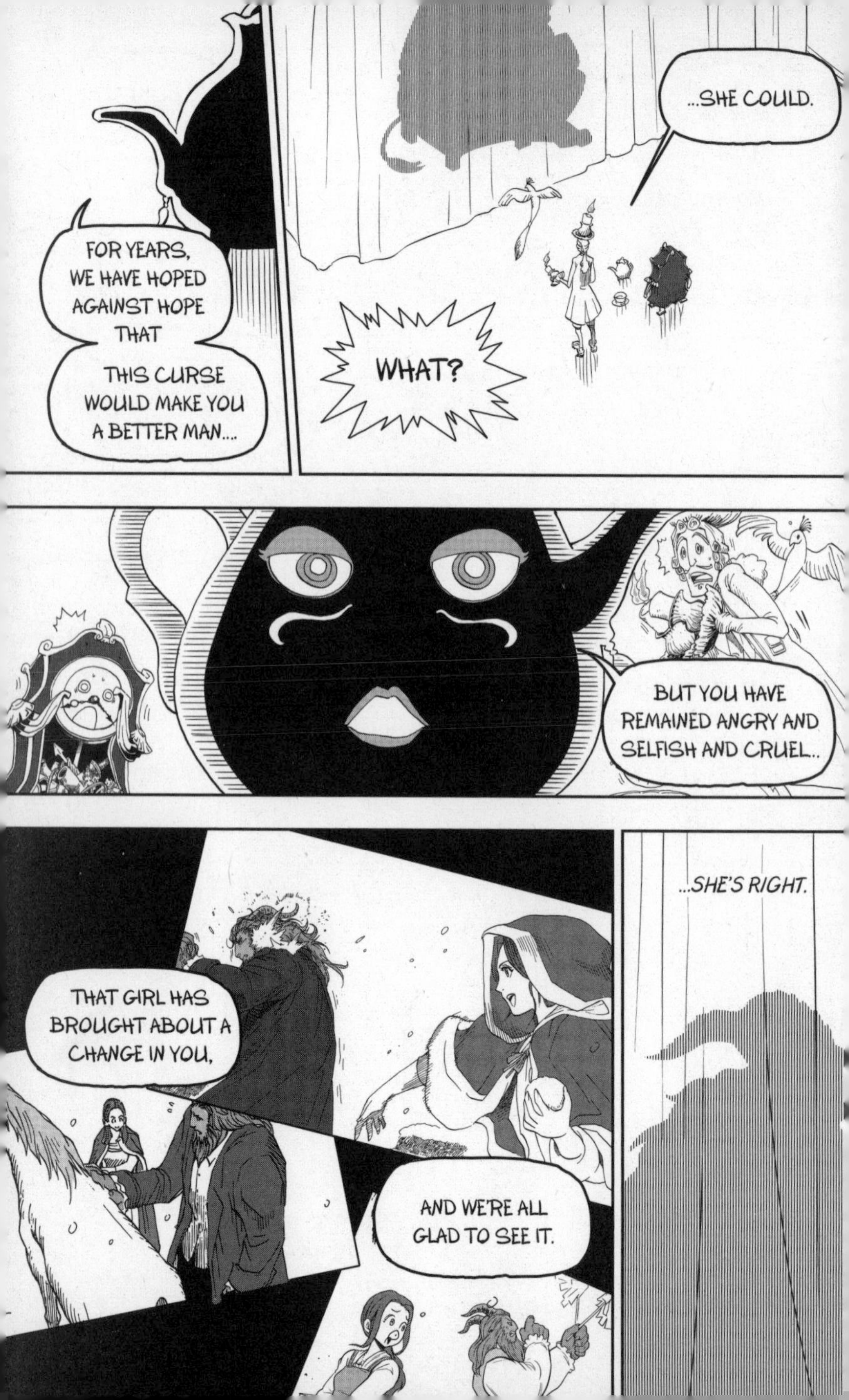
...SHE COULD.
WHAT?
FOR YEARS, WE HAVE HOPED AGAINST HOPE THAT
THIS CURSE WOULD MAKE YOU A BETTER MAN....
BUT YOU HAVE REMAINED ANGRY AND SELFISH AND CRUEL..
...SHE'S RIGHT.
THAT GIRL HAS BROUGHT ABOUT A CHANGE IN YOU,
AND WE'RE ALL GLAD TO SEE IT.

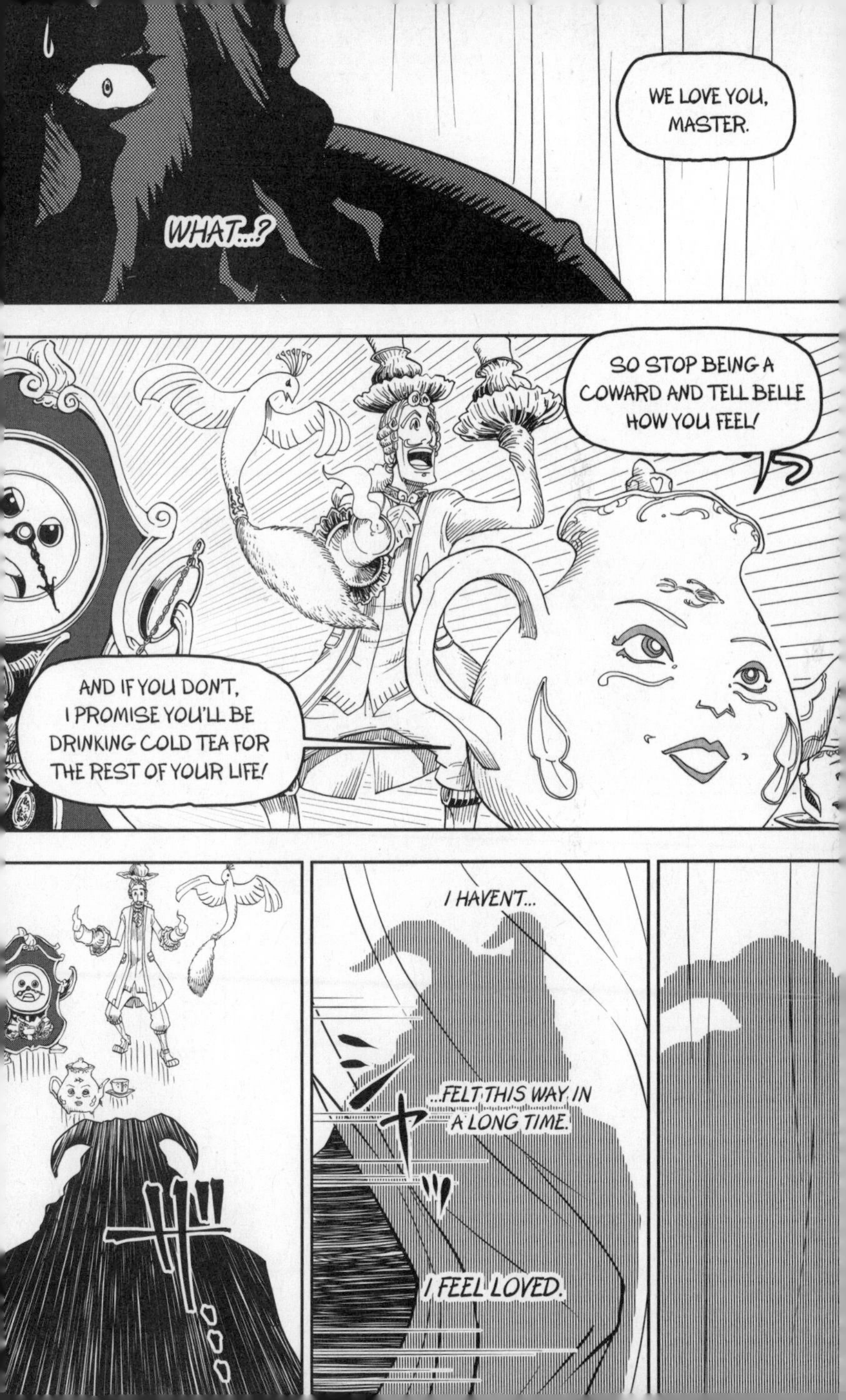
WE LOVE YOU, MASTER.
WHAT...?
SO STOP BEING A COWARD AND TELL BELLE HOW YOU FEEL!
AND IF YOU DON'T, I PROMISE YOU'LL BE DRINKING COLD TEA FOR THE REST OF YOUR LIFE!
I HAVEN'T...
...FELT THIS WAY IN A LONG TIME.
I FEEL LOVED.

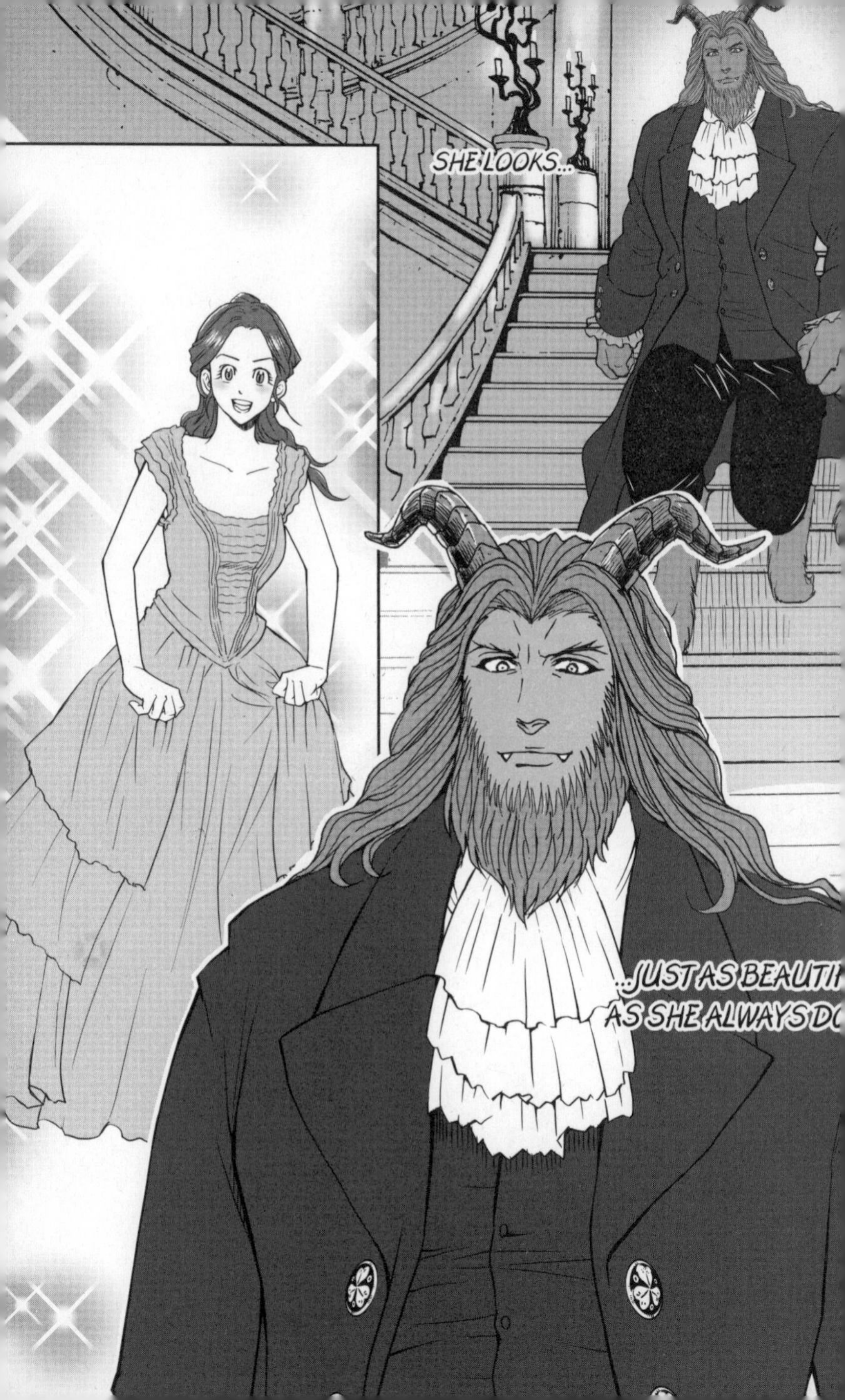
SHE LOOKS...
...JUST AS BEAUTI
AS SHE ALWAYS DO

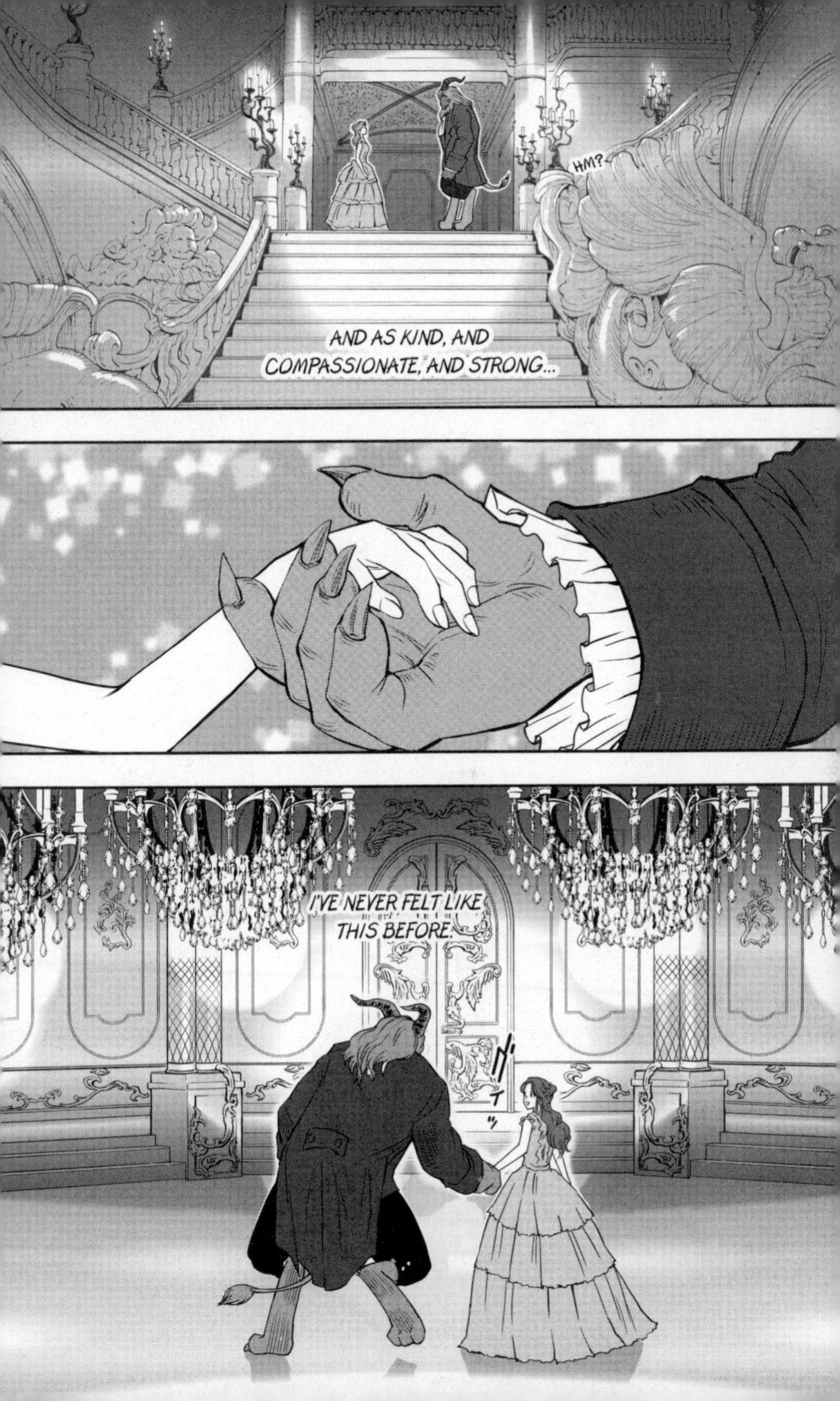
HM?
AND AS KIND, AND COMPASSIONATE, AND STRONG...
I'VE NEVER FELT LIKE THIS BEFORE.

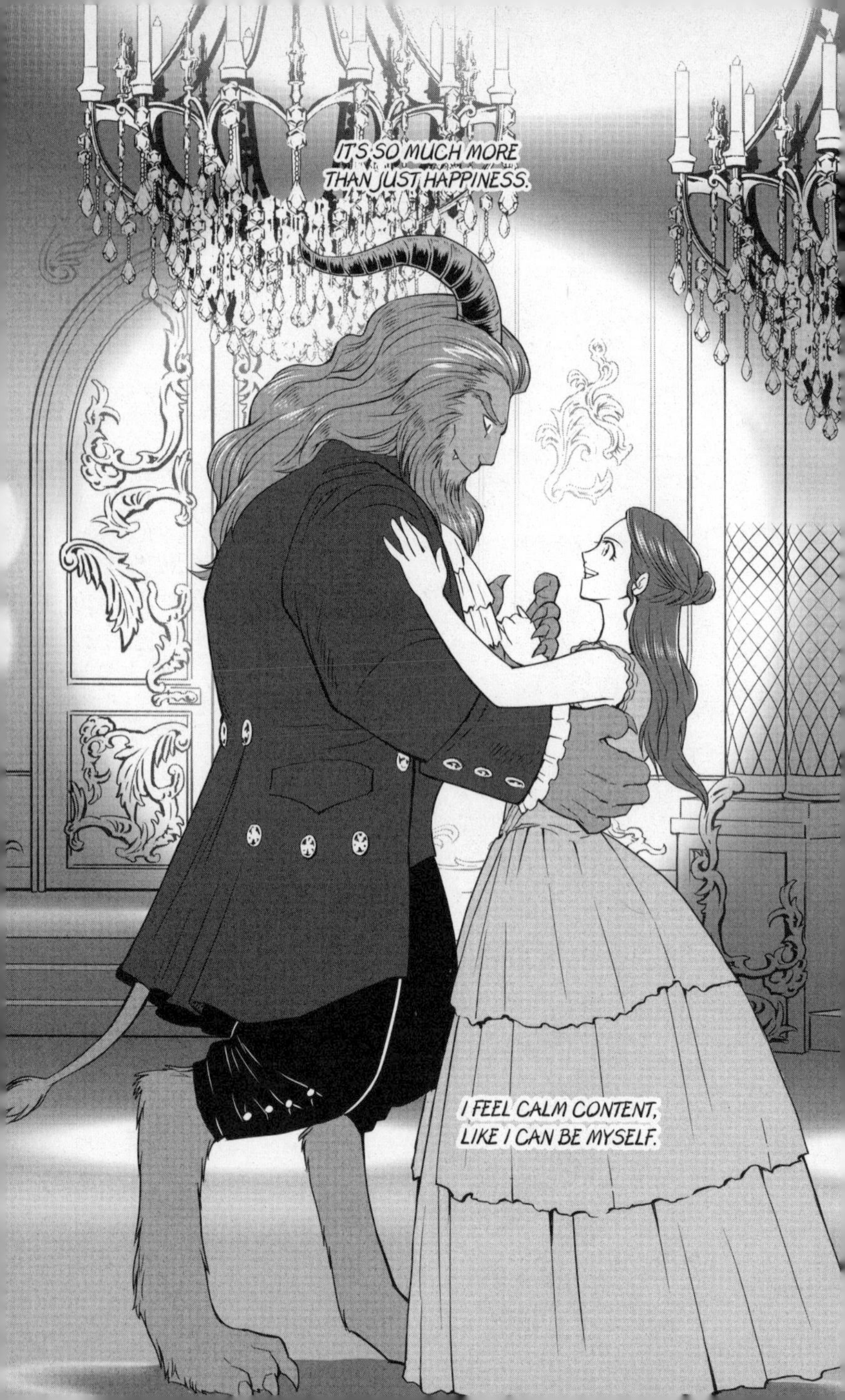
IT'S SO MUCH MORE THAN JUST HAPPINESS.
I FEEL CALM CONTENT, LIKE I CAN BE MYSELF.

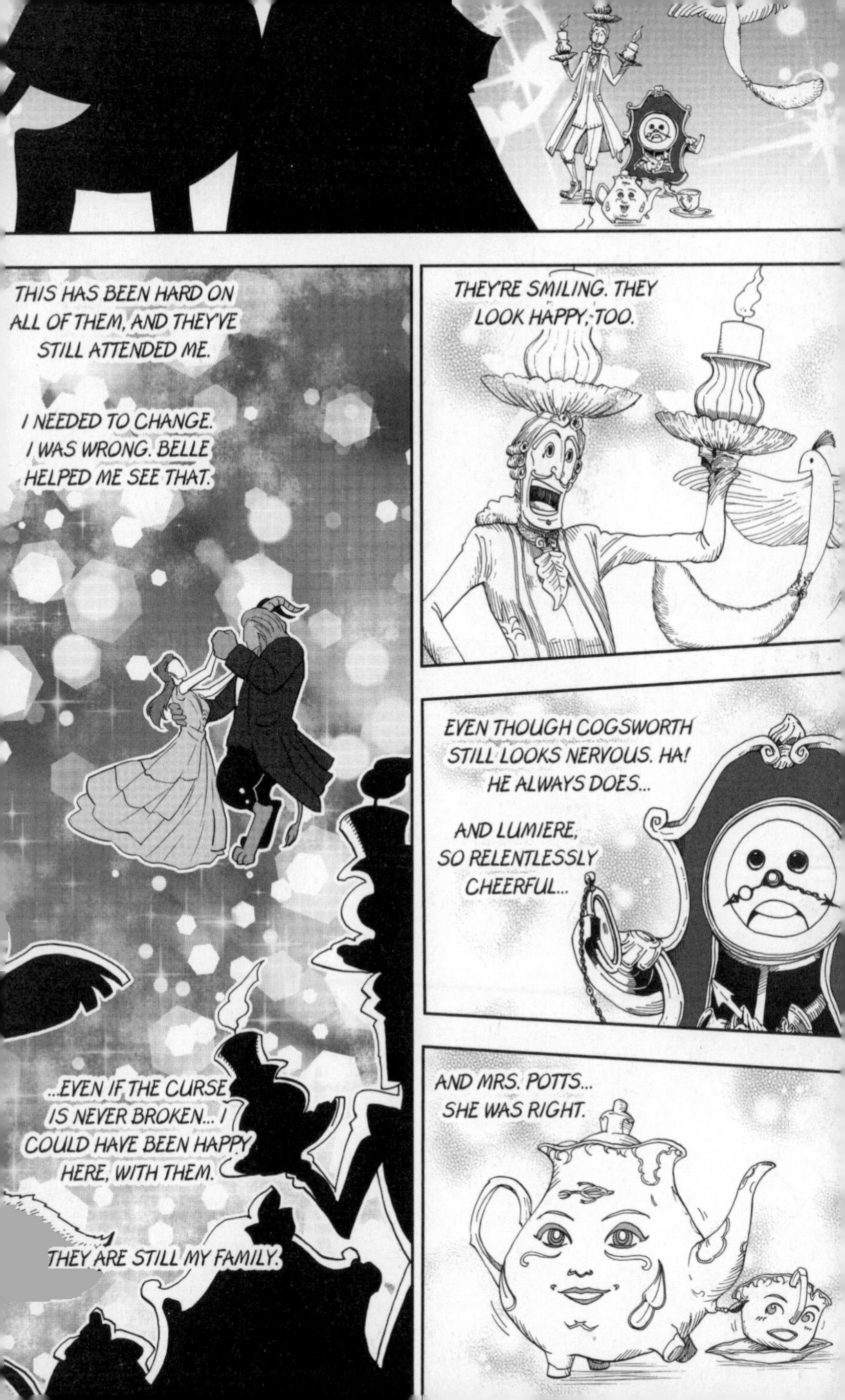
THEY'RE SMILING. THEY LOOK HAPPY, TOO.
EVEN THOUGH COGSWORTH STILL LOOKS NERVOUS. HA! HE ALWAYS DOES...
AND LUMIERE, SO RELENTLESSLY CHEERFUL...
AND MRS. POTTS... SHE WAS RIGHT.
THIS HAS BEEN HARD ON ALL OF THEM, AND THEY'VE STILL ATTENDED ME.
I NEEDED TO CHANGE. I WAS WRONG. BELLE HELPED ME SEE THAT.
...EVEN IF THE CURSE IS NEVER BROKEN... I COULD HAVE BEEN HAPPY HERE, WITH THEM.
THEY ARE STILL MY FAMILY.

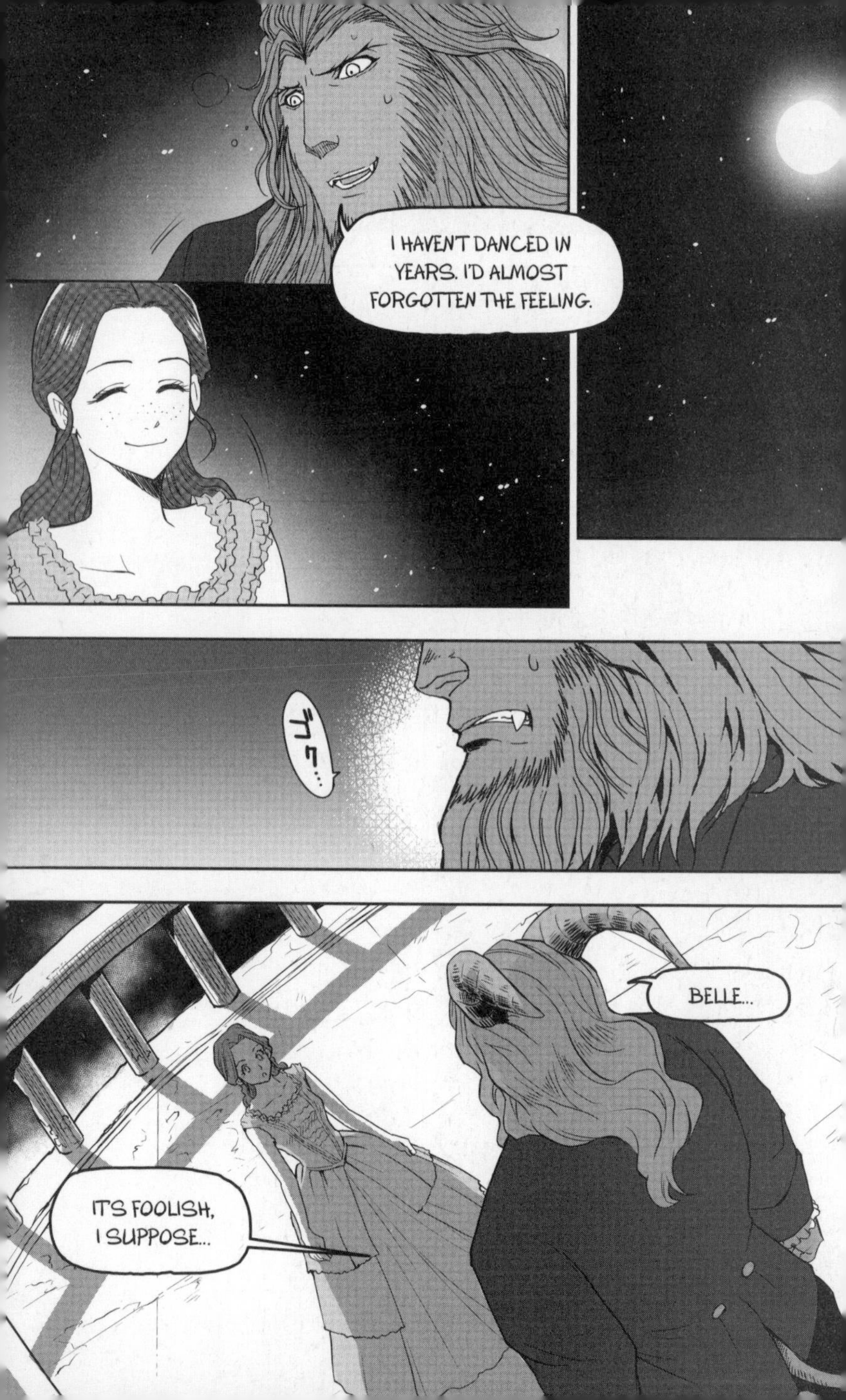
I HAVEN'T DANCED IN YEARS. I'D ALMOST FORGOTTEN THE FEELING.
グッ…
BELLE...
IT'S FOOLISH, I SUPPOSE...

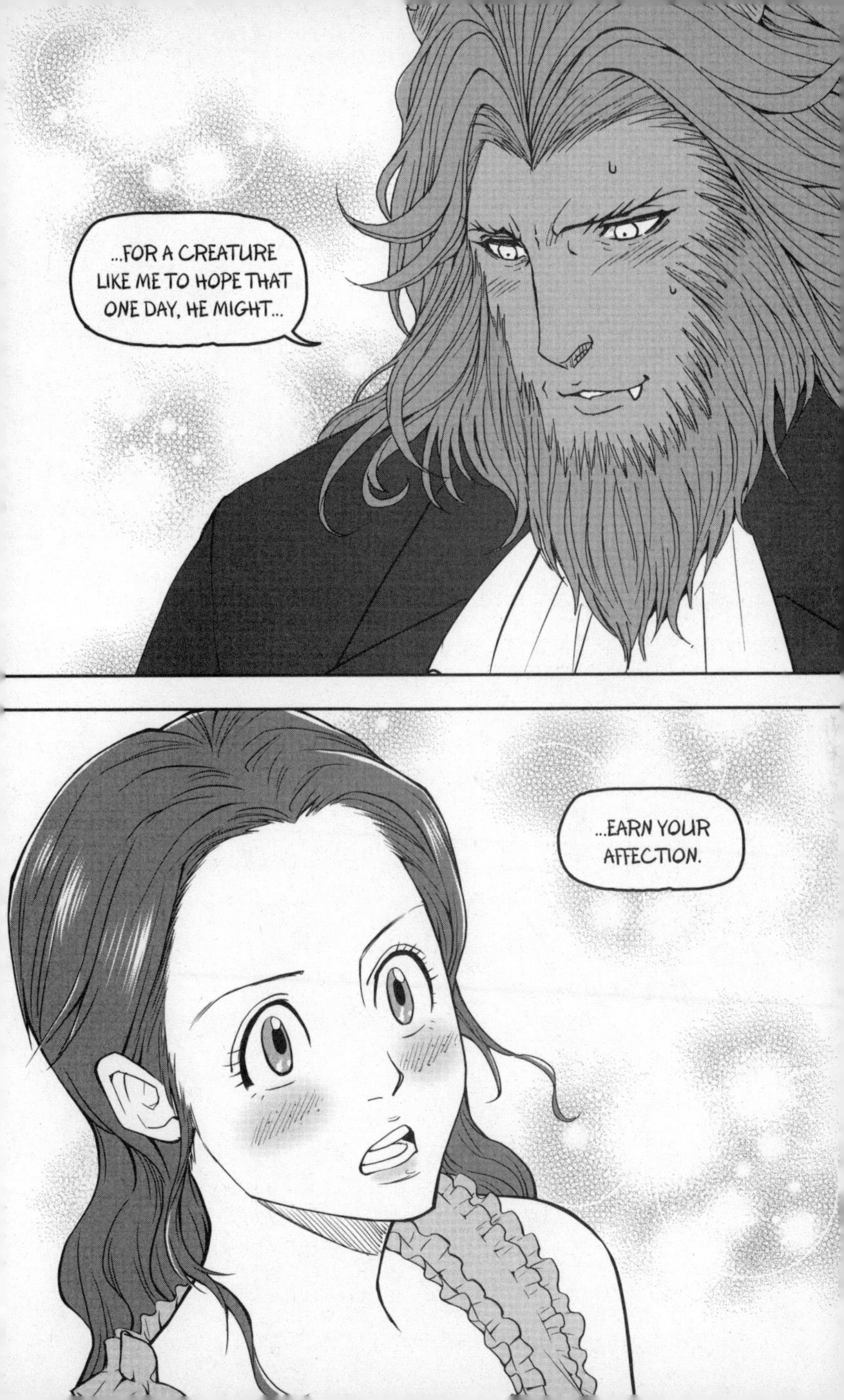
...FOR A CREATURE LIKE ME TO HOPE THAT ONE DAY, HE MIGHT...
...EARN YOUR AFFECTION.

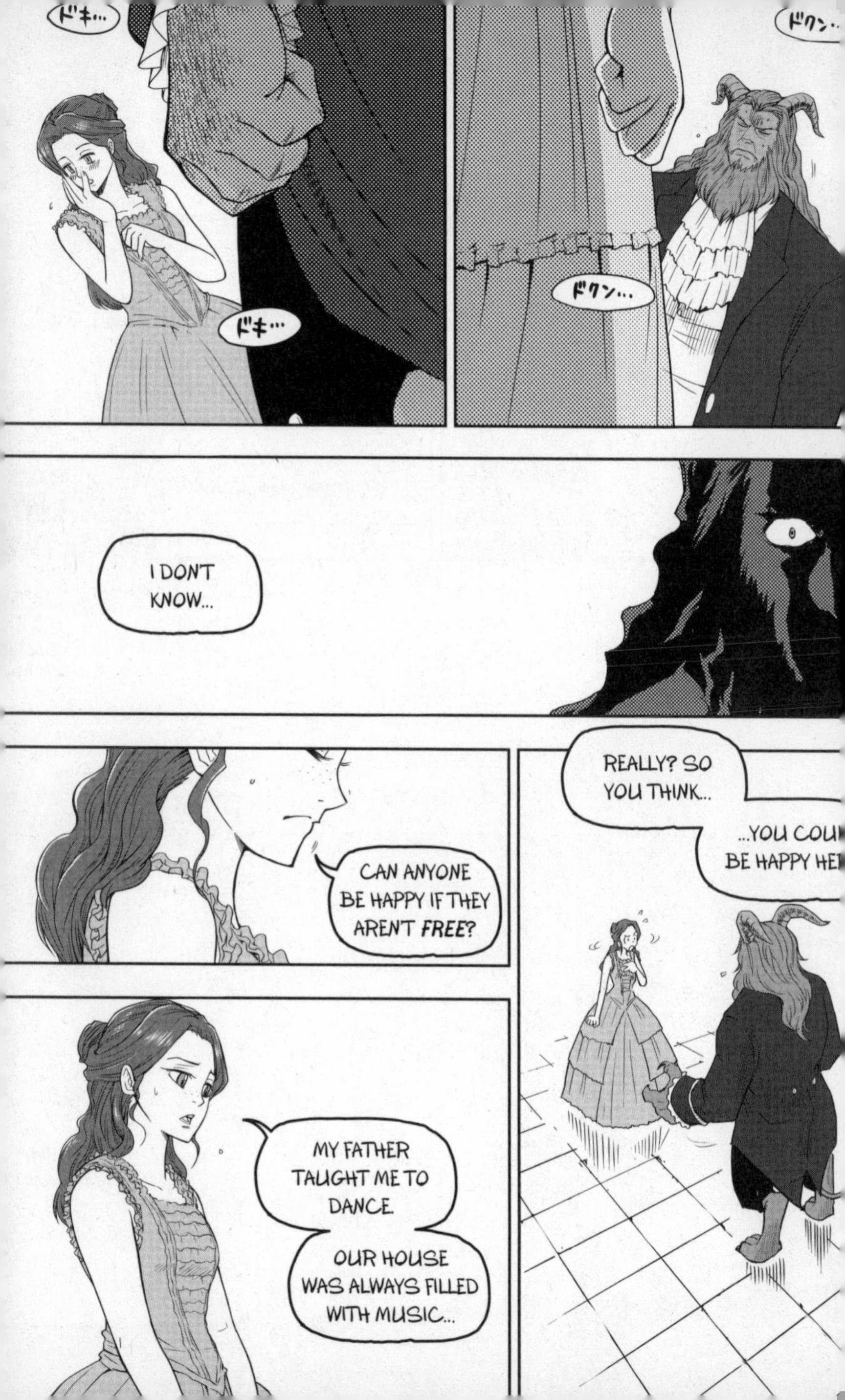
ドクン…
ドクン…
ドキ…
ドキ…
I DON'T KNOW...
REALLY? SO YOU THINK...
...YOU COU BE HAPPY HE
CAN ANYONE BE HAPPY IF THEY AREN'T FREE?
MY FATHER TAUGHT ME TO DANCE.
OUR HOUSE WAS ALWAYS FILLED WITH MUSIC...

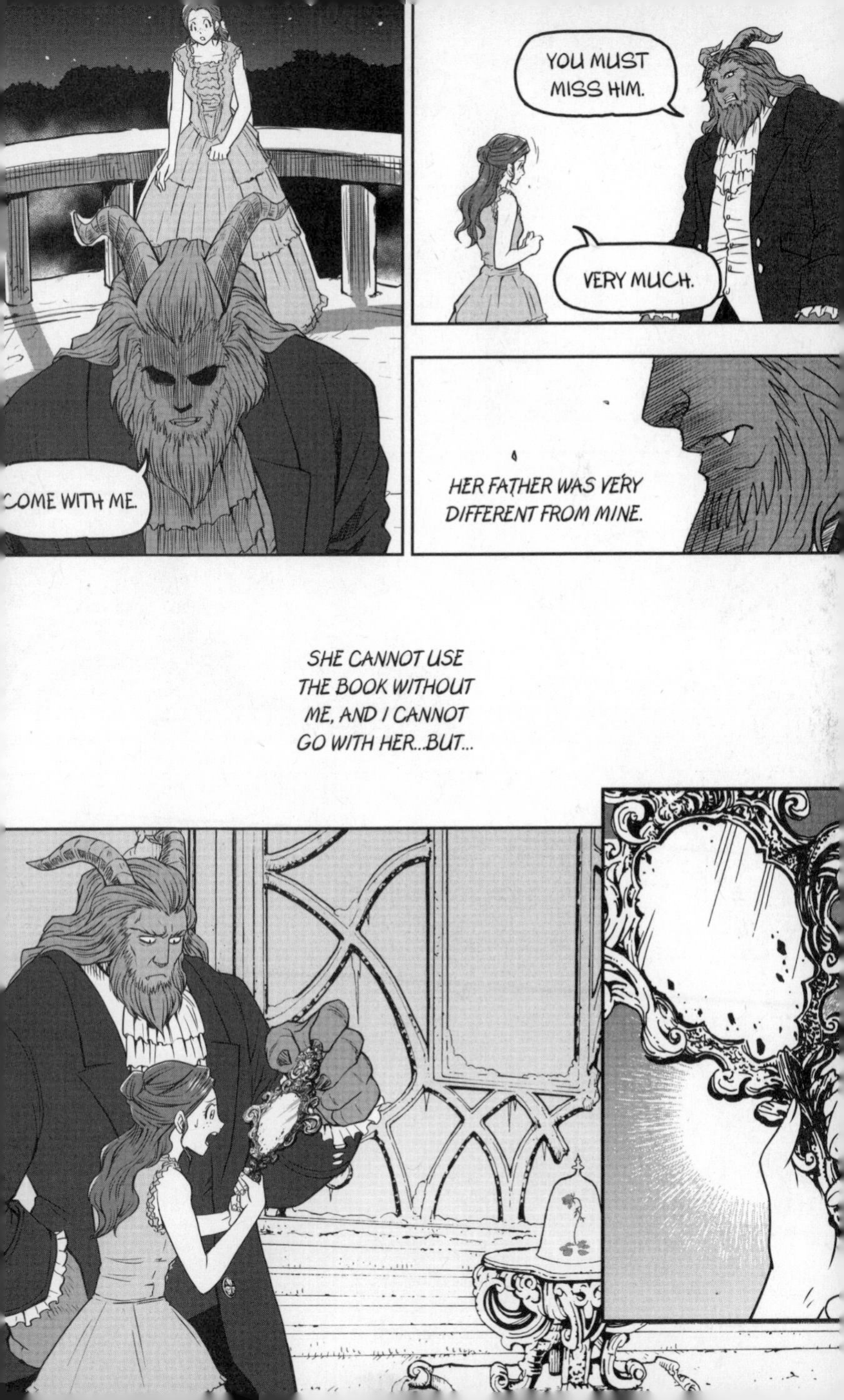
YOU MUST MISS HIM.
VERY MUCH.
HER FATHER WAS VERY DIFFERENT FROM MINE.
COME WITH ME.
SHE CANNOT USE THE BOOK WITHOUT ME, AND I CANNOT GO WITH HER...BUT...

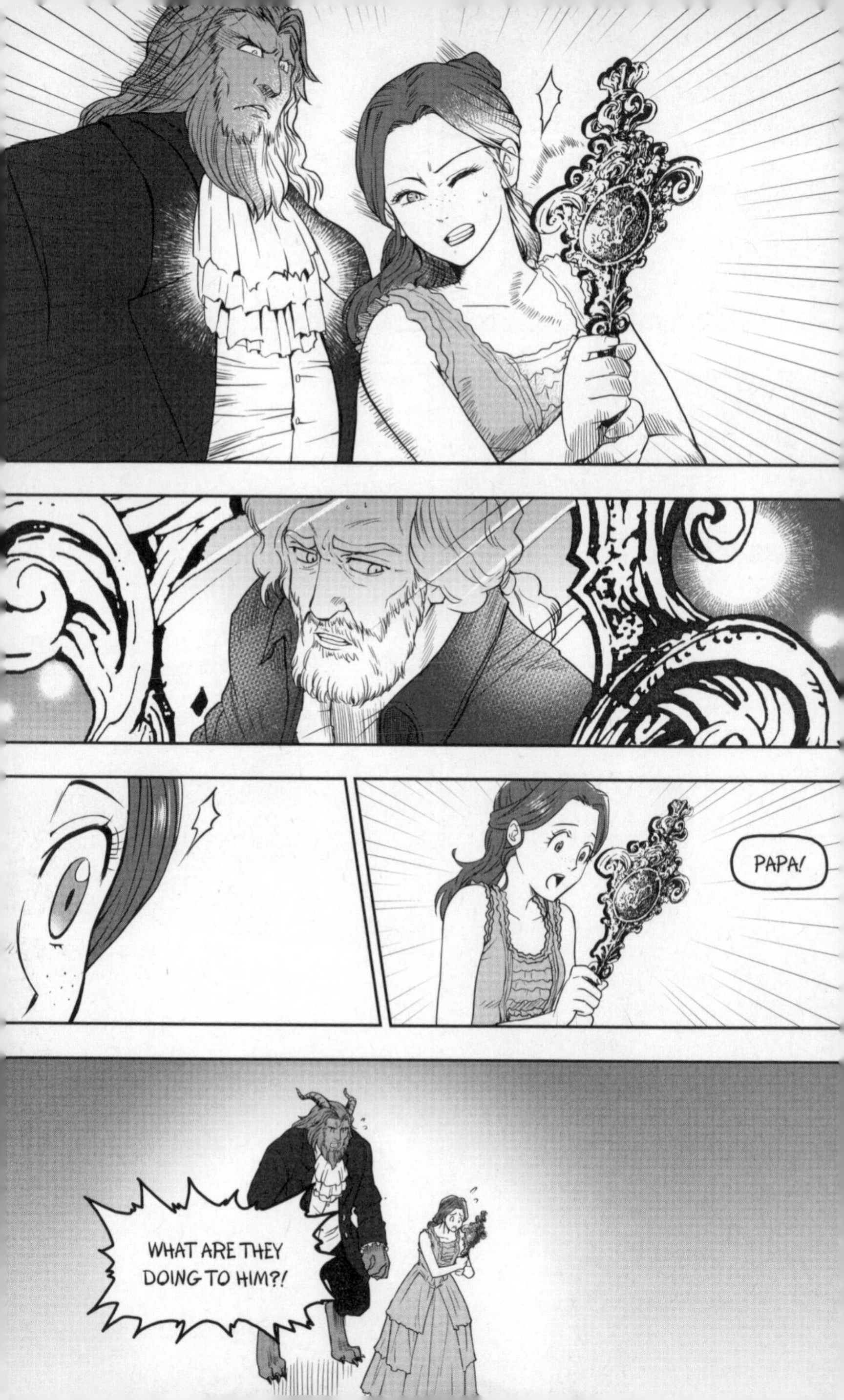
PAPA!
WHAT ARE THEY DOING TO HIM?!

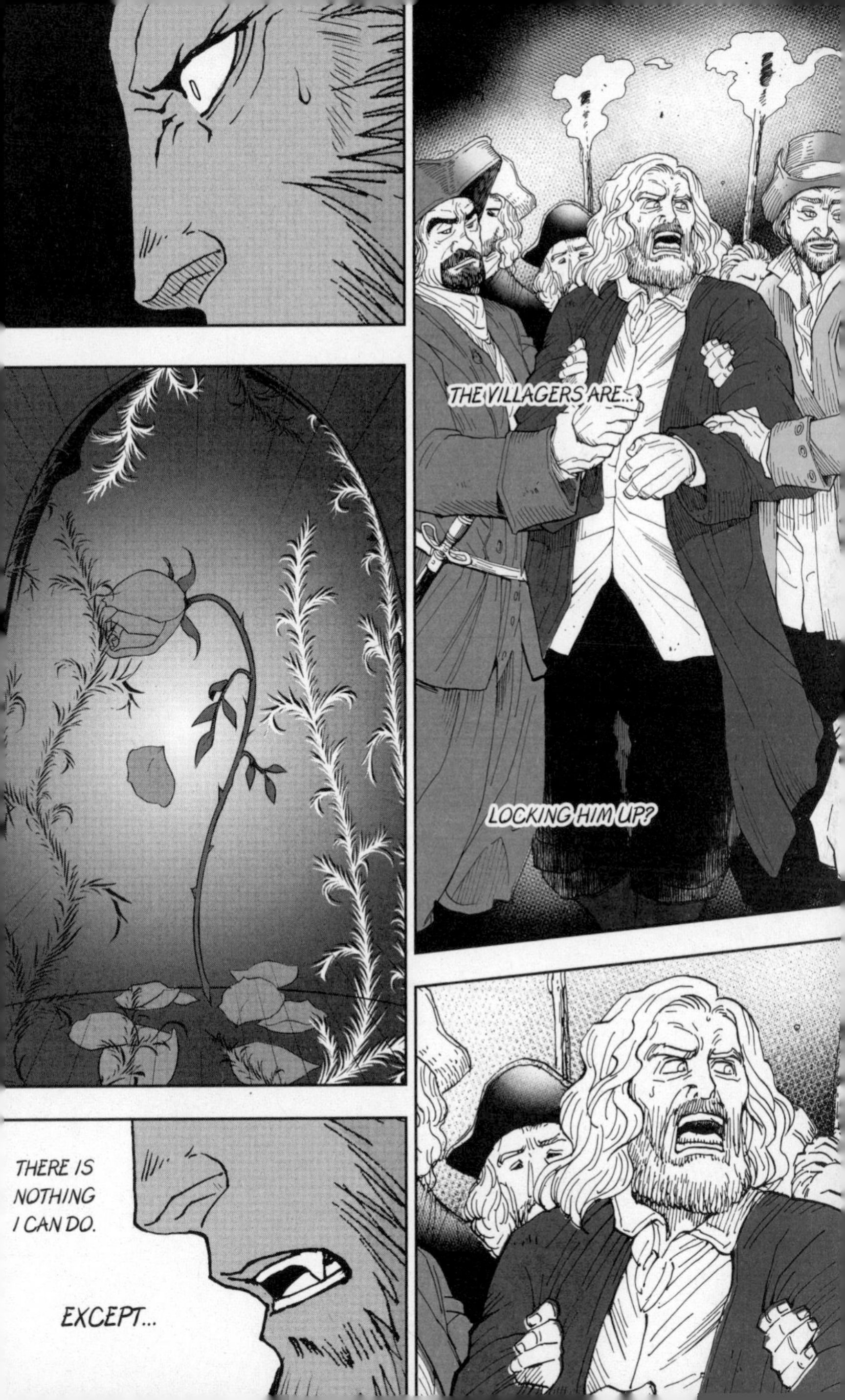
THE VILLAGERS ARE...
LOCKING HIM UP?
THERE IS NOTHING I CAN DO.
EXCEPT...

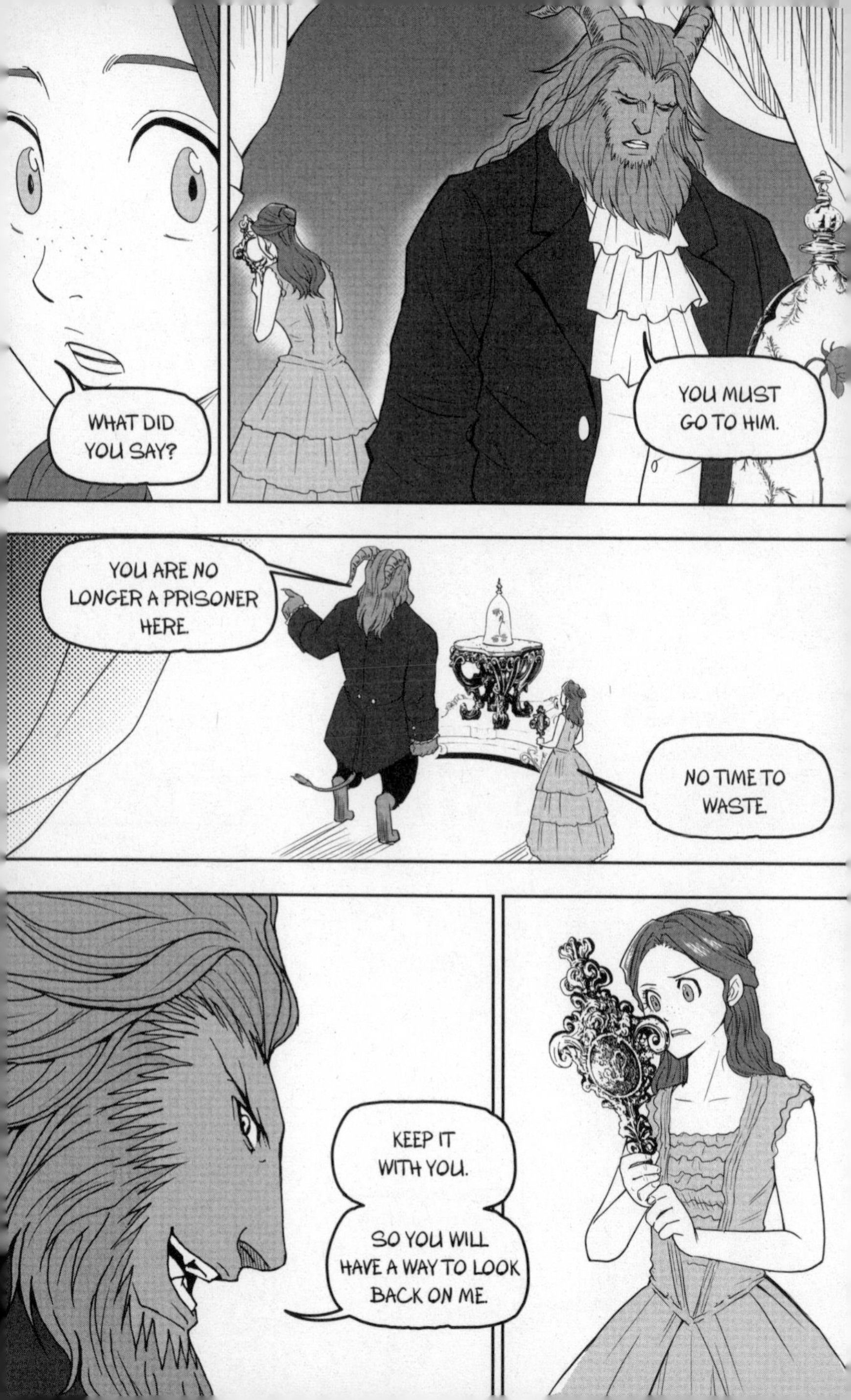
YOU MUST GO TO HIM.
WHAT DID YOU SAY?
YOU ARE NO LONGER A PRISONER HERE.
NO TIME TO WASTE.
KEEP IT WITH YOU.
SO YOU WILL HAVE A WAY TO LOOK BACK ON ME.

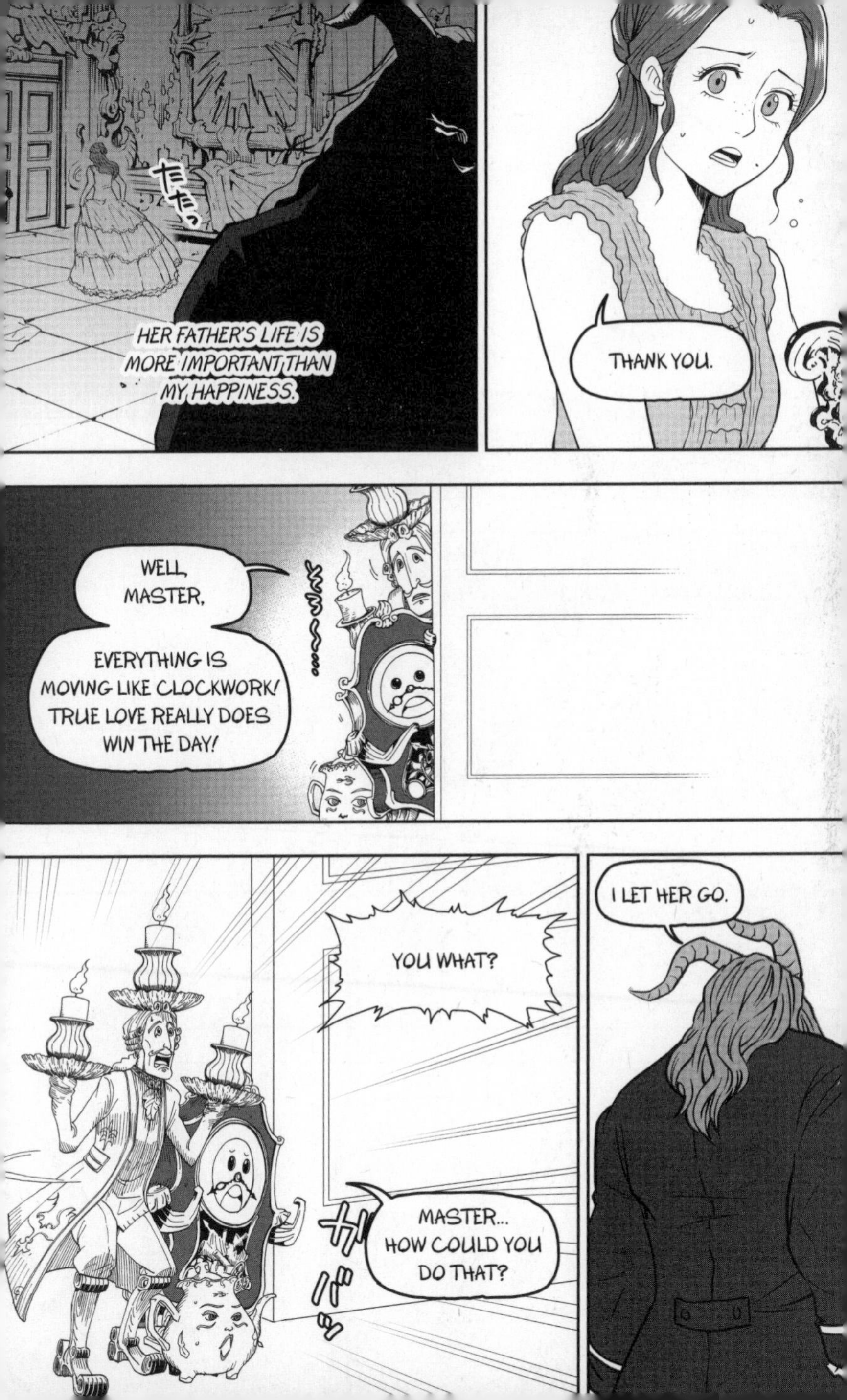
THANK YOU.
HER FATHER'S LIFE IS MORE IMPORTANT THAN MY HAPPINESS.
たたっ
WELL, MASTER,
EVERYTHING IS MOVING LIKE CLOCKWORK! TRUE LOVE REALLY DOES WIN THE DAY!
I LET HER GO.
YOU WHAT?
MASTER... HOW COULD YOU DO THAT?

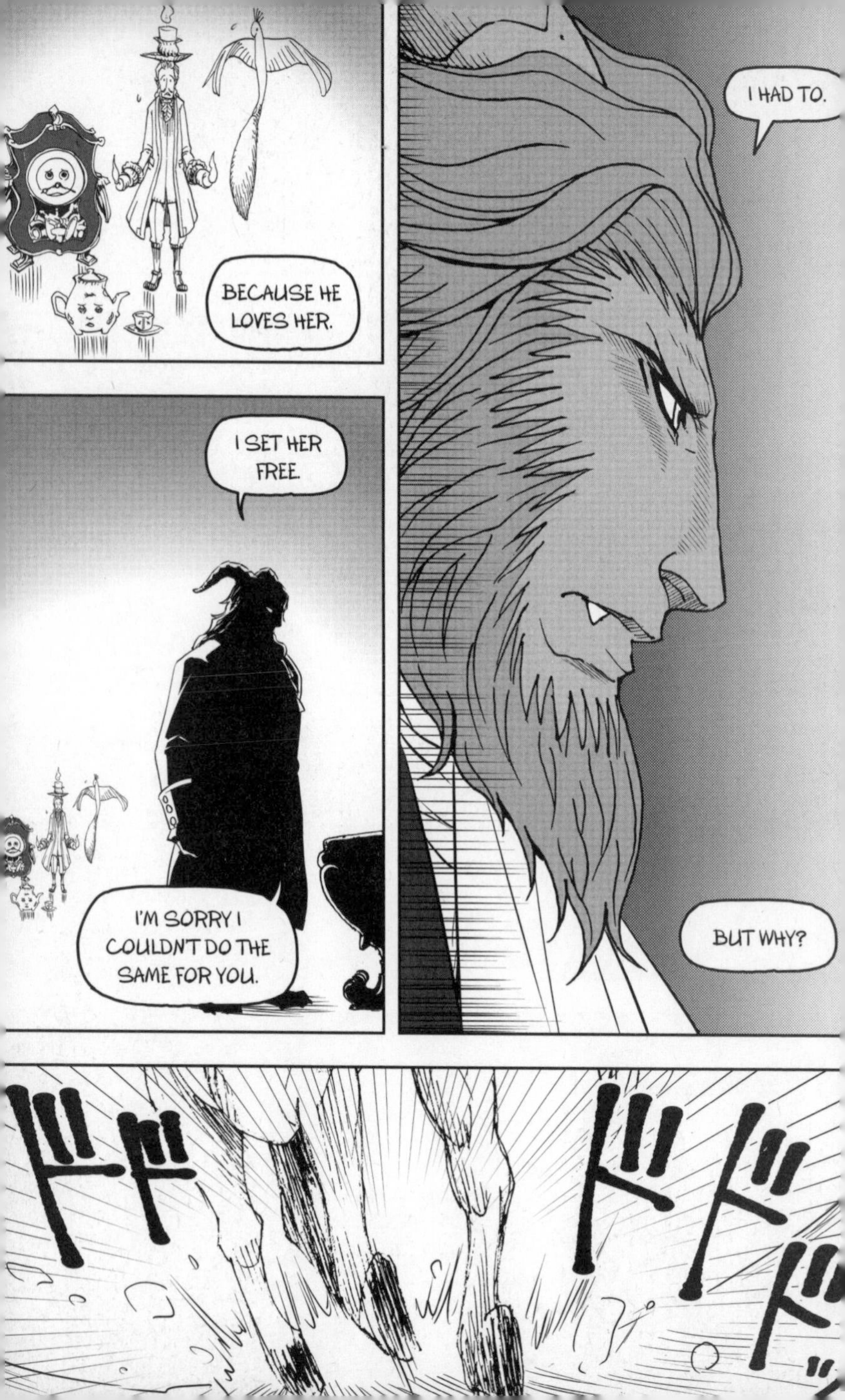
I HAD TO.
BUT WHY?
BECAUSE HE LOVES HER.
I SET HER FREE.
I'M SORRY I COULDN'T DO THE SAME FOR YOU.
ドドド
ドド

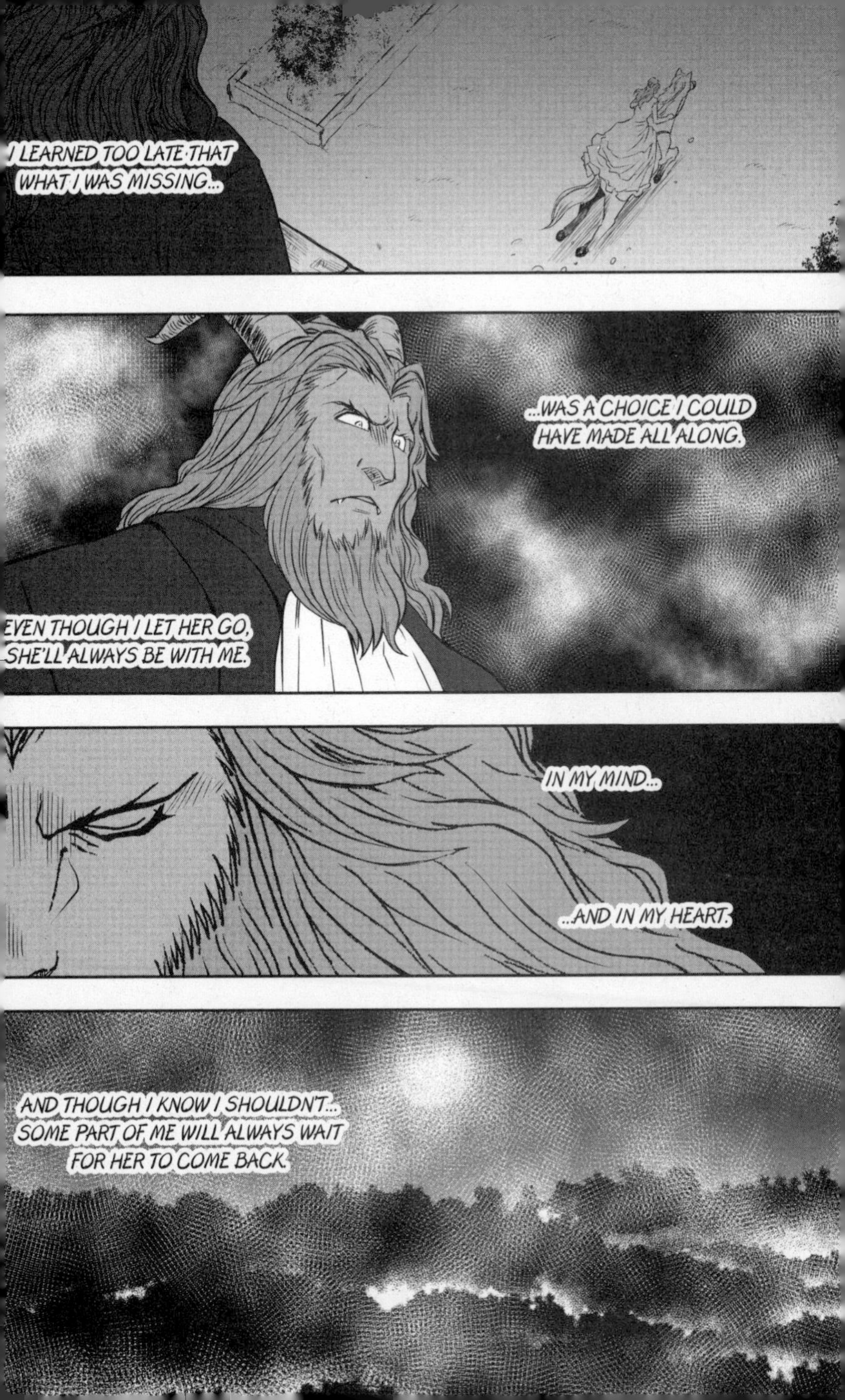
I LEARNED TOO LATE THAT WHAT I WAS MISSING...
...WAS A CHOICE I COULD HAVE MADE ALL ALONG.
EVEN THOUGH I LET HER GO, SHE'LL ALWAYS BE WITH ME.
IN MY MIND...
...AND IN MY HEART.
AND THOUGH I KNOW I SHOULDN'T... SOME PART OF ME WILL ALWAYS WAIT FOR HER TO COME BACK.

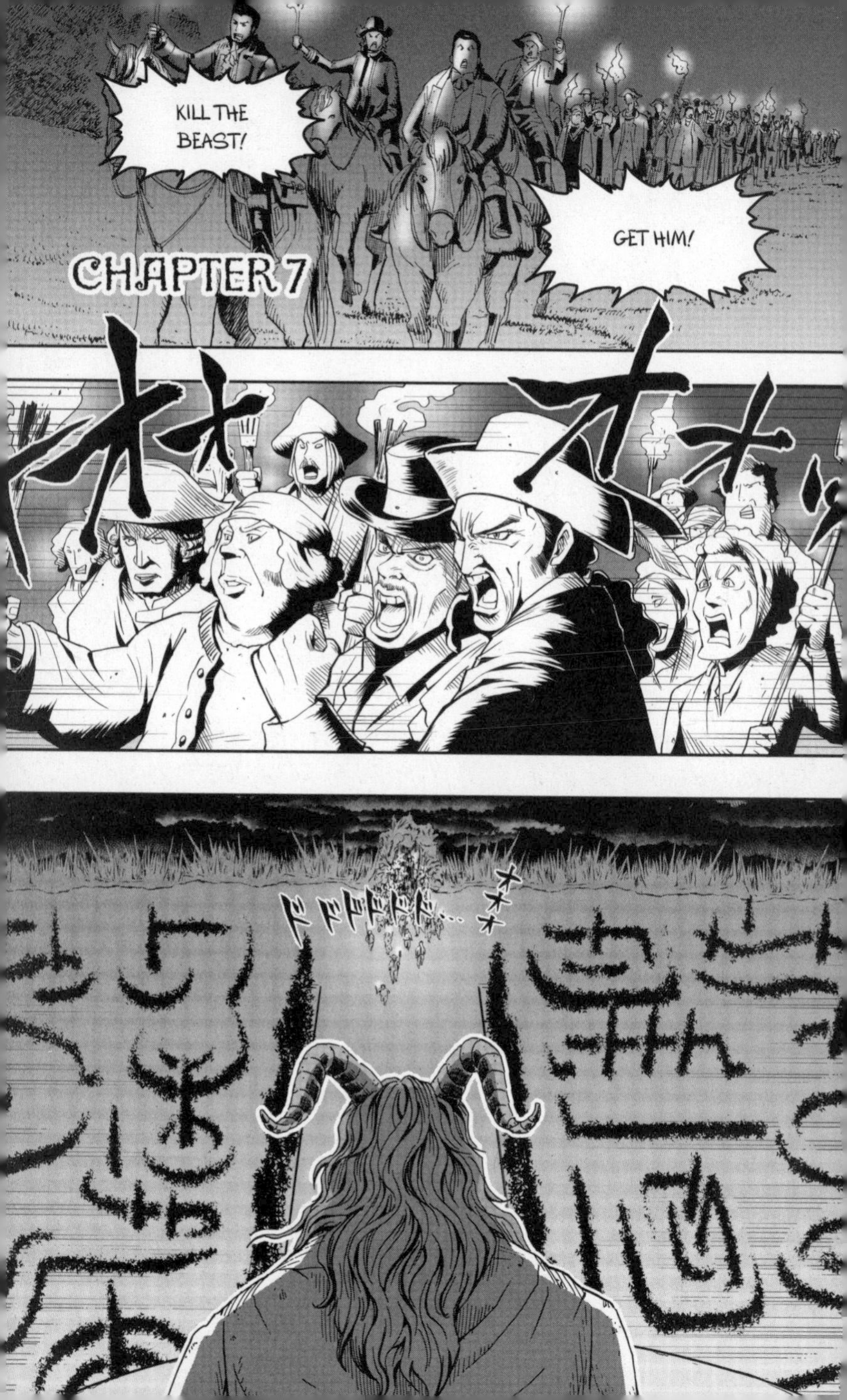
KILL THE BEAST!
GET HIM!
CHAPTER 7
オオオオッ
オオオ
ドドドドド…

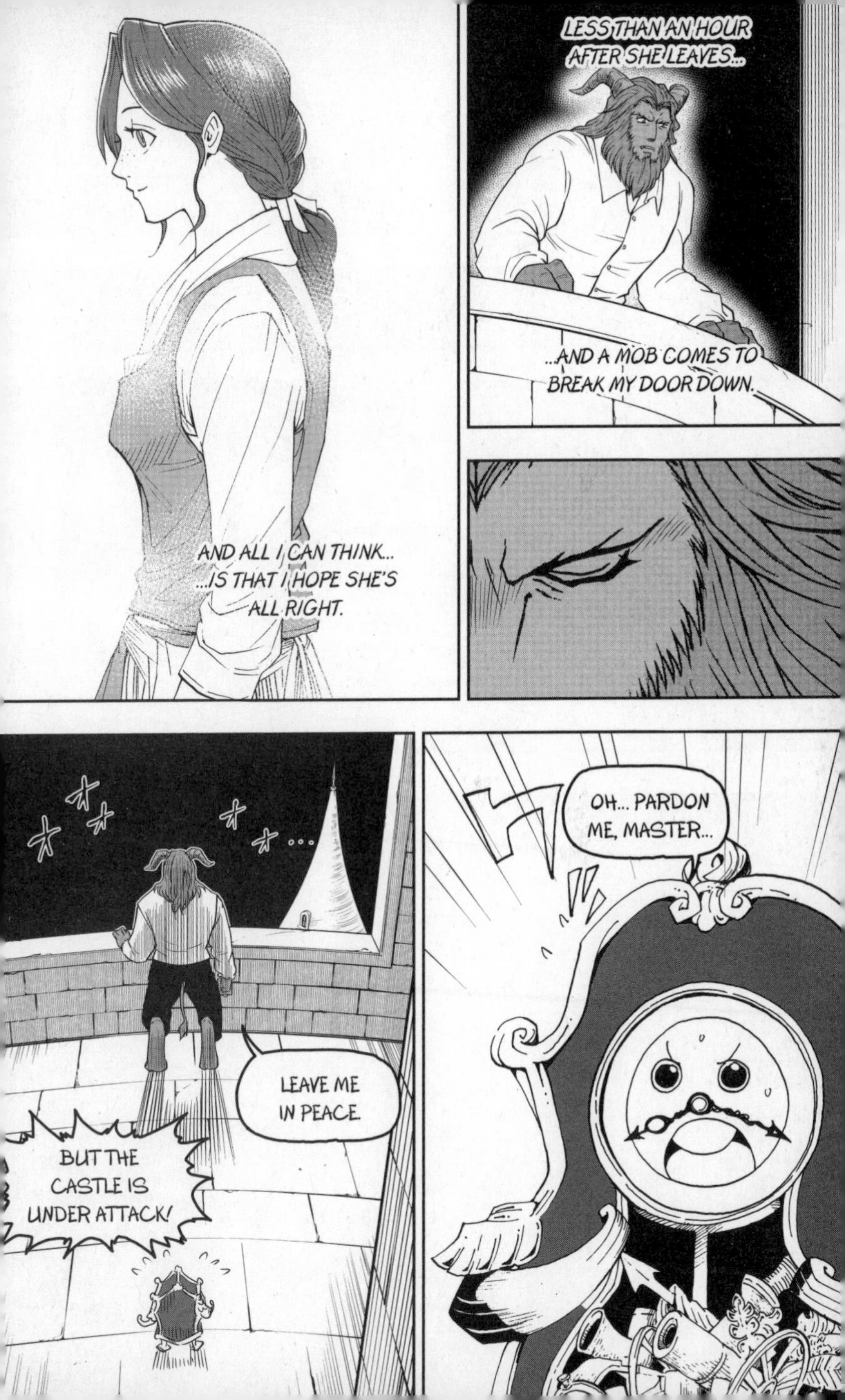
LESS THAN AN HOUR AFTER SHE LEAVES...
...AND A MOB COMES TO BREAK MY DOOR DOWN.
AND ALL I CAN THINK... ...IS THAT I HOPE SHE'S ALL RIGHT.
OH... PARDON ME, MASTER...
...
LEAVE ME IN PEACE.
BUT THE CASTLE IS UNDER ATTACK!

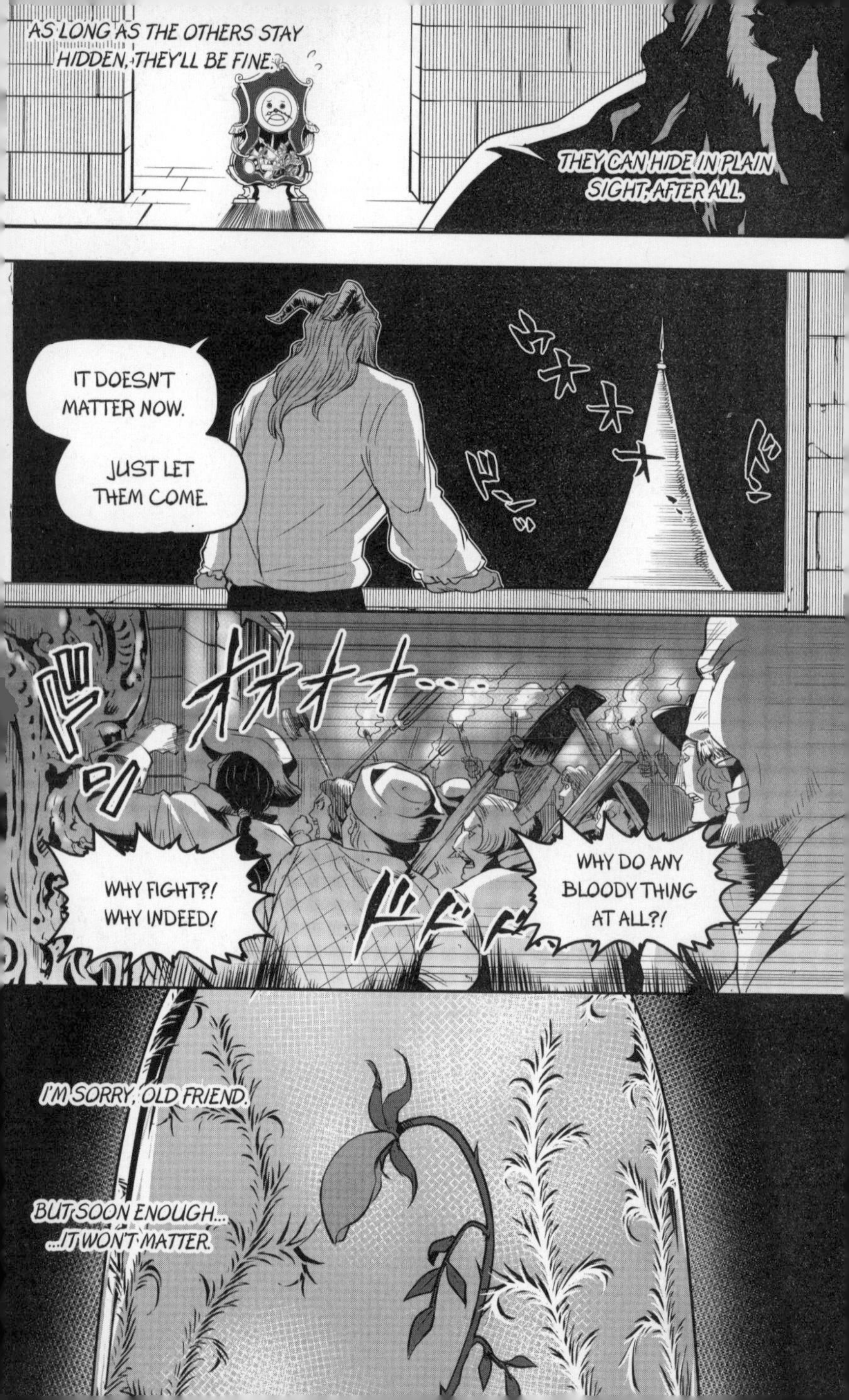
THEY CAN HIDE IN PLAIN SIGHT, AFTER ALL.
AS LONG AS THE OTHERS STAY HIDDEN, THEY'LL BE FINE.
IT DOESN'T MATTER NOW.
JUST LET THEM COME.
WHY DO ANY BLOODY THING AT ALL?!
WHY FIGHT?! WHY INDEED!
I'M SORRY, OLD FRIEND.
BUT SOON ENOUGH... ...IT WON'T MATTER.

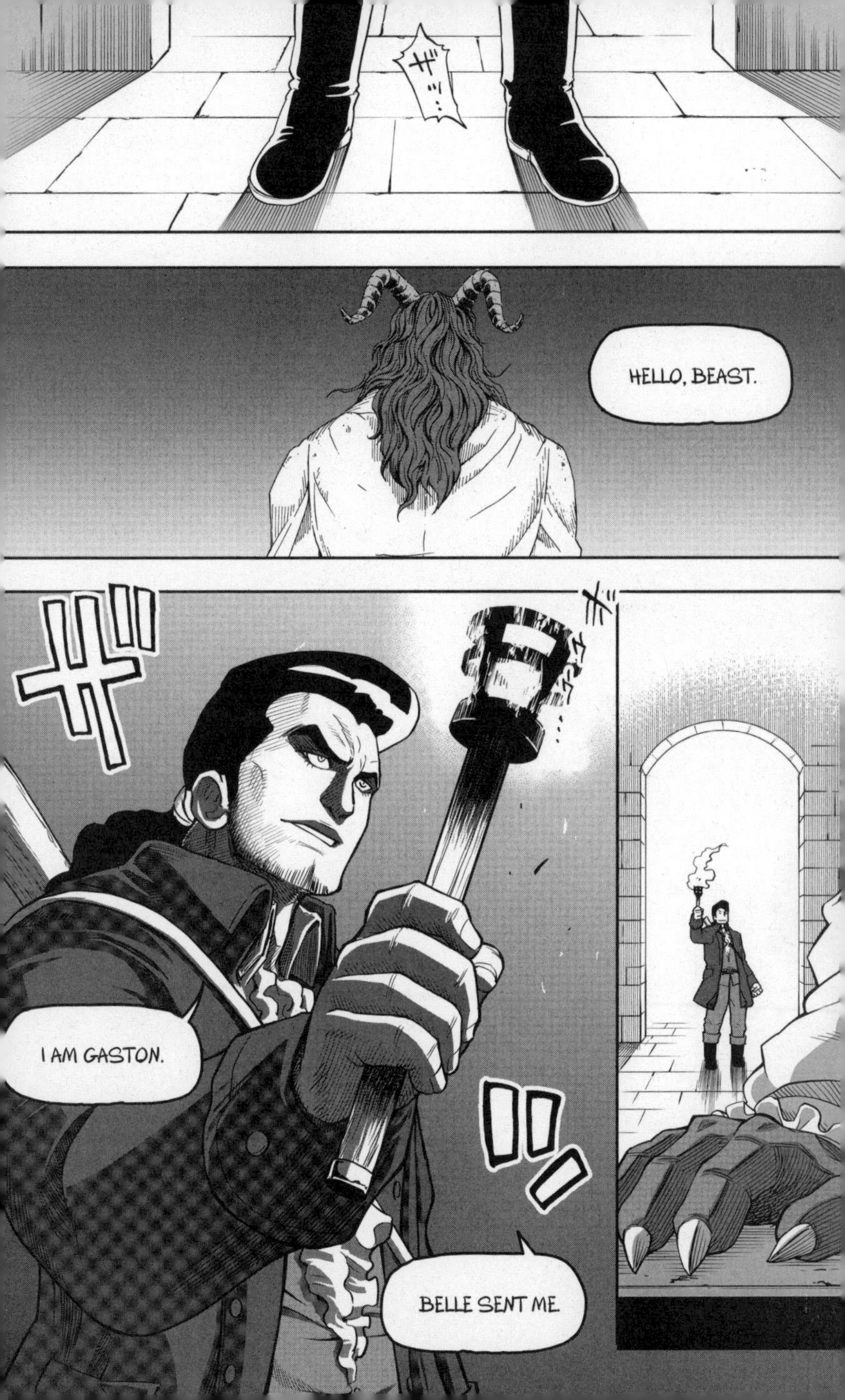
ザッ…
HELLO, BEAST.
I AM GASTON.
BELLE SENT ME.

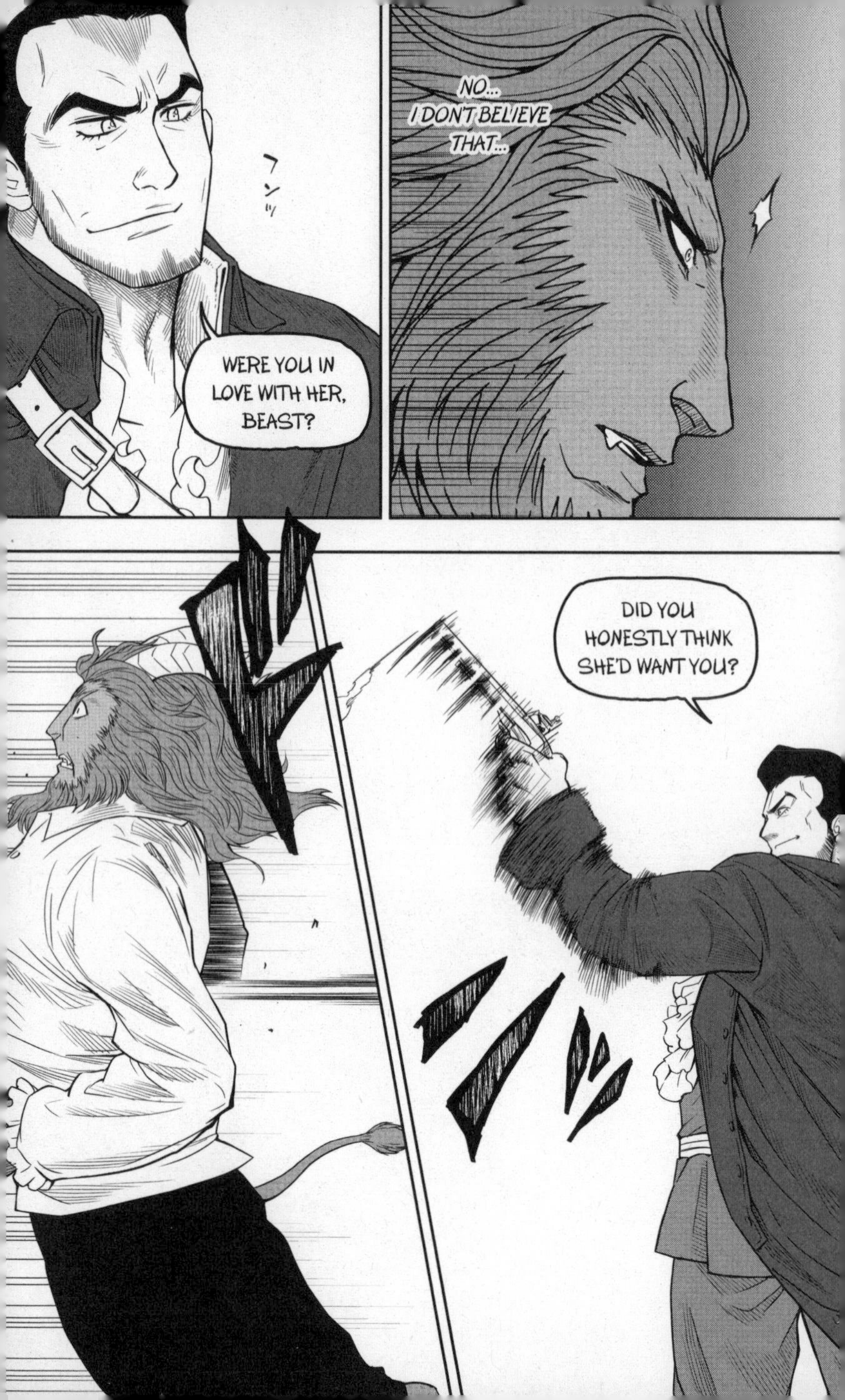
NO... I DON'T BELIEVE THAT...
フンッ
WERE YOU IN LOVE WITH HER, BEAST?
DID YOU HONESTLY THINK SHE'D WANT YOU?

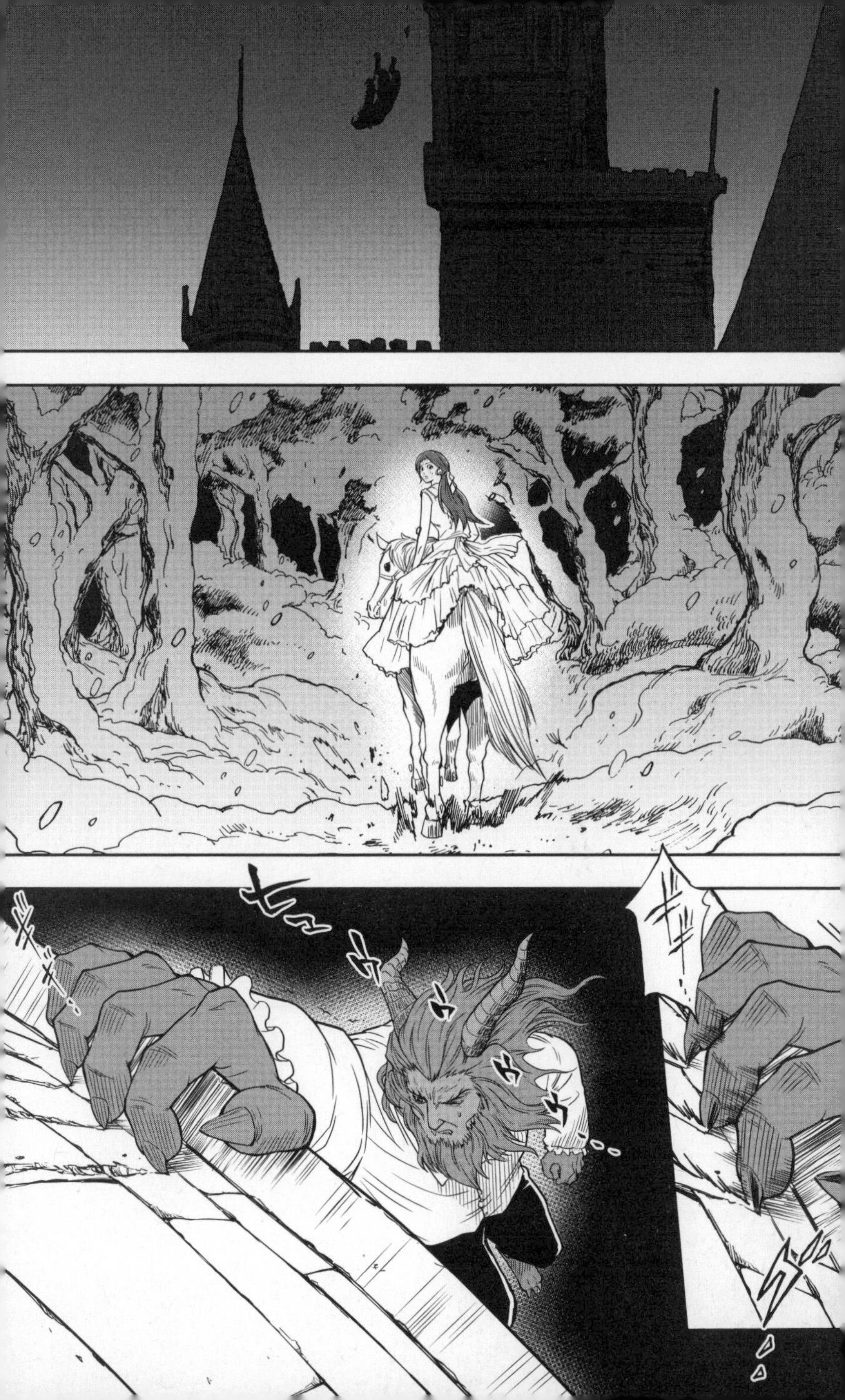

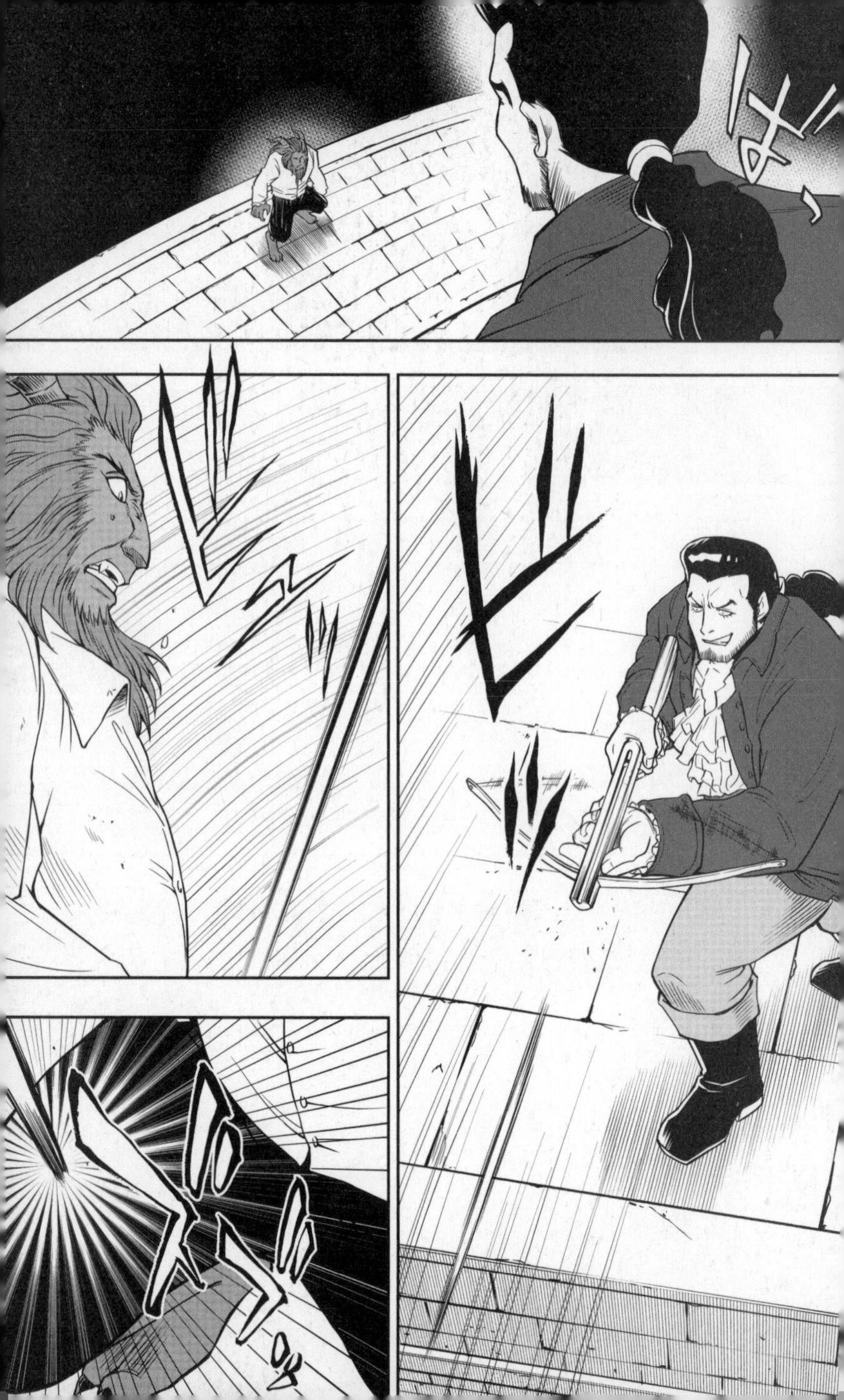
はっ

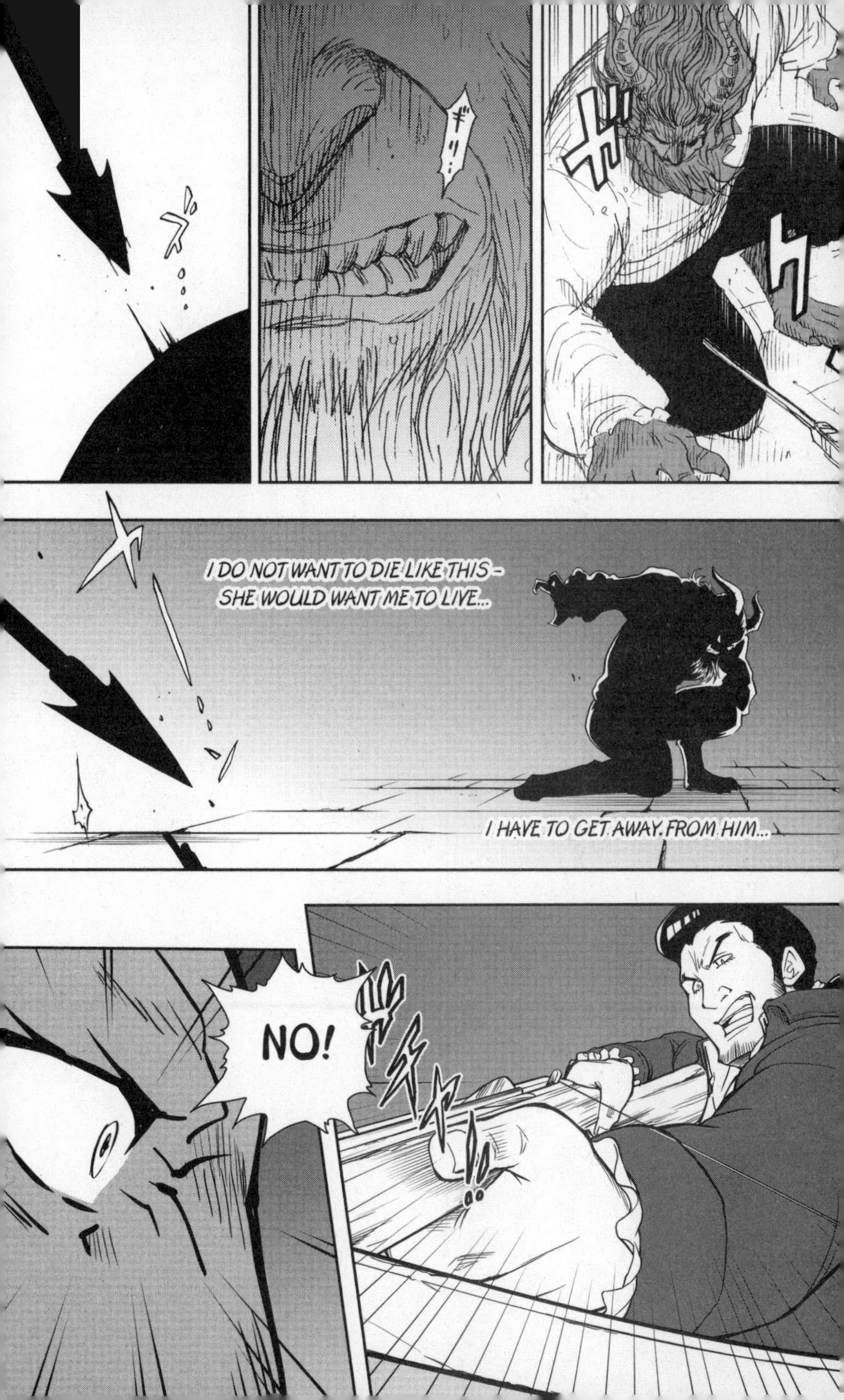
ギリ…
ズ
I DO NOT WANT TO DIE LIKE THIS – SHE WOULD WANT ME TO LIVE...
I HAVE TO GET AWAY FROM HIM...
NO!

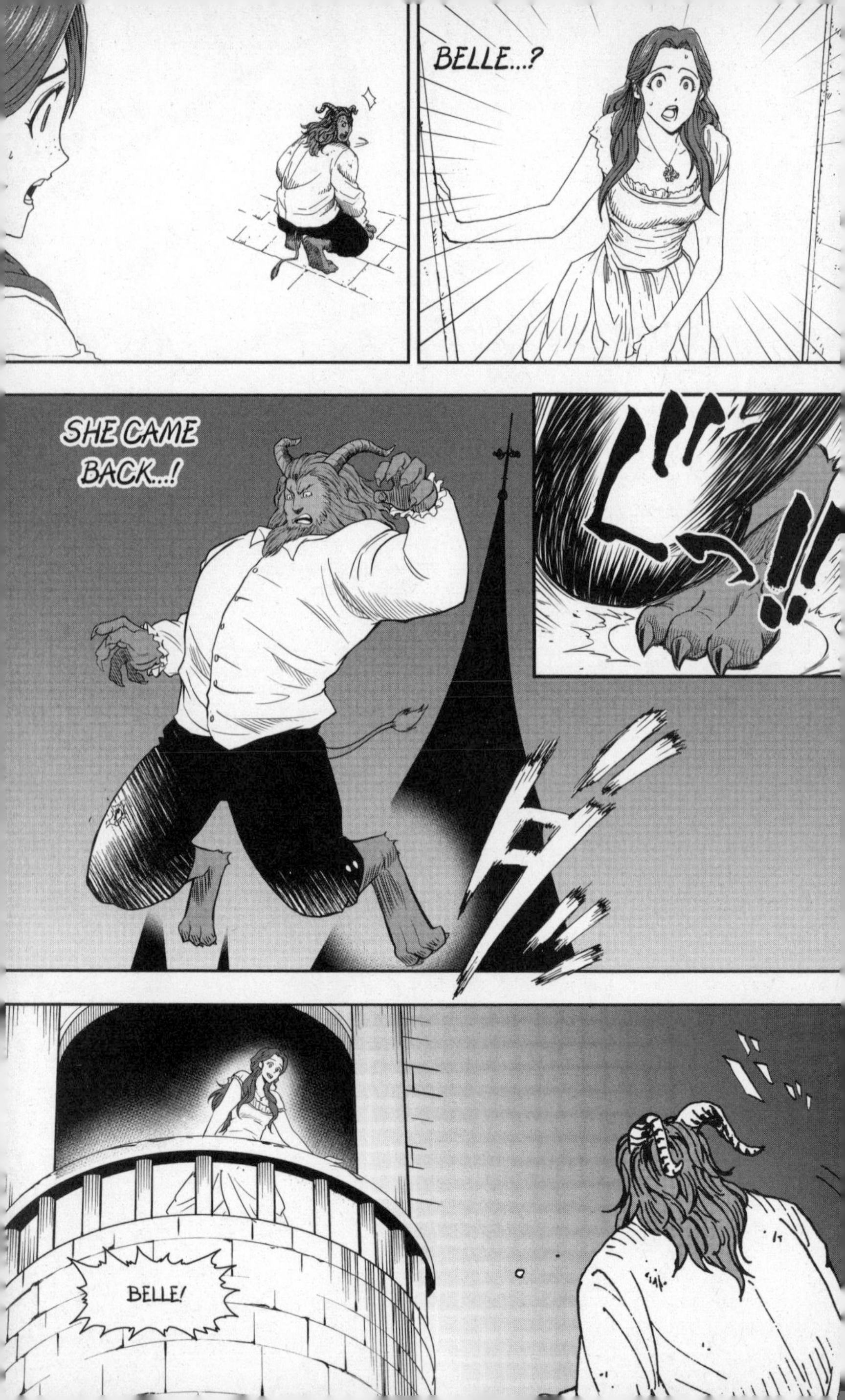
BELLE...?
SHE CAME BACK...!
BELLE!

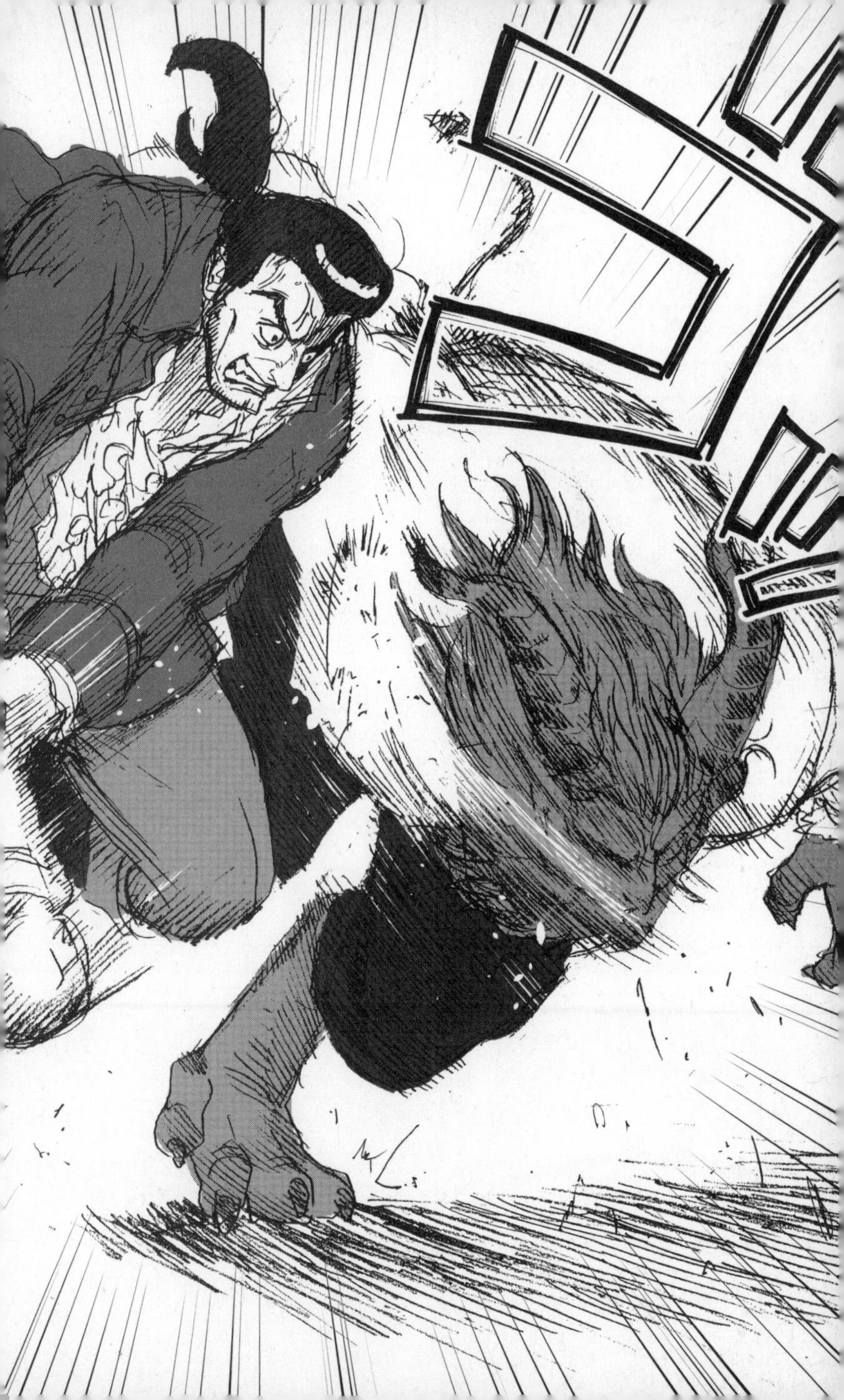

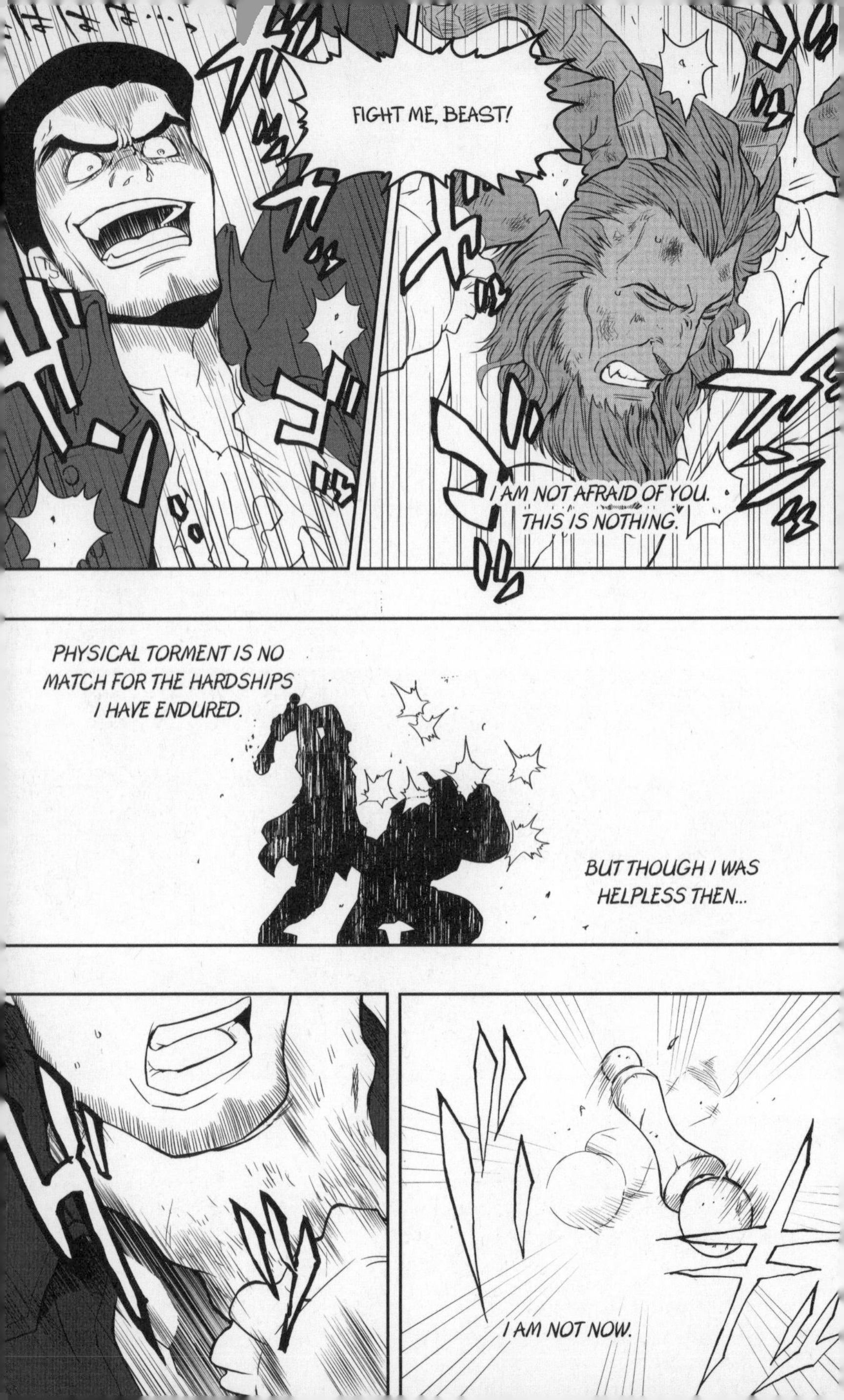
FIGHT ME, BEAST!
I AM NOT AFRAID OF YOU. THIS IS NOTHING.
PHYSICAL TORMENT IS NO MATCH FOR THE HARDSHIPS I HAVE ENDURED.
BUT THOUGH I WAS HELPLESS THEN...
I AM NOT NOW.

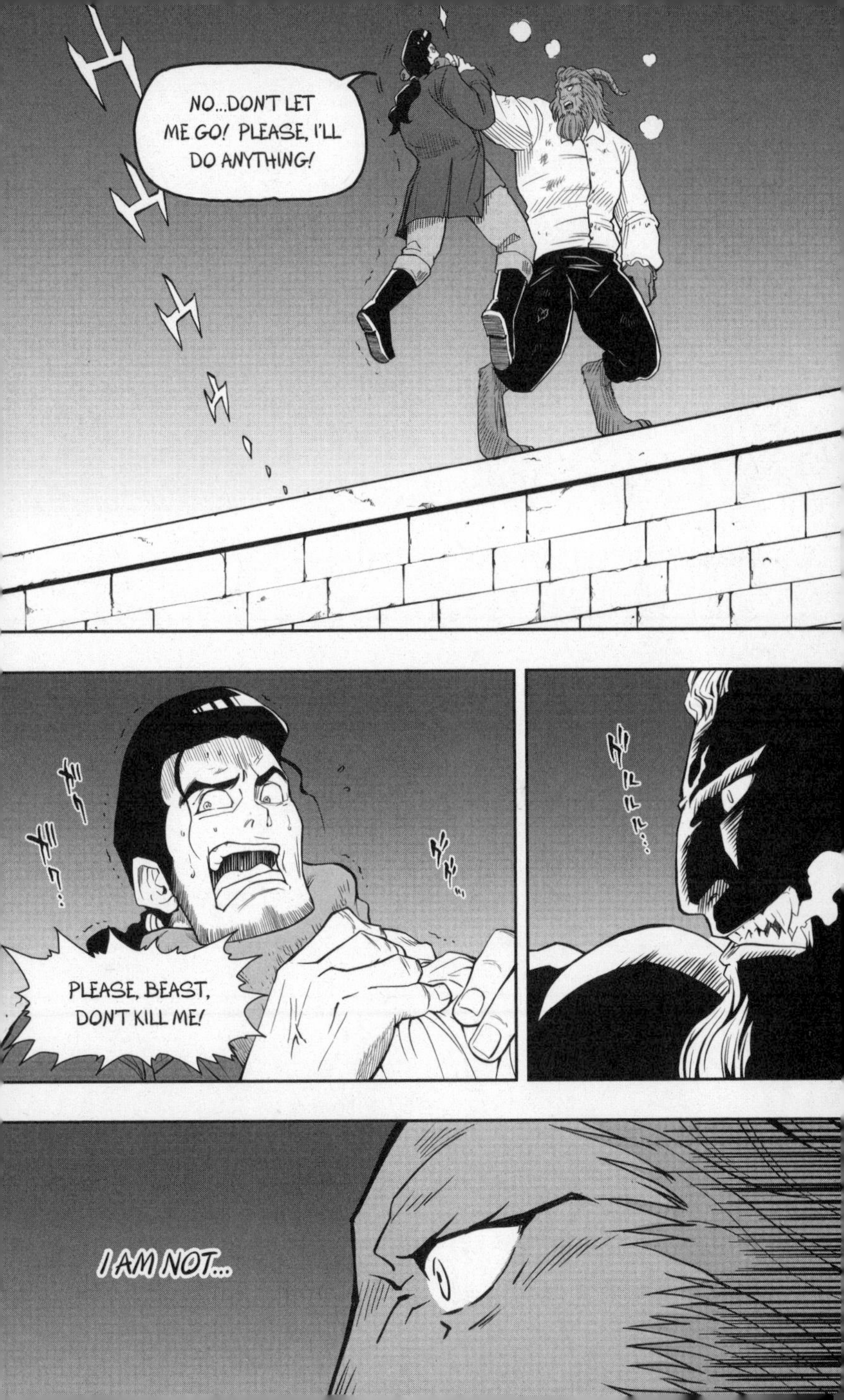
NO...DON'T LET ME GO! PLEASE, I'LL DO ANYTHING!
PLEASE, BEAST, DON'T KILL ME!
I AM NOT...

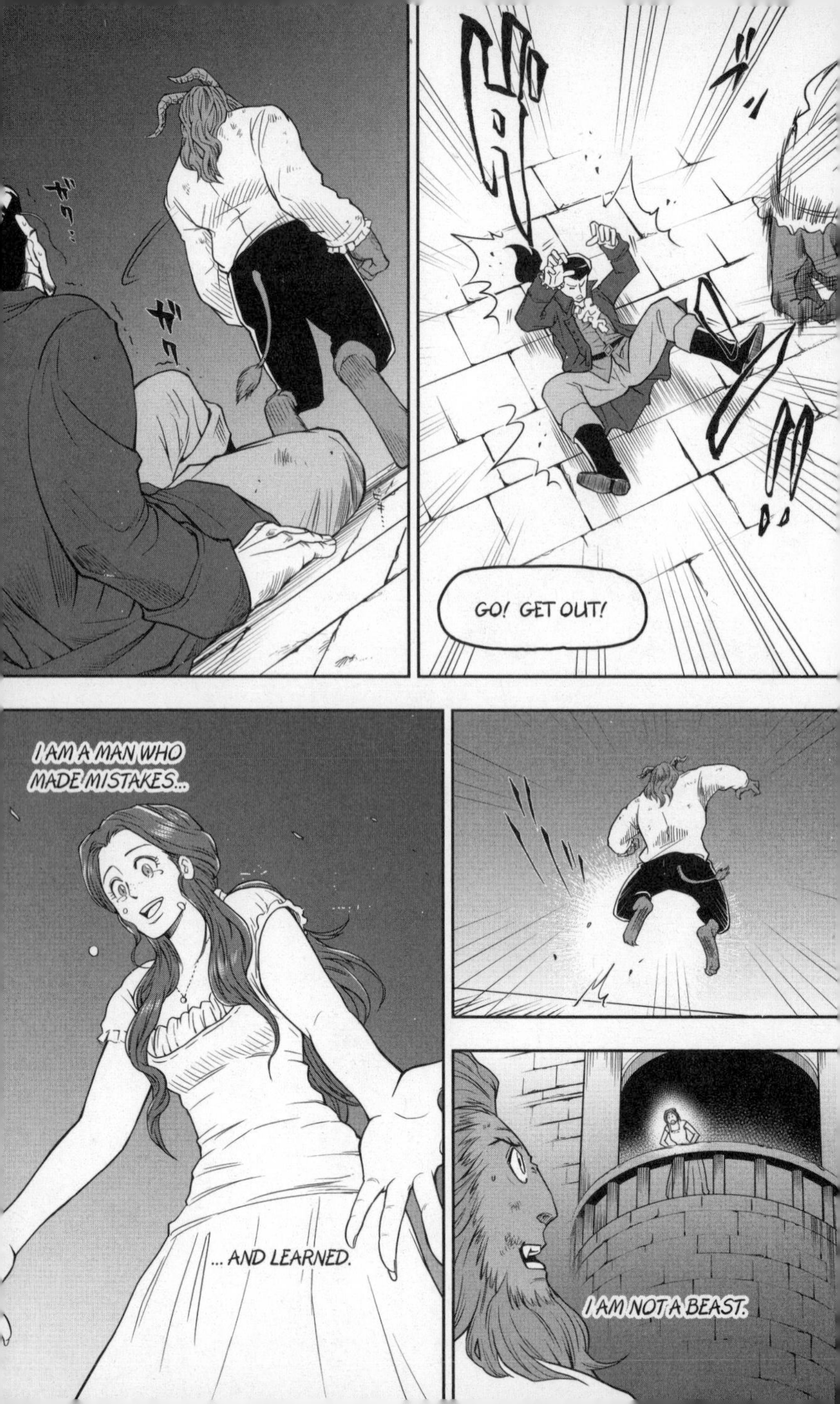
GO! GET OUT!
I AM NOT A BEAST.
I AM A MAN WHO MADE MISTAKES...
... AND LEARNED.

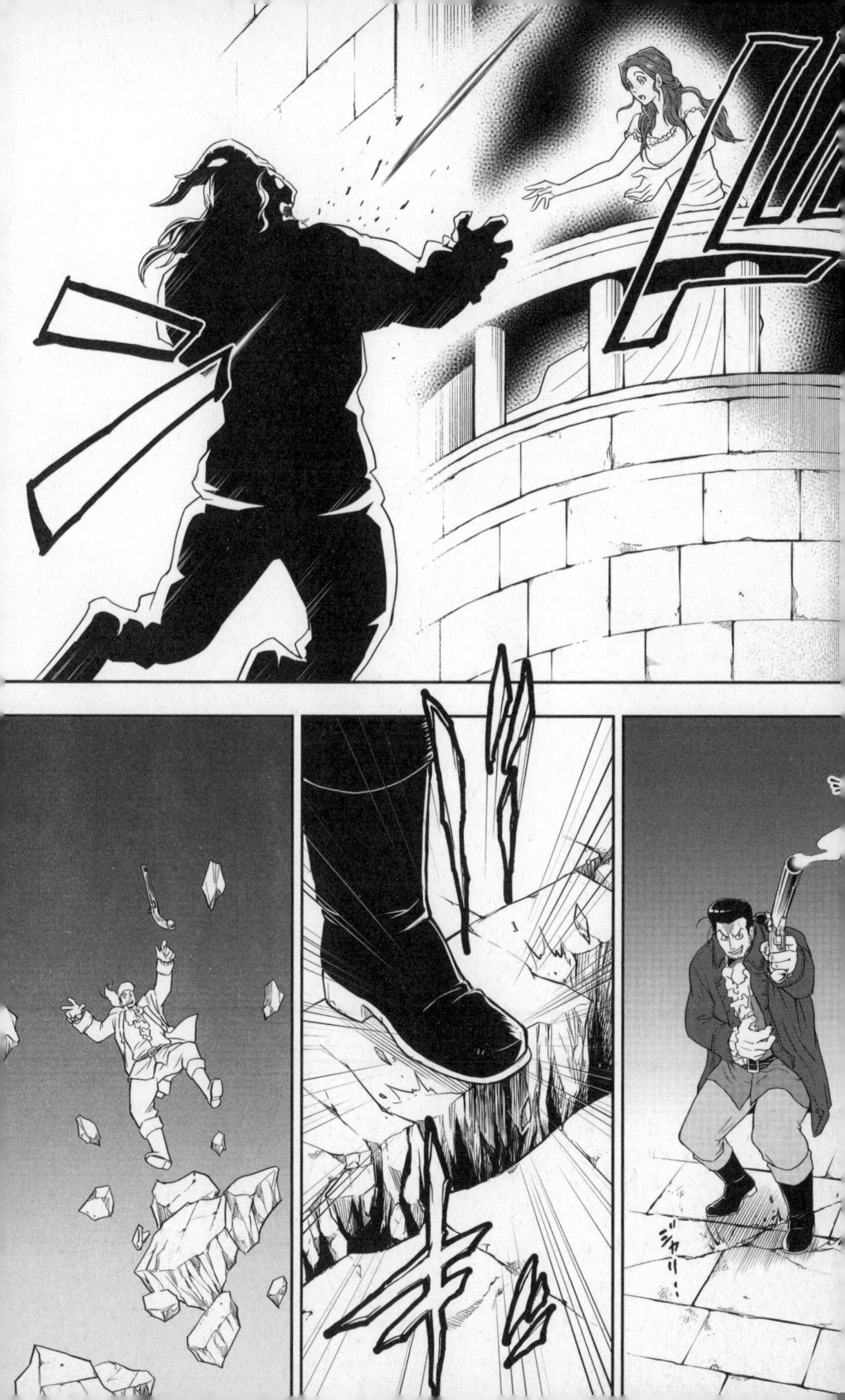
ジャリ‥

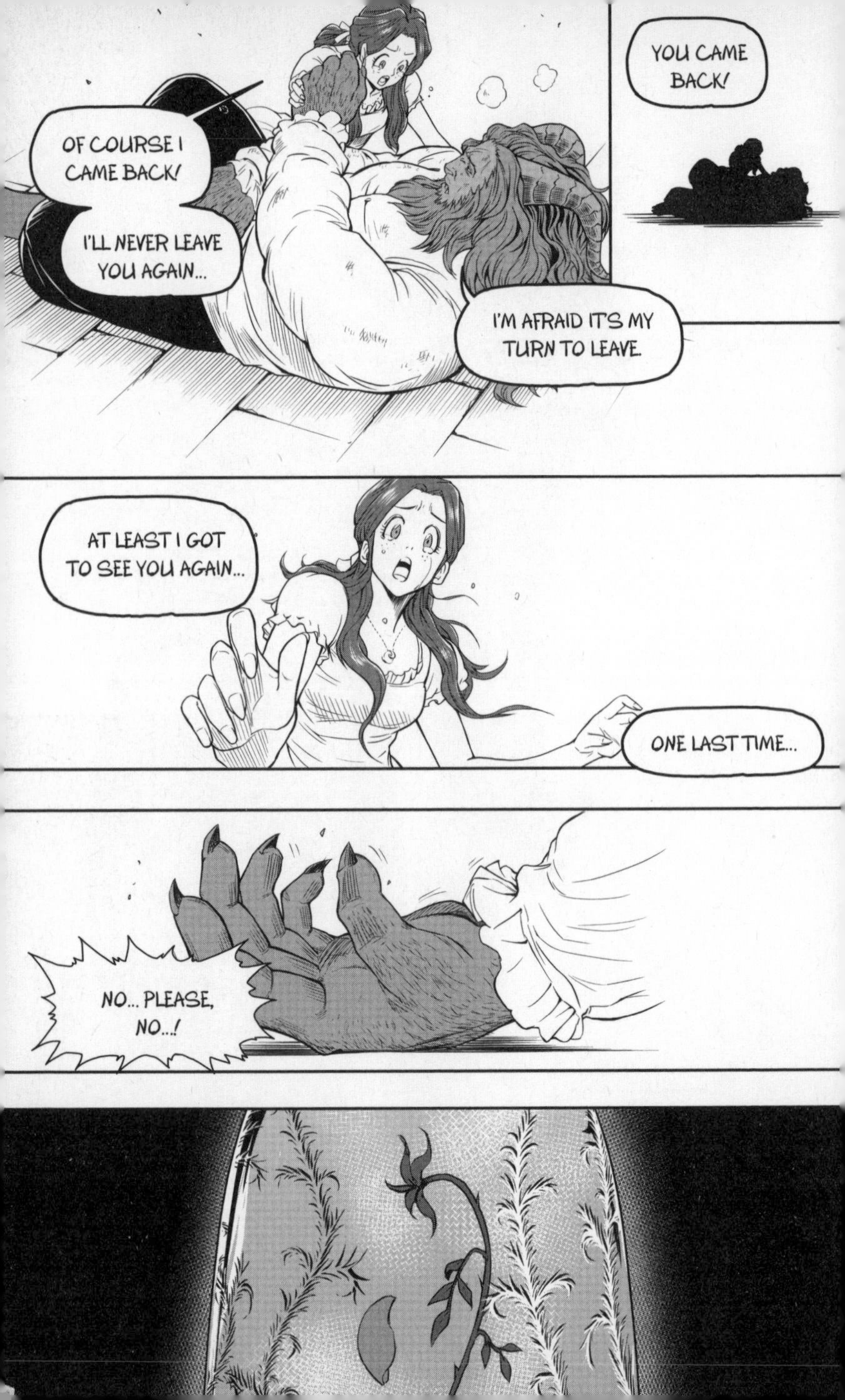
YOU CAME BACK!
OF COURSE I CAME BACK!
I'LL NEVER LEAVE YOU AGAIN...
I'M AFRAID IT'S MY TURN TO LEAVE.
AT LEAST I GOT TO SEE YOU AGAIN...
ONE LAST TIME...
NO... PLEASE, NO...!

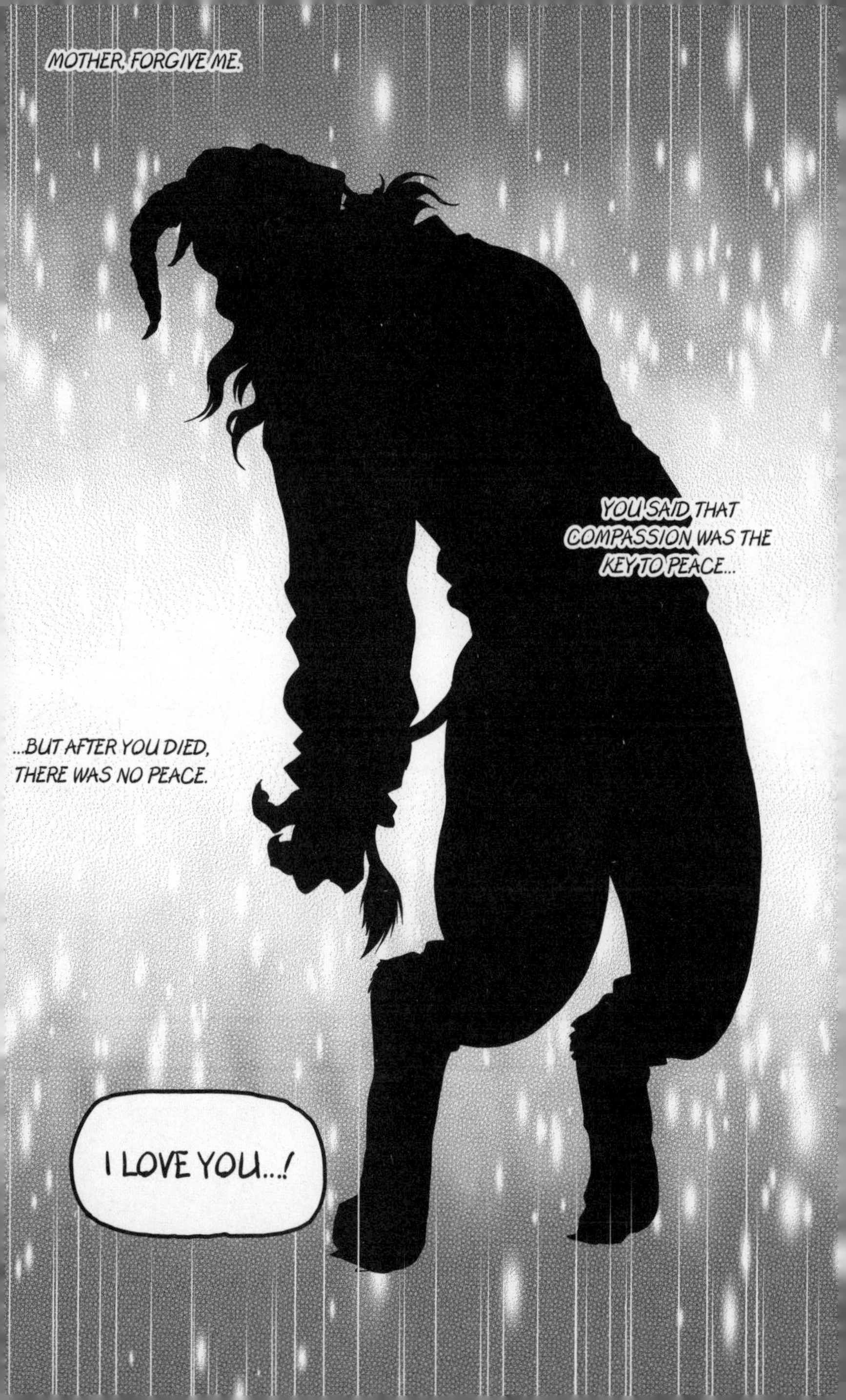
MOTHER, FORGIVE ME.
YOU SAID THAT COMPASSION WAS THE KEY TO PEACE...
...BUT AFTER YOU DIED, THERE WAS NO PEACE.
I LOVE YOU...!

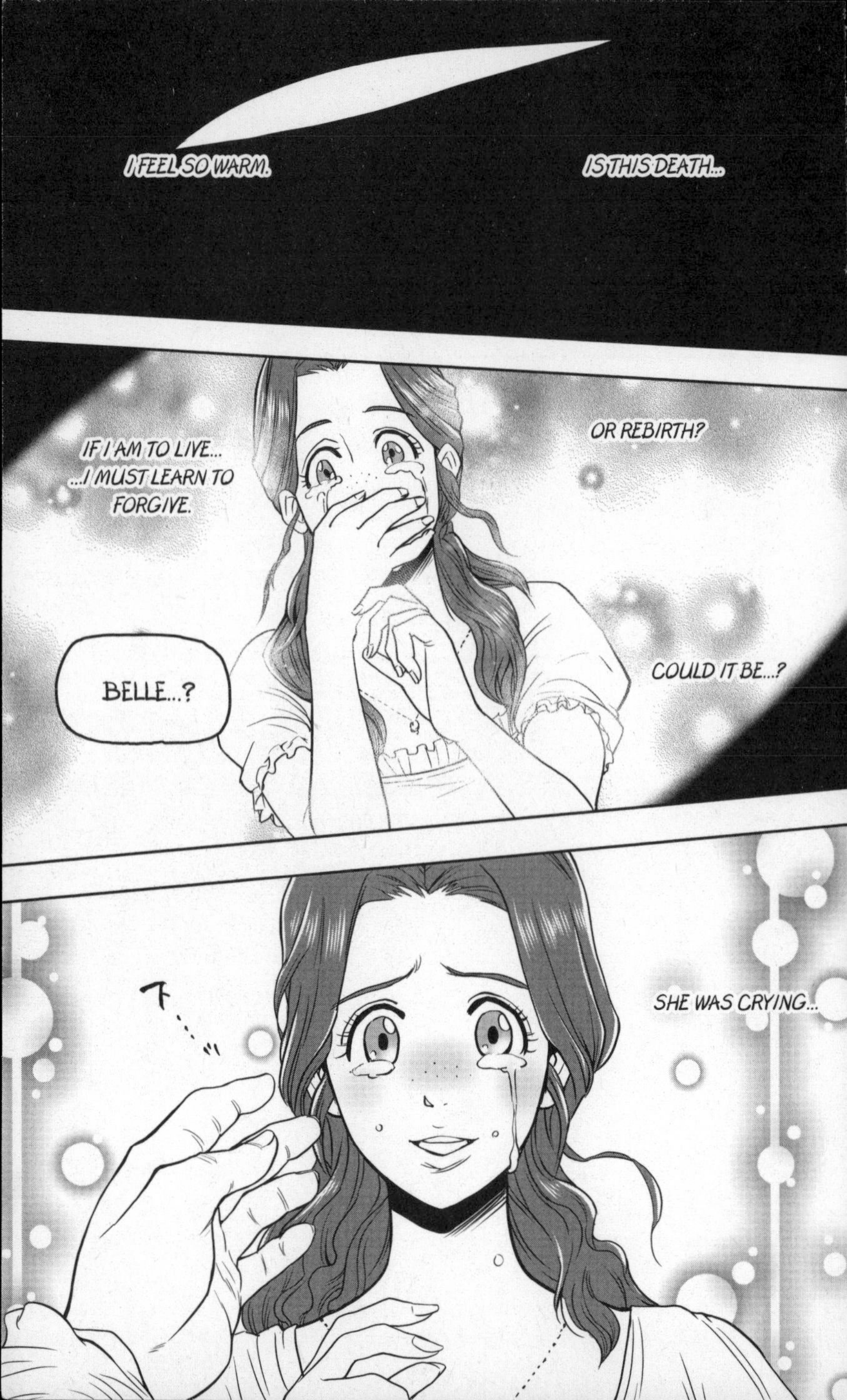
IS THIS DEATH...
I FEEL SO WARM.
OR REBIRTH?
IF I AM TO LIVE... ...I MUST LEARN TO FORGIVE.
COULD IT BE...?
BELLE...?
SHE WAS CRYING...

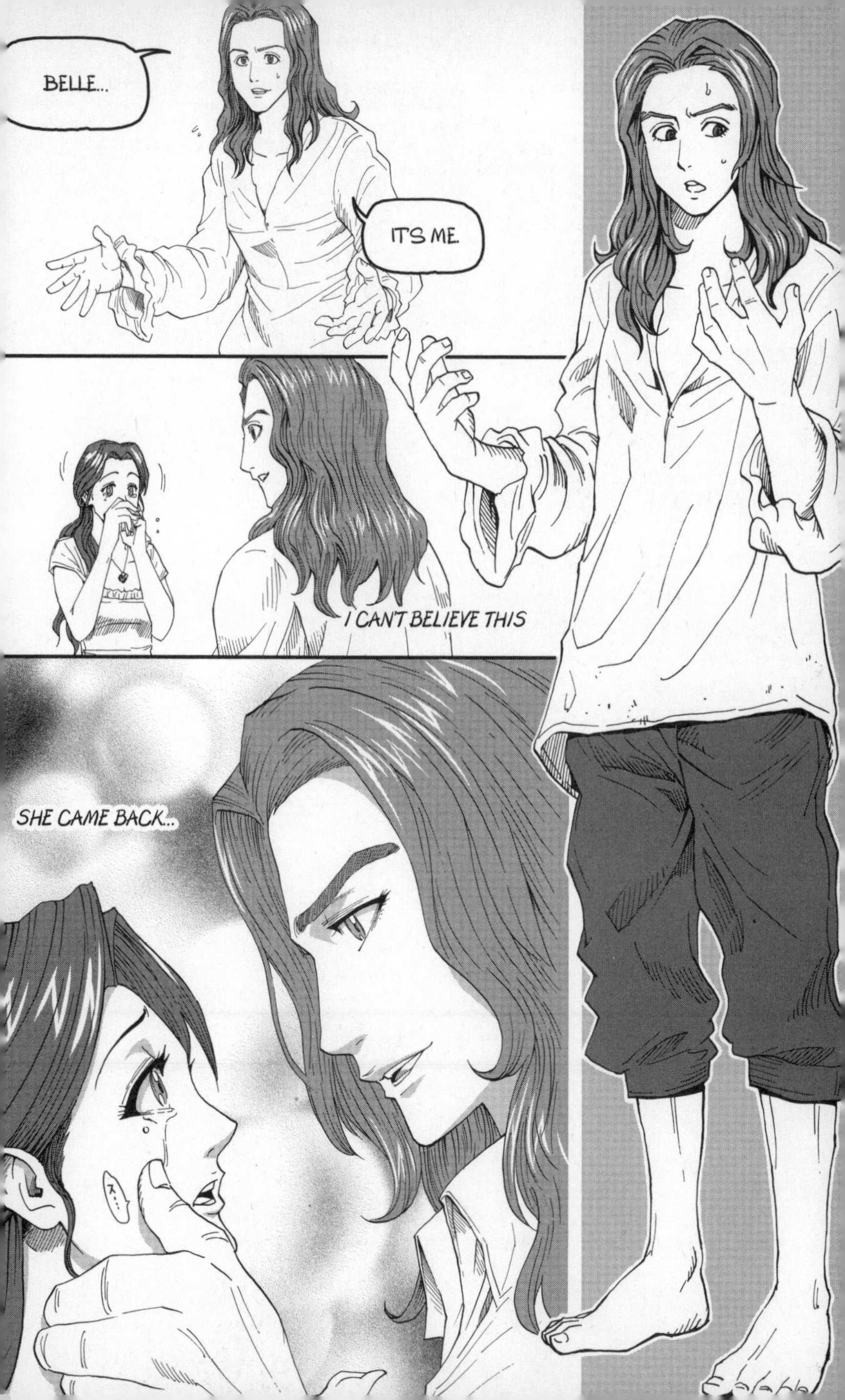
BELLE...
IT'S ME.
I CAN'T BELIEVE THIS
SHE CAME BACK...
ス…

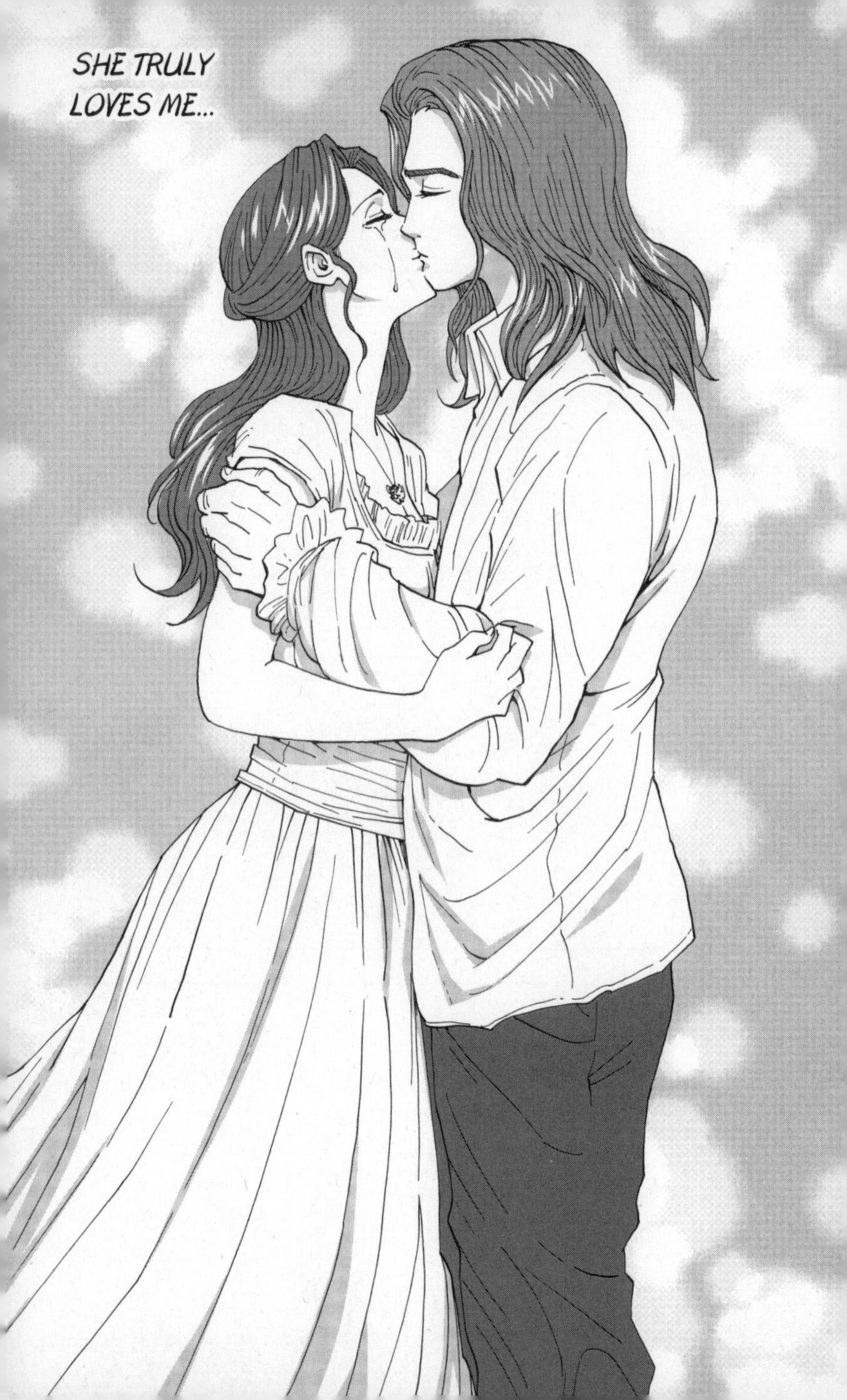
SHE TRULY LOVES ME...

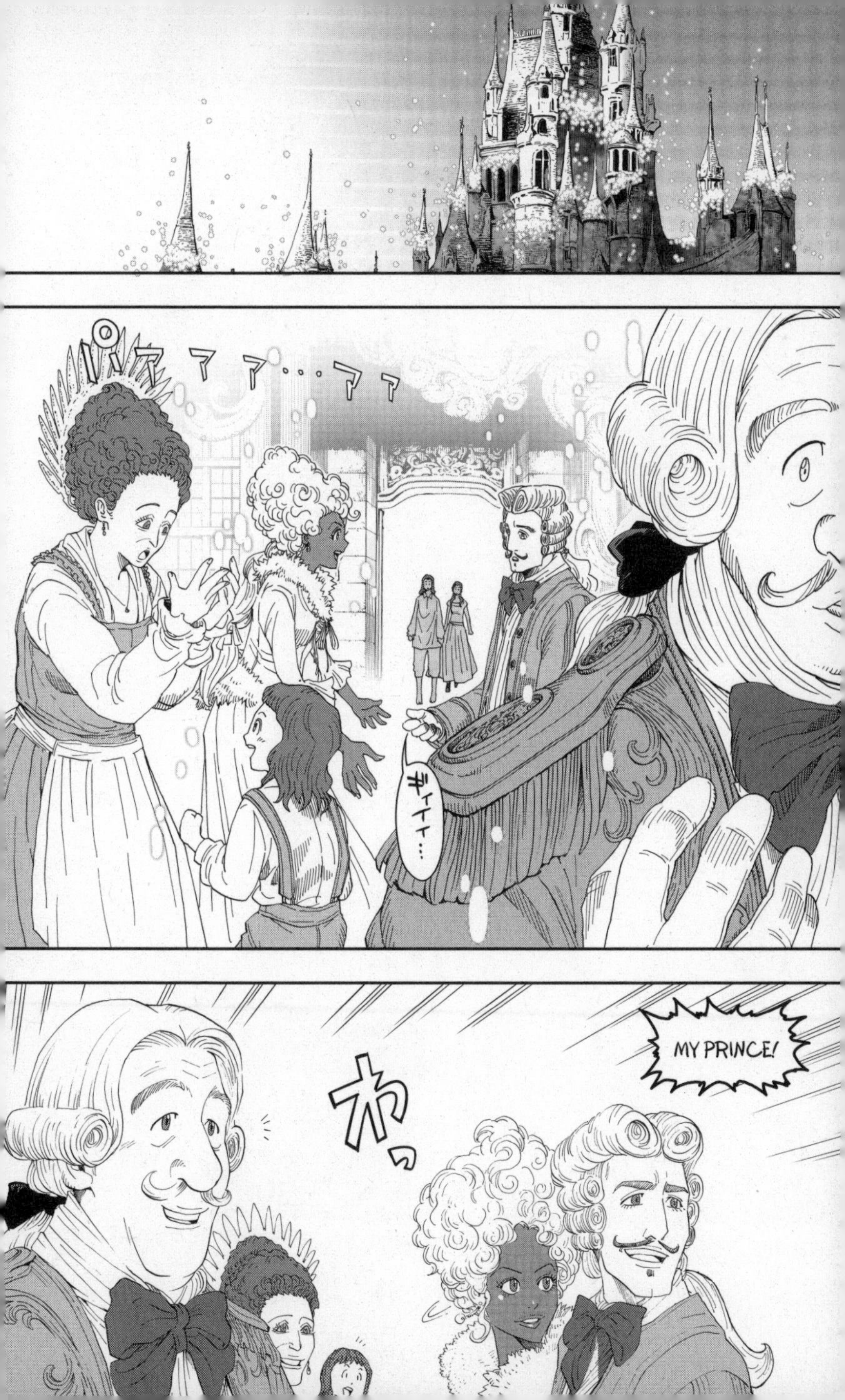
パアアア…アア
ギイイイ…
MY PRINCE!
わっ

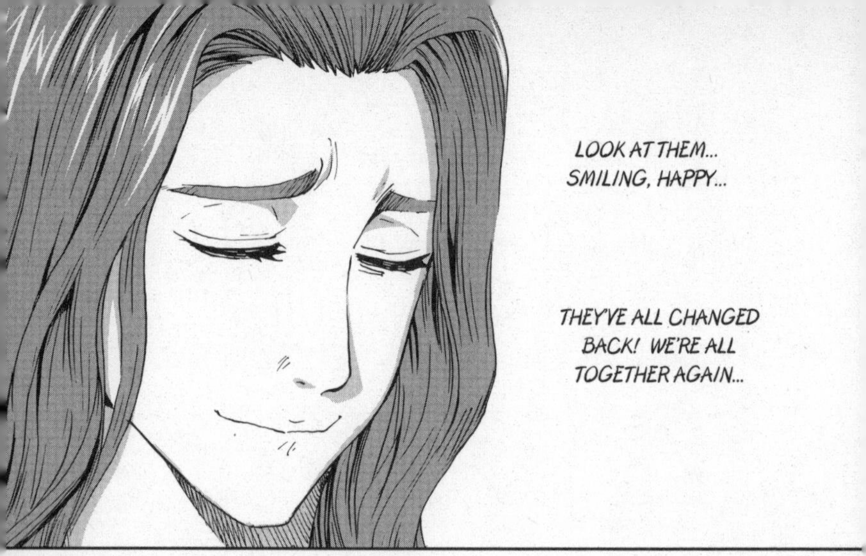
LOOK AT THEM... SMILING, HAPPY...
THEY'VE ALL CHANGED BACK! WE'RE ALL TOGETHER AGAIN...
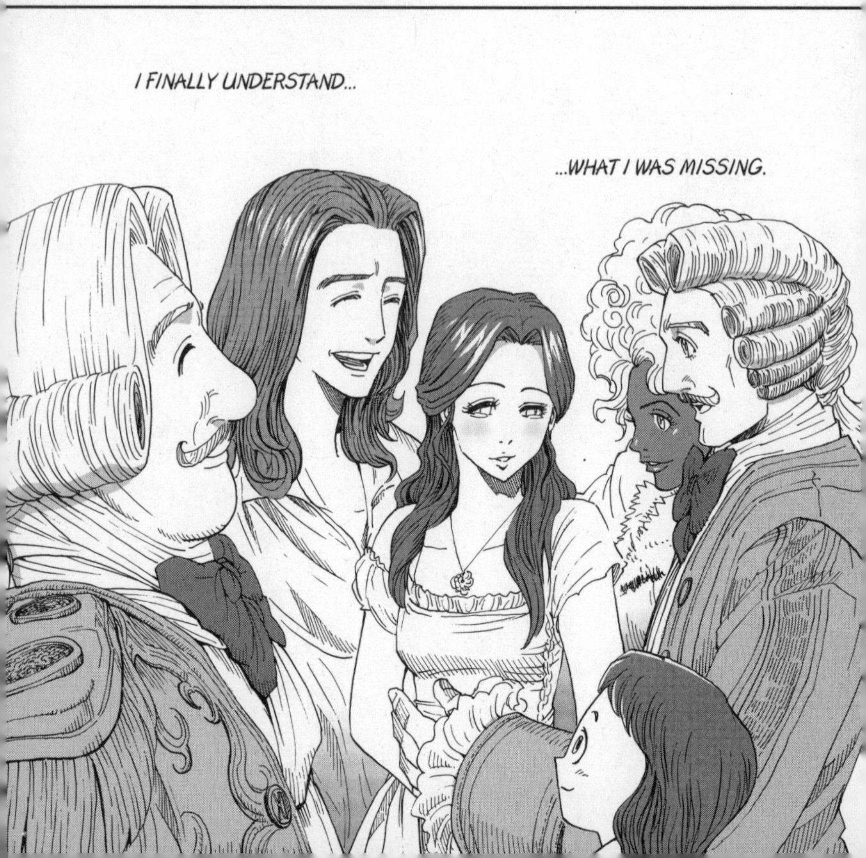
I FINALLY UNDERSTAND...
...WHAT I WAS MISSING.

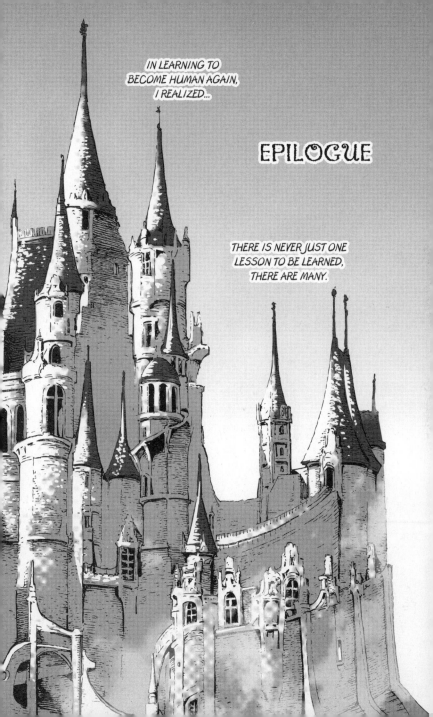

IN LEARNING TO
BECOME HUMAN AGAIN,
I REALIZED...

EPILOGUE

THERE IS NEVER JUST ONE
LESSON TO BE LEARNED,
THERE ARE MANY.

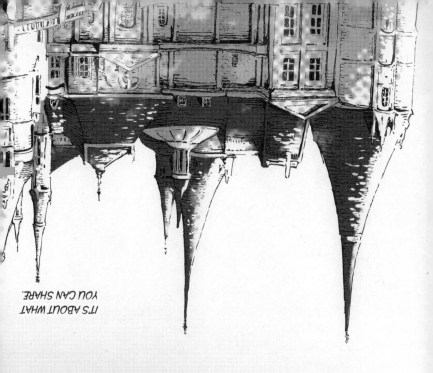

GROWING IS A PROCESS.
IT NEVER STOPS.

BEAUTY ISN'T ABOUT
WHAT YOU HAVE...

IT'S ABOUT WHAT
YOU CAN SHARE.

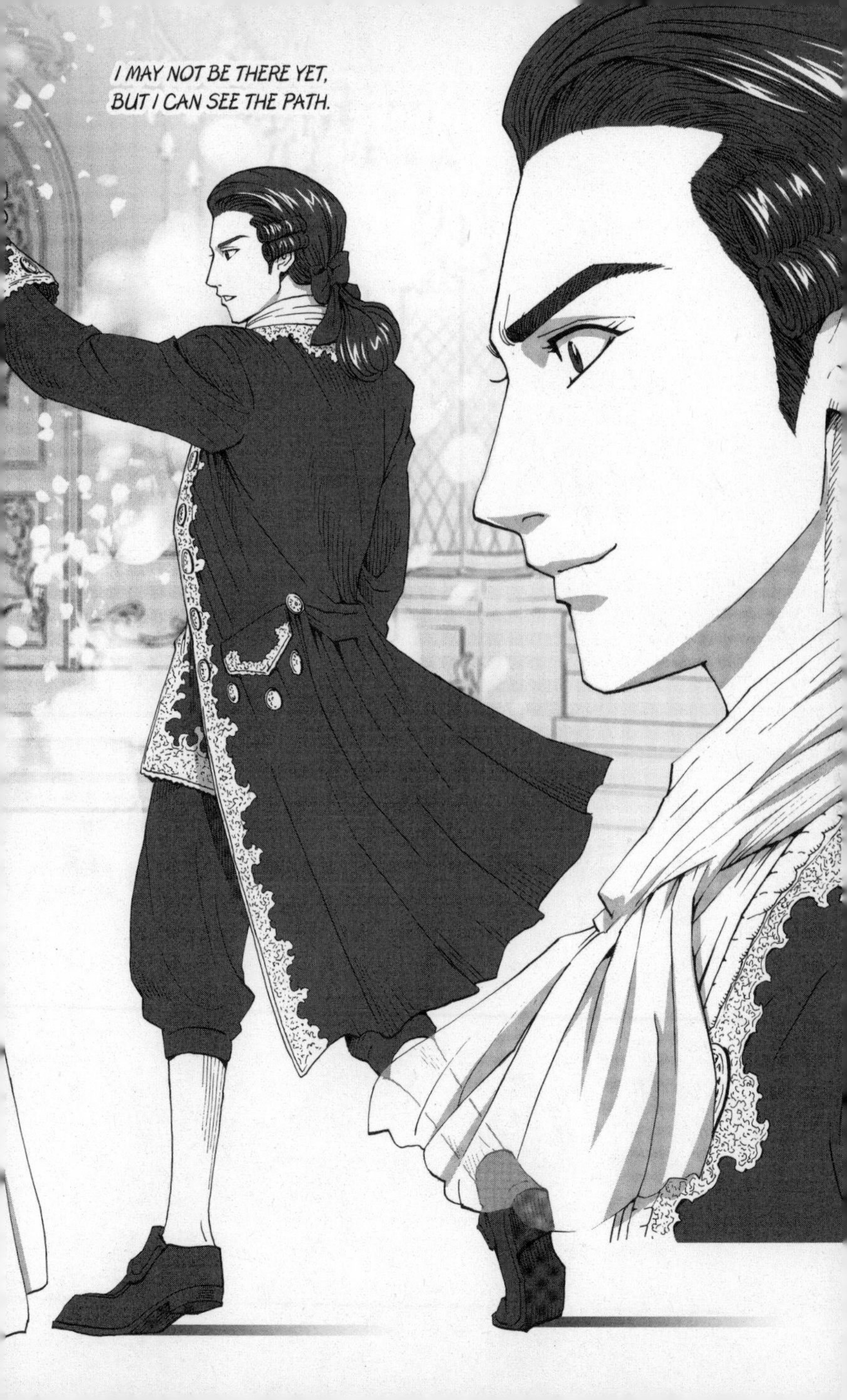
I MAY NOT BE THERE YET, BUT I CAN SEE THE PATH.

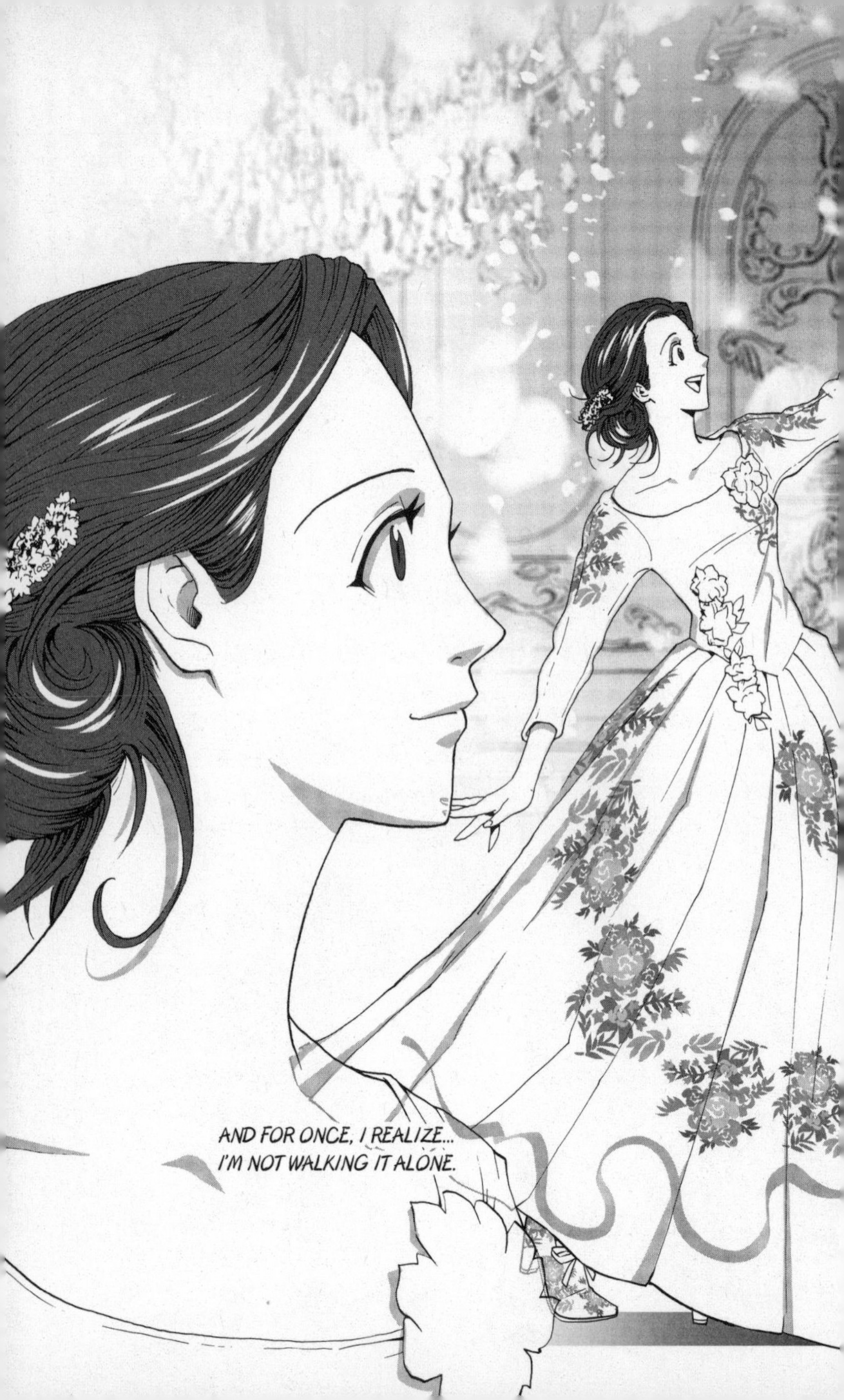
AND FOR ONCE, I REALIZE...
I'M NOT WALKING IT ALONE.

Disney

Beauty and the Beast

MANGA CONCEPT ART

It took many variations of rough concepts to find the best version that best captured the essence of the film character while maintaining a manga look and feel. Enjoy a few examples here!

王子 THE PRINCE

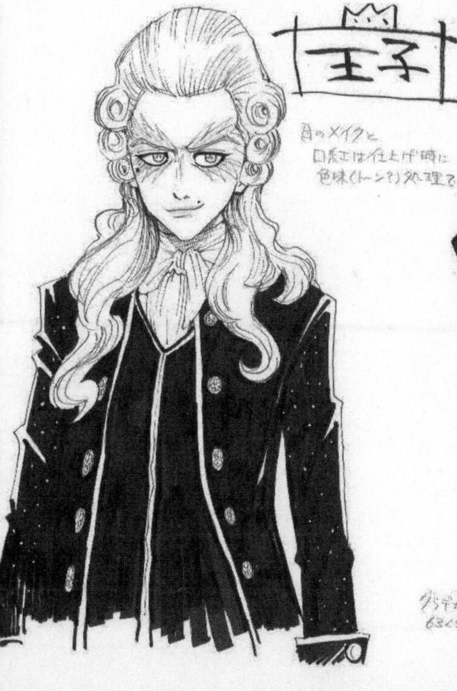
目のメイクと
口紅は仕上げ時に
色味(トーン?)処理で

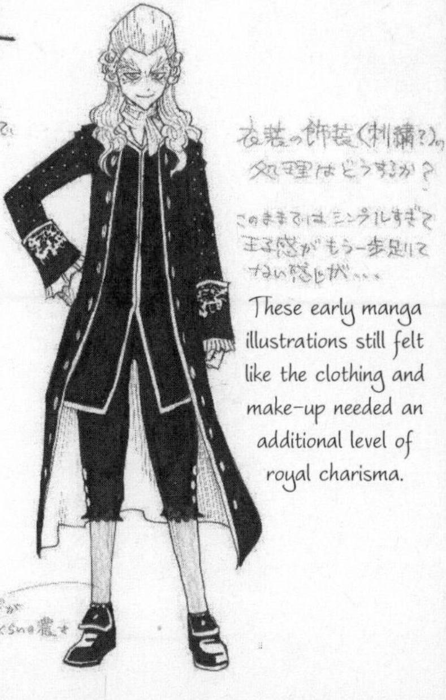
衣装の飾装(刺繍?)の
処理はどうするか?
このままではシンプルすぎて
王子感がもう一歩足りて
ない感じが…
グラデが
63くらいの濃さ

These early manga illustrations still felt like the clothing and make-up needed an additional level of royal charisma.

THE PRINCE - Make-Up

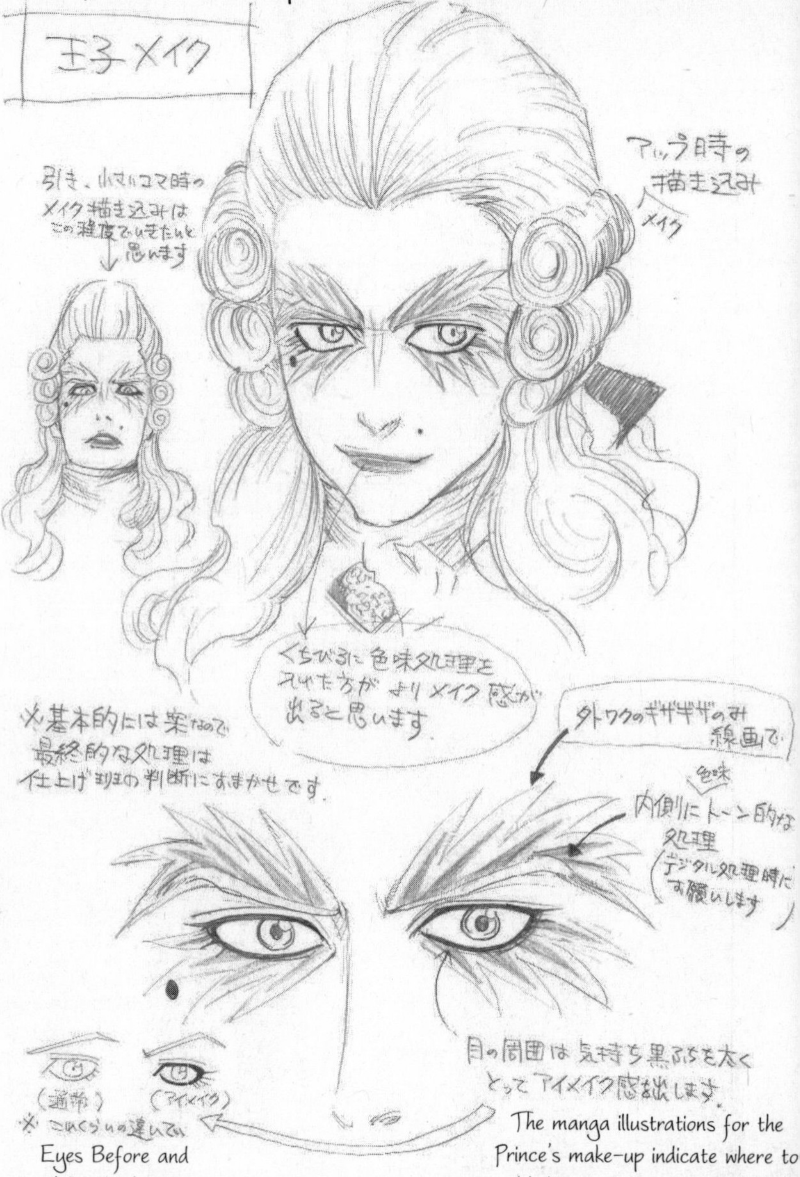
王子メイク
引き、小さいコマ時のメイク描き込みはこの程度でいきたいと思います
アップ時の描き込み
メイク
くちびるに色味処理を入れた方がよりメイク感が出ると思います
※基本的には案なので最終的な処理は仕上げ班の判断におまかせです。
外ワクのギザギザのみ線画で
色味
内側にトーン的な処理
(デジタル処理時にお願いします)
目の周囲は気持ち黒ぶちを太くとってアイメイク感出します。
(通常)
(アイメイク)
※これくらいの違いで

Eyes Before and After Make-up

The manga illustrations for the Prince's make-up indicate where to add digital screentones and which lines to thicken for emphasis.

These work-in-progress
llustrations show early first
tempts to adapt the Beast's
look to manga style.

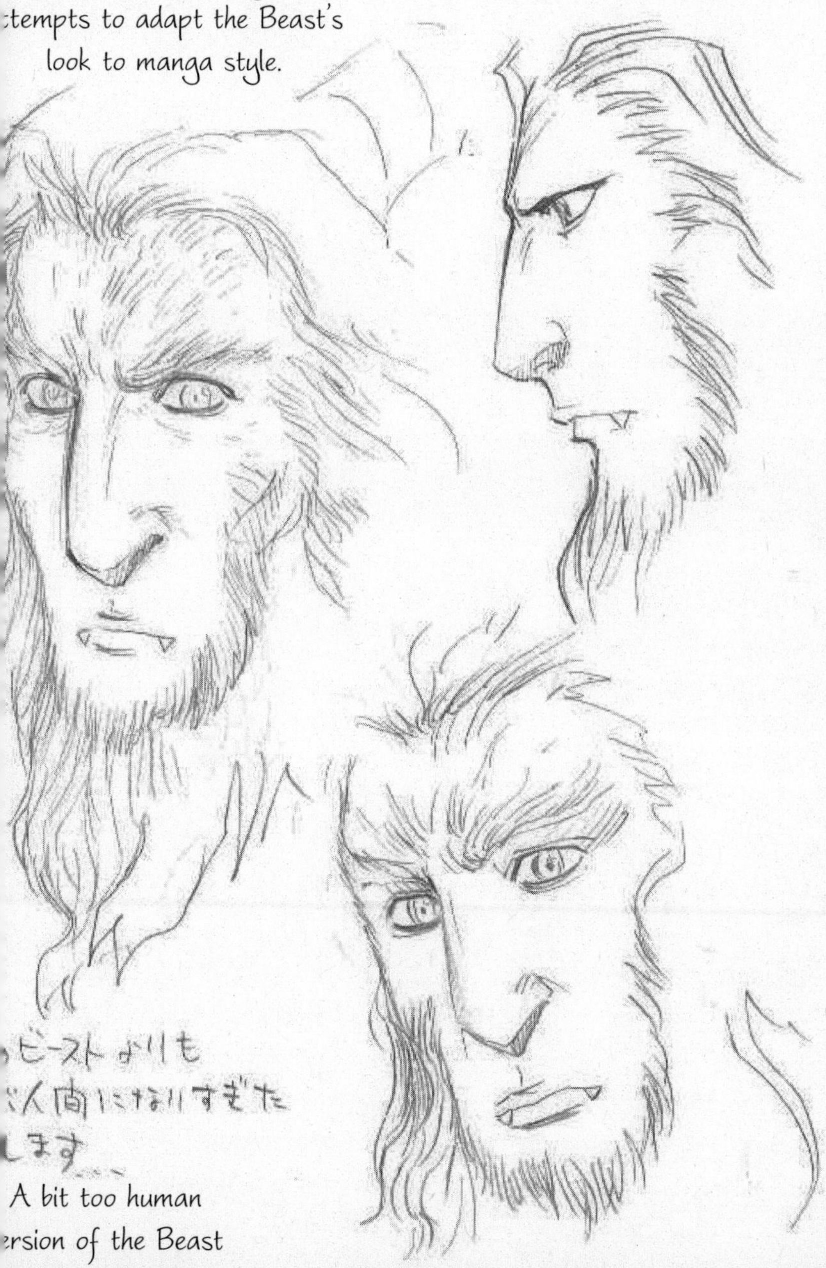

ビーストよりも
人向になりすぎた
します

A bit too human
ersion of the Beast

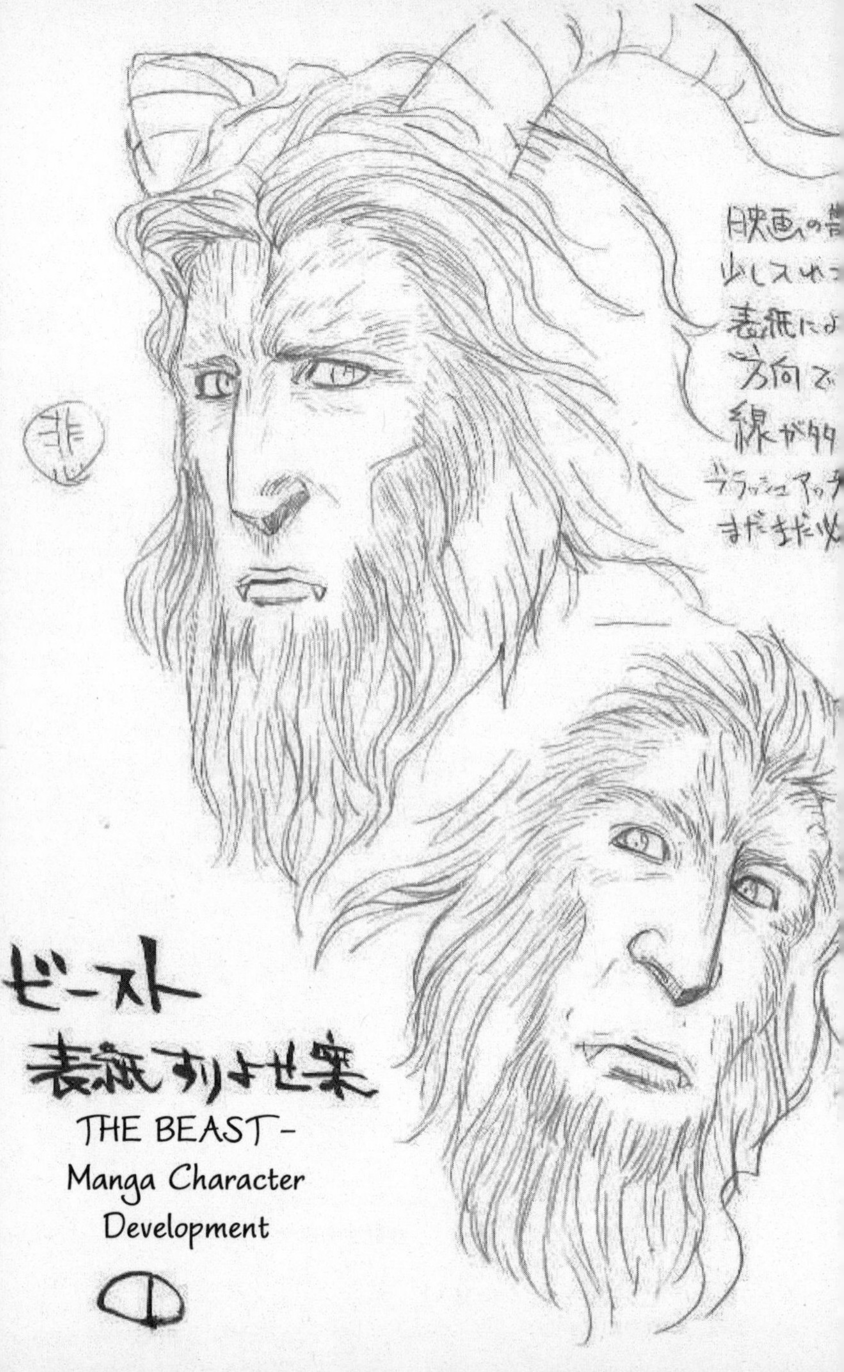
映画の
少しスせ
表紙によ
方向で
線が多
ブラッシュアッ
まだまだ必
ビースト
表紙すりよせ案
THE BEAST -
Manga Character
Development

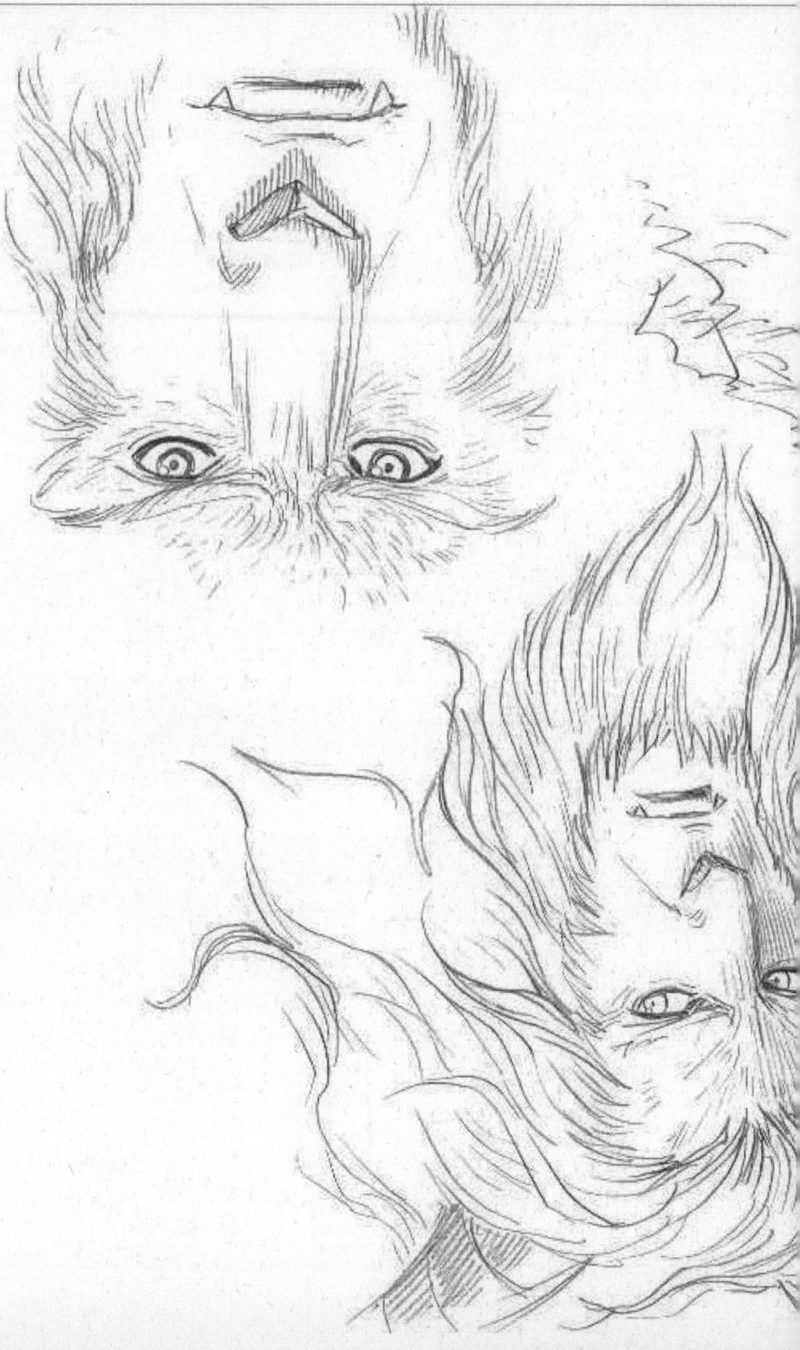

THE BEAST -
rough sketch of the
Beast with emotion

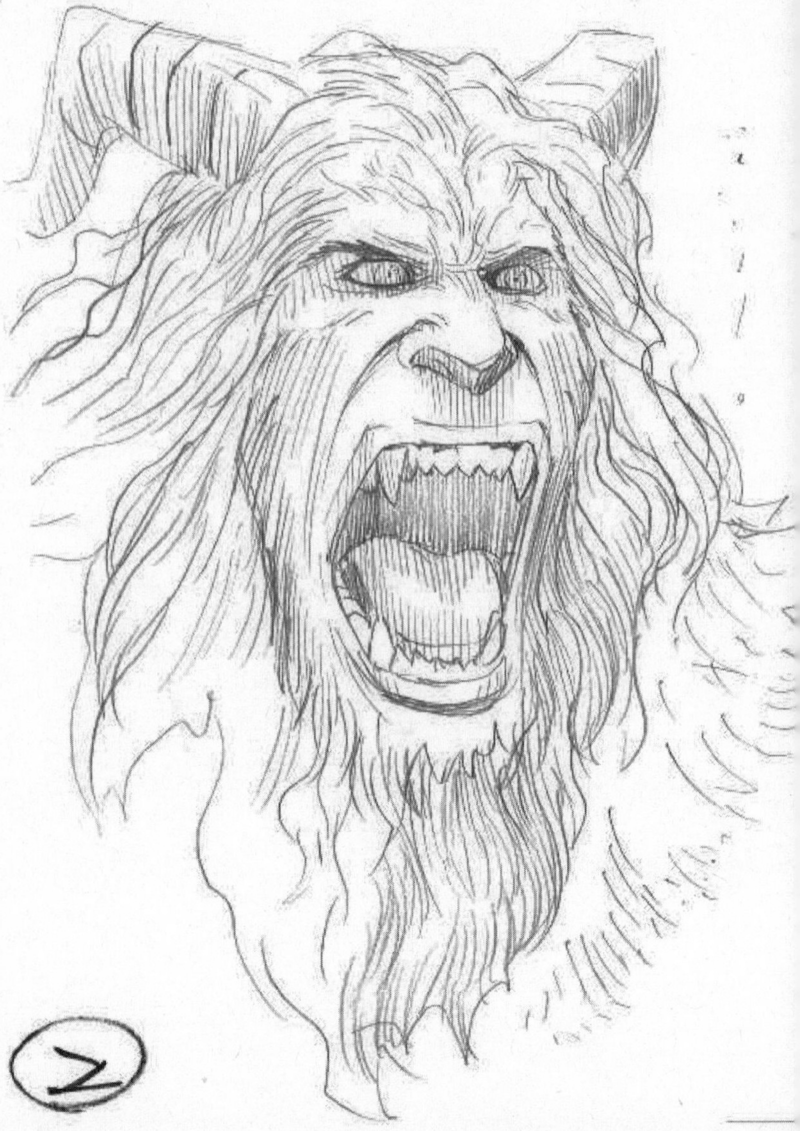

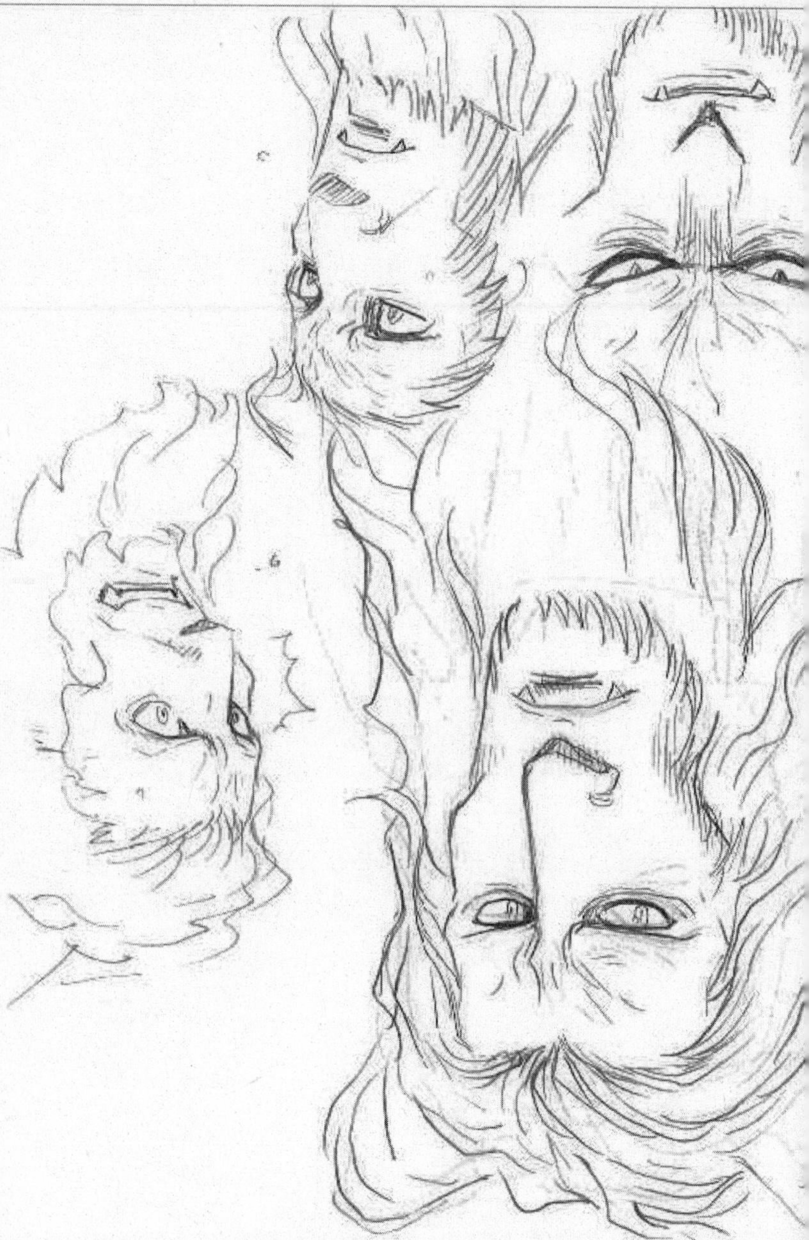

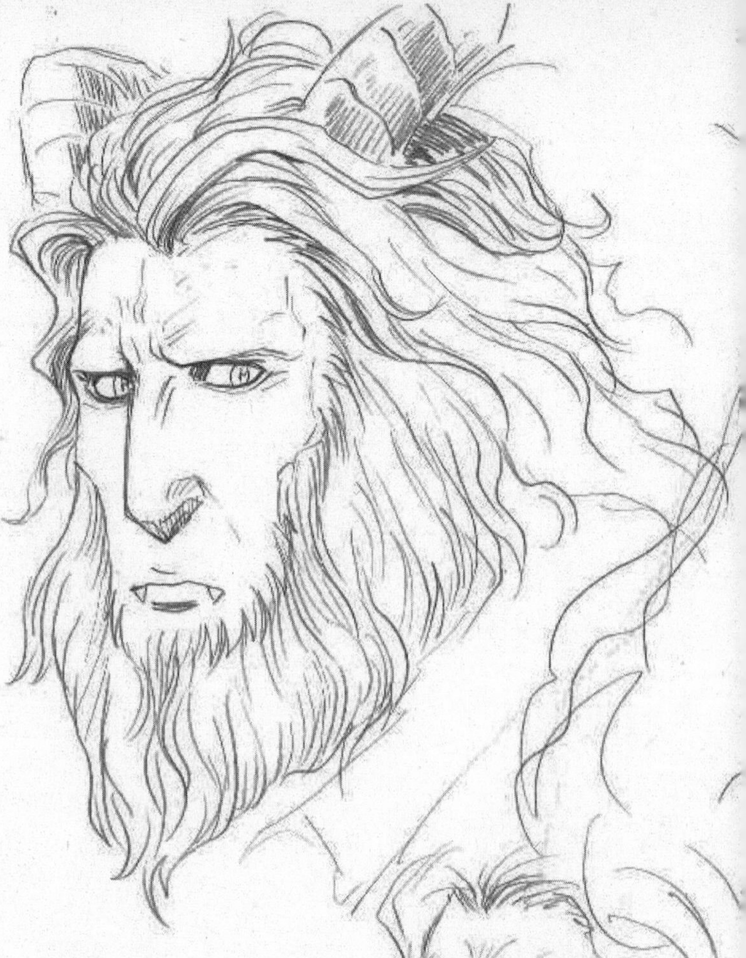

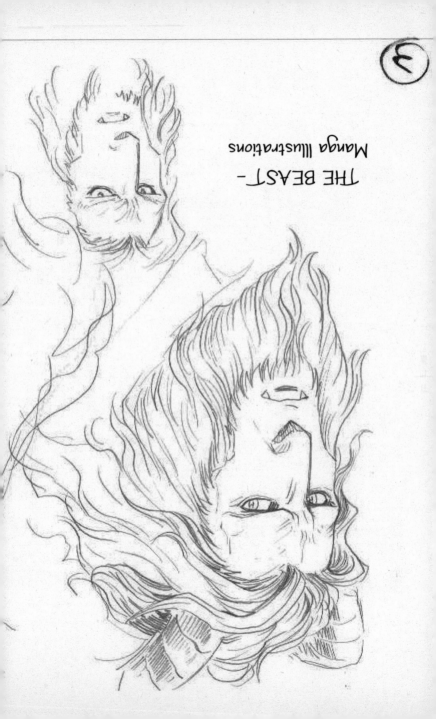

THE BEAST -
Manga Illustrations

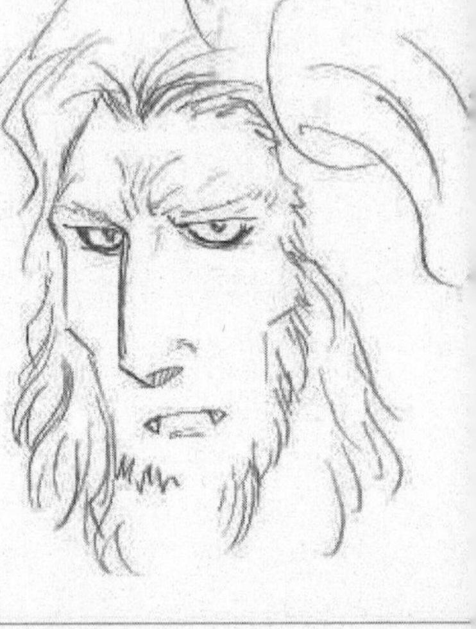

BEAST'S LAIR – In front of the rose jar

ビースト部屋 バラケース前

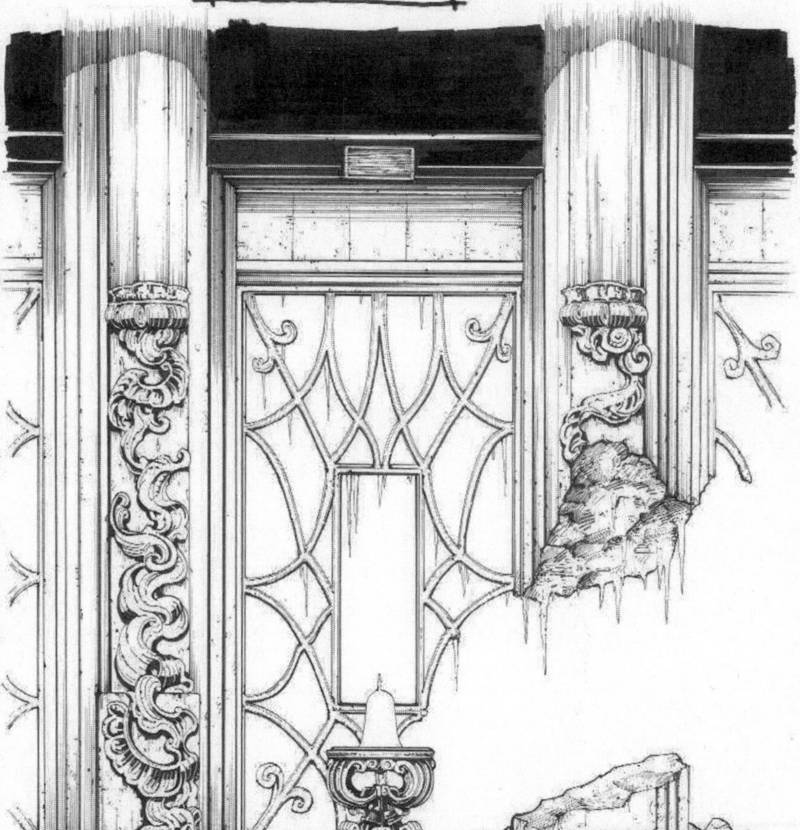

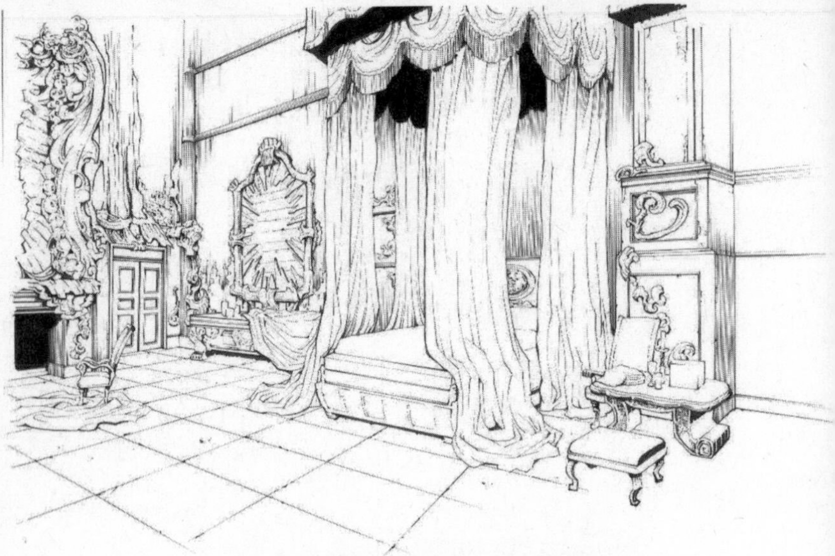

BEAST'S LAIR ビースト部屋

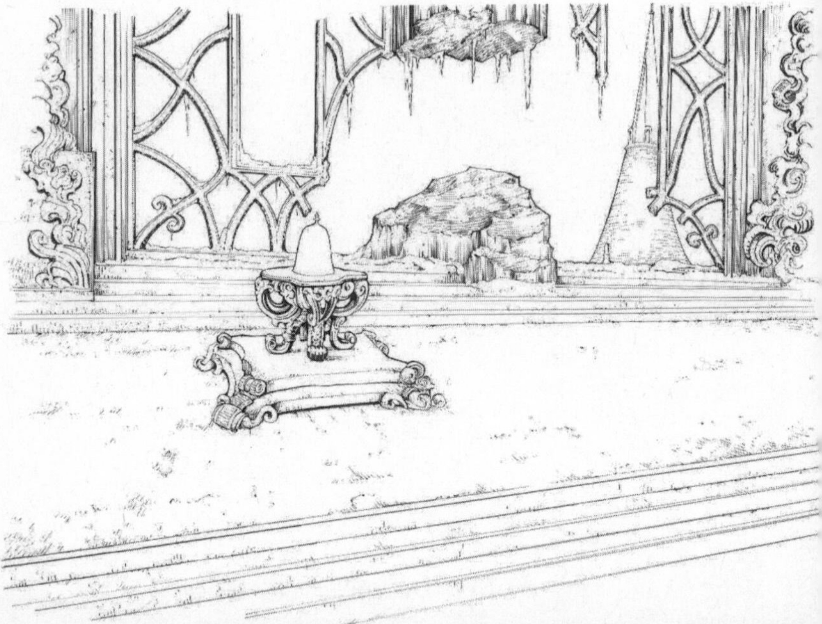

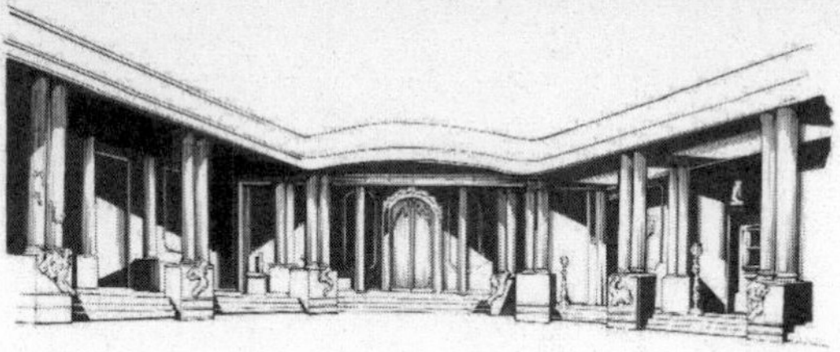

ダンスホール (トレース・フリーハンド) BALLROOM - Freehand Trace

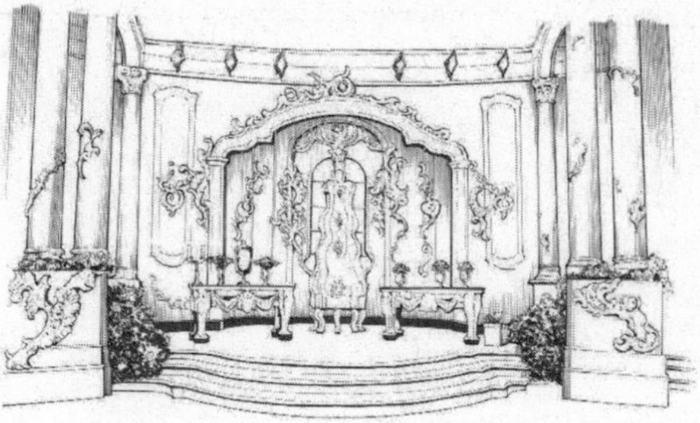

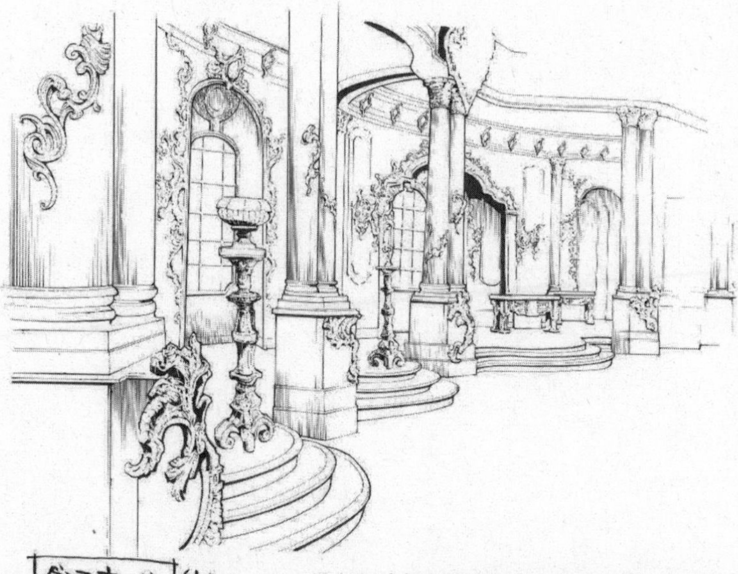

ダンスホール (トレース・フリーハンド) BALLROOM: Freehand Trace

CASTLE - Entrance way ビースト城 城門

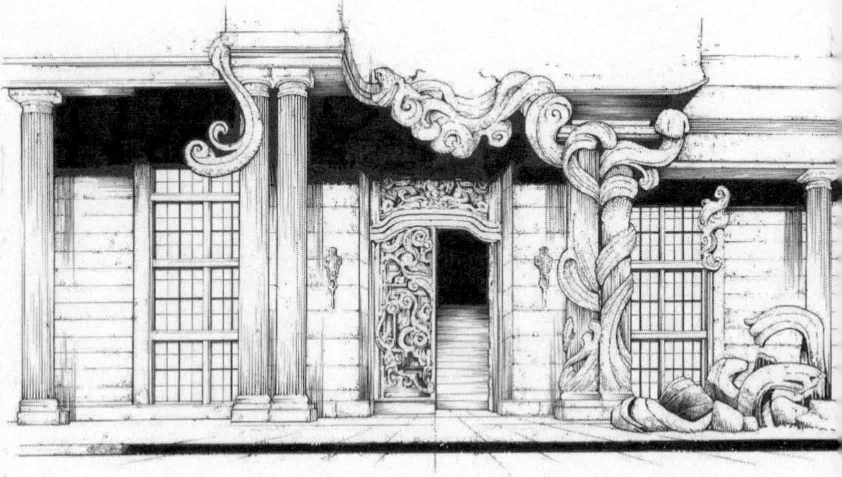

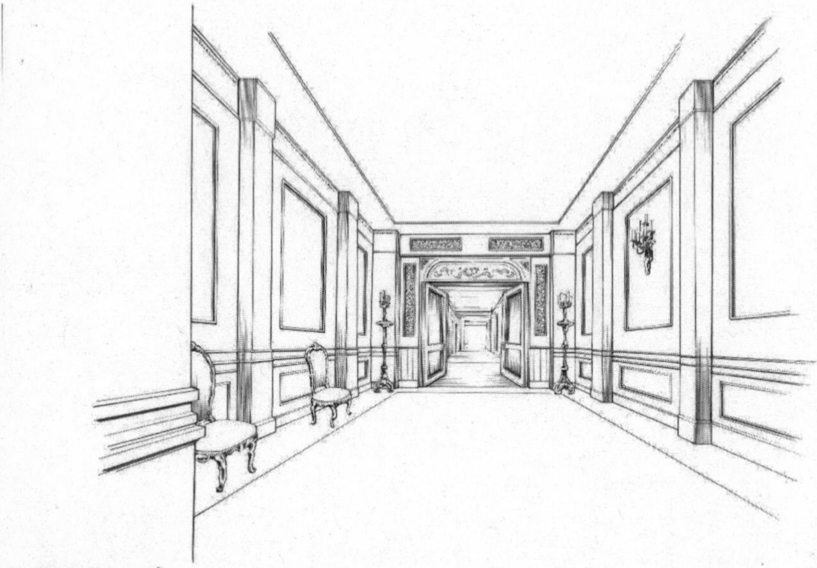

城・ろう下 CASTLE: hallway

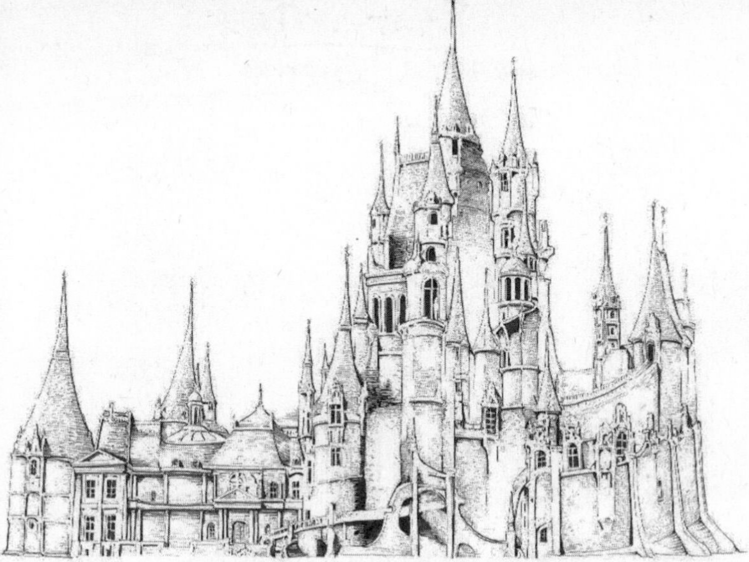

城 トレース・フリーハンド（参考用）

CASTLE - Freehand Trace (for reference)

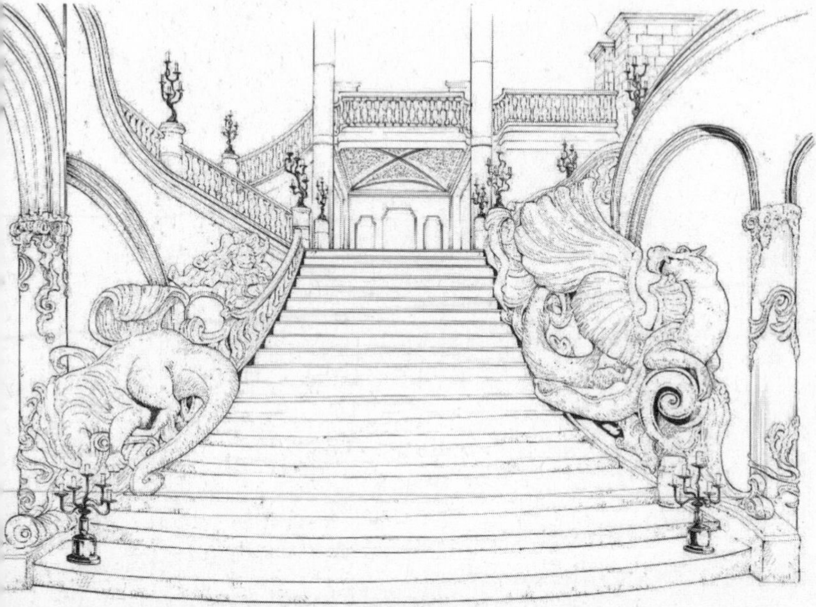

ルミエール修正案

Lumiere

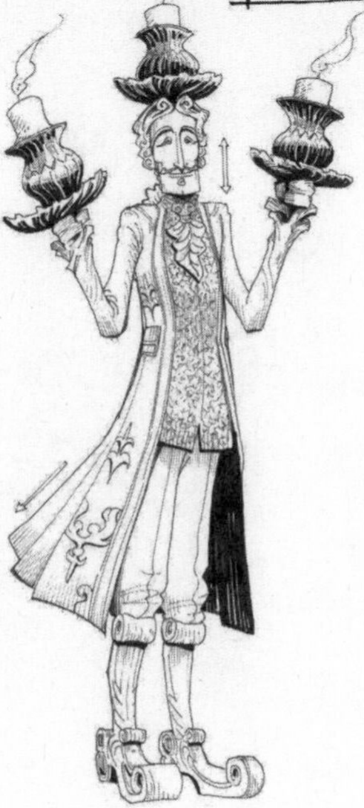

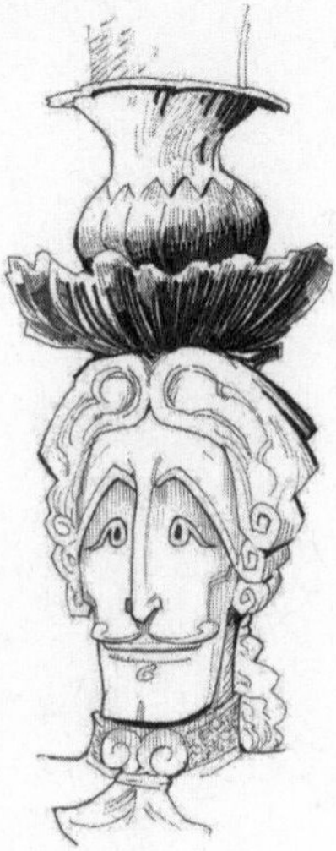

ポット&チップ

Mrs. Potts & Chip

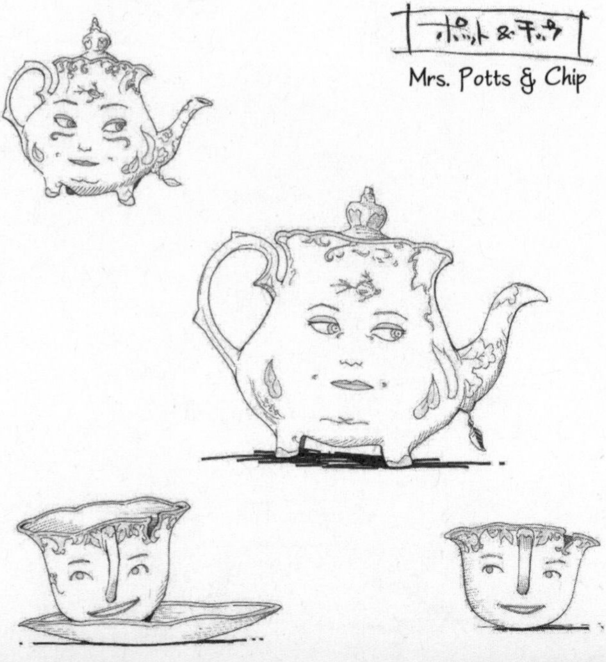

コグスワース

Cogsworth

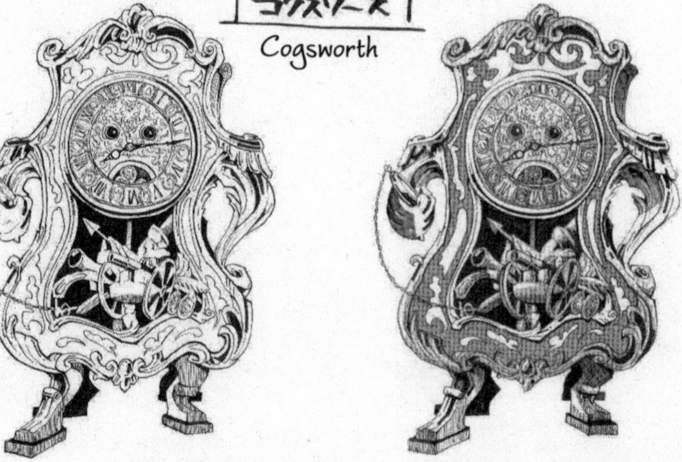

タンス

Madame de Garderobe

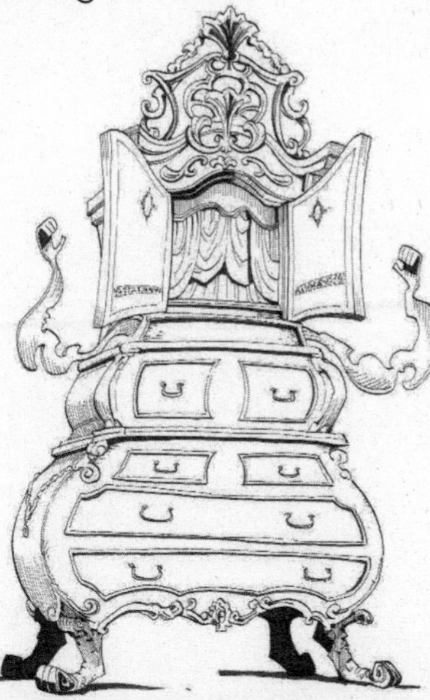

Disney Beauty and the Beast: Beast's Tale
Art by: Studio Dice
Story Adapted by: Mallory Reaves

Publishing Assistant - Janae Young
Marketing Assistant - Kae Winters
Technology and Digital Media Assistant - Phillip Hong
Retouching and Lettering - Vibrraant Publishing Studio
Cover designer - Cody Matheson
Editor - Janae Young & Julie Taylor
Editor-in-Chief & Publisher - Stu Levy

Studio DICE

Hachi Mizuno
Kousuke Takezawa
Pon Tachibana

Rie Osanai
Masashi Kuju
Eriko Terao
Hisashi Nosaka

Tatsuyuki Maeda
Sachika Aoyama
Aya Nakamura

Concept Art by Hachi Mizuno
Cover Art by Hisashi Nosaka

Coordination by MITCHELL PRODUCTION, LLC
http://mitchellprod.com/en

A TOKYOPOP® Manga

TOKYOPOP and 🐸 are trademarks or registered trademarks of TOKYOPOP Inc.

TOKYOPOP Inc.
5200 W. Century Blvd. Suite 705
Los Angeles, 90045

E-mail: info@TOKYOPOP.com
Come visit us online at www.TOKYOPOP.com

f www.facebook.com/TOKYOPOP
🐦 www.twitter.com/TOKYOPOP
▶ www.youtube.com/TOKYOPOPTV
📌 www.pinterest.com/TOKYOPOP
📷 www.instagram.com/TOKYOPOP
t. TOKYOPOP.tumblr.com

ISBN: 978-1-4278-5685-2

First TOKYOPOP Printing: March 2017
10 9 8 7 6 5 4 3 2 1
Printed in the USA

STOP

THIS IS THE BACK OF THE BOOK!

How do you read manga-style? It's simple! To learn, just start in the top right panel and follow the numbers:

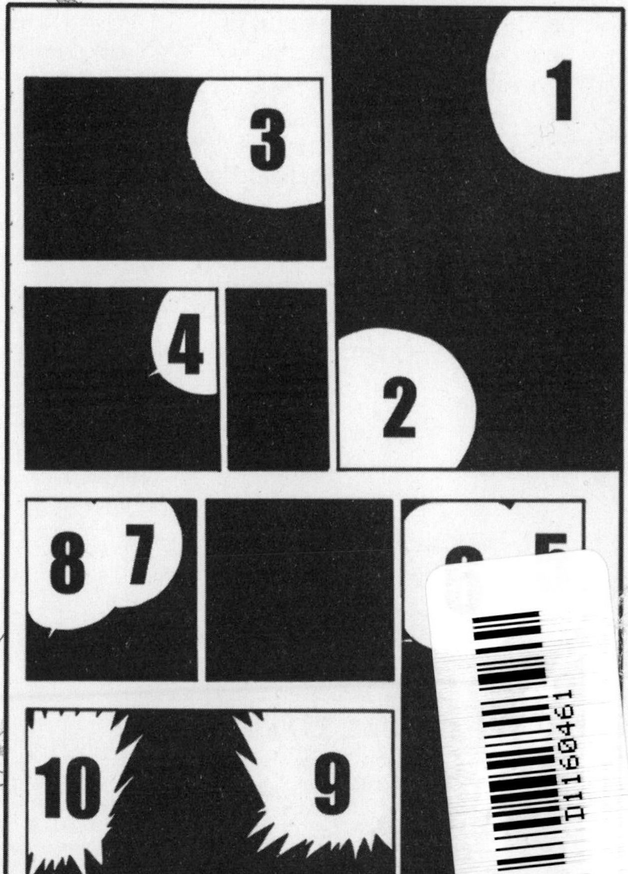
1
2
3
4
7
8
9
10